Continuities
in
Popular
Culture

CONTINUITIES IN POPULAR CULTURE

THE PRESENT IN THE PAST & THE PAST IN THE PRESENT AND FUTURE

Edited by Ray B. Browne and Ronald J. Ambrosetti

Bowling Green State University Popular Press
Bowling Green, OH 43403

Library of Congress Catalogue Card No: 93-70931

ISBN: 0-87972-592-3 Clothbound
       0-87972-593-1 Paperback

Cover design by Laura Darnell-Dumm

CONTENTS

Introduction

There is an apparent paradox in culture, especially popular culture, which on the one hand says that there is nothing deader than yesterday but also, on the other hand, nothing with more lasting vitality. Though some individuals among us may be reasonably indifferent to the past, all swim in a sea that has washed the banks of history and absorbed the flotsam and jetsam of previous cultures. Yet the sea world constantly changes its waters, and all of us—paradoxically—must live in and be a part of the paraphernalia of today.

Realization of the continuity of culture gives a special poignancy to George Santayana's caution that we must learn the lessons of the past or be condemned to re-experience them. This is especially important as the whole dynamic of the past reasserts itself in a new re-experiencing of the past in the newfound vitality of ethnic, racial, and nationalistic developments in the folk cultures that they drive and motivate. They are a recapitulation of the past with modern technologies, with therefore new opportunities and new hazards.

It seems that if we have not learned the lessons of history in the present-day blind outbreaks of racial and nationalistic prejudices and hates we will see cultures torn apart by ignorant armies and selfish politicians, like that currently being experienced in what was once Yugoslavia and in South Africa. And, lest we in the U.S. be too smug, the same kinds of explosions have seeds in our own society and threaten our own future.

From the beginning America was to be the "melting pot" of the people of the world, where the persecuted, the poor and oppressed were allowed to rise above or at least overcome their ethnic and nationalistic prejudices and become a part of what revolutionary Tom Paine and Thomas Jefferson envisioned as a new world and a new nation conceived on the principle of liberty, justice and equality for all, no matter what the origin and degree of enslavement. Such a "city on a hill," as the Puritans liked to see America, such a paradise has not yet come to be, though much progress has been made, perhaps because of the evil of great numbers of people, all fleeing from other great numbers of people—and the curse of the rigidity of language labels and stereotypes. Even in America people did not manage to shake them.

1

2 Continuities in Popular Culture

It is one thing for a group of people—even a large percentage of a whole nation—to flee the curses of the nation and try to become a part of a new civilization—as the Irish did. But there was a built-in bind that apparently people did not recognize or were unable to overcome. If a "melting pot" of peoples is to succeed it must remove the exterior husk of ethnicity and nationality and expose the individual underneath so the individual can grow in the new climate with the new conditions of nurture.

But such was not to be. The Irish became not American-Irish but Irish-Americans, the migrating Germans became not American-Germans but German-Americans. The culture of the place of origin wherever possible directed lifestyles in the new world. The only cultures that were immediately, though superficially, Americanized were African slaves and native Americans. The former, being chattel, were assumed to have no culture and therefore had to take on the "husks" of the white cultures they worked in. Native Americans, likewise, were assumed to have only savage attributes of a way of life that must immediately be changed for the better, that is, made American-European.

Perhaps cultures are too superficial, too much a part of a way of life, ever to overcome the bone-and-muscle heredity of a group of people. Homer's Ulysses was, in Tennyson's memorable phrase, "a part of all that [he] had met," but he remained Greek still. When people become self-conscious, worried about their present and their future, they dig in the past for security. In doing so they revitalize the old way of life, often to the hazard of the present. Cultures that have been suppressed will, when given the power, rise again. In so doing they change the status quo, driving it through the pangs of birth and rebirth through quiet or open revolution, until all have what passes for equal chance in the sun.

Some one hundred and fifty nations and ethnic groups have contributed to the cultures of America as practiced by some 250 million citizens. Thousands of cultures make up the varied cultures of the upcoming 5-10 billion peoples of the world, all developing their rights as citizens of the world, and many eventually with the power to enforce them. Americans too easily and quickly changed their concept of "melting pot" for the glib notion of "Brunswick stew," with all peoples identifiably maintaining their separateness and merely floating in the common water culture. If Abraham Lincoln's famous dictum that no nation can exist half slave and half free is valid, then its terrible corollary surely must hold: No world can exist with 5-10 billion people and thousands of conflicting cultures. Neither the edges nor the middle can hold under those circumstances.

What is needed in the ever-growing complexity is not discontinuity but enlightened continuity, not a forgetting of roots and tribal loyalties but a proper application of those ties to the past that can contribute positively to a new future—if it ever comes—and a "New World," not of the Western Hemisphere but of the whole globe, extending Lincoln's vision to a world "conceived in liberty, and dedicated to the proposition that all men [and women] are created equal."

Though cultures may seem to differ dramatically one from another, they all have in common humanity and the Humanities, the greatest stabilizing forces in all people and all societies. The Humanities are those elements in culture which respond to the basic human needs in all of us; the common threads in all individuals and all societies, the ties that bind us all together as *homo sapiens*. The Humanities are a people's inheritance, their history, the totality of the present as well as of the past. The Humanities are what the tribe's sages teach by word of mouth and by example, by book, television or any other medium, and what everybody sees on the streets of his or her daily existence. The present-day Humanities are, as they have always been, the popular culture of everyday life—the mass media, entertainments, diversions, heroes, icons, rituals, psychology, religion, love-hate—the whole swirl of a nation's various mixes of attitudes and actions. Popular culture, serving the basic drive of the Humanities, has always tried to democratize society, to make all people equal participants in life and in the cultures it generates. "The mass of mankind has not been born with saddles on their backs, nor a favored few booted and spurred," observed Thomas Jefferson. Popular Culture is the stable of horses all can ride. The Humanities are what humanity is and what it might become. As such it is, of course, international. Humanity is world-wide, the Humanities cover the same peoples.

The world, it is clear to all who look, has a new imperative, the need for a new accommodation that will allow 5-10 billion people to move into the electronic age, which is just over the horizon in all sections of the world. Precisely what that age will be nobody at the moment can foresee. Writers of science-fiction are concerned with grasping the technology of the future. Developers of that technology can only develop their technology, as one development opens up the way for the next, but providing no map into the future.

In groping for answers we might learn much from the American microcosm. Inasmuch as we Americans have found ourselves in a global economy in the last ten years (actually the global market goes back at least to Columbus' discovery), we must come to equal terms of recognition, acceptance and valorization of a global culture. This "global culture" or "global literacy" constitutes an expressive culture which at the same time belongs to no one and everyone, and at times it says nothing and yet everything. In more specific, and perhaps acceptable terminology, global culture transcends the old familiar boundaries of nationalism, geography, race, gender, and class. Like the border ballads of old, true provenience hovers in the metaphysics of the expressive culture. Place and space have been relegated to less significant roles as the hegemonic forces in the forming and reshaping of the key elements and trends in this global culture. The old centers of power—the power of the word and the image, that is—like New York and Los Angeles, must now compete with the word, the image and the ballad from Nashville, Soweto, Prague and Kuwait. The camcorder and the fax machine have provided a stupendous democratization of the power of the word and image—in short, a new multi-sensory literature has been created, and it is a literature that is being "read" synchronously and instantly around the globe. This democratization is the most basic of common denominators in the popular culture of all periods and places.

One of the great ironies in the emergence of this global culture is that while American energies and vision have influenced so much of the whole phenomenon—inadvertently perhaps, by exporting our popular culture and way of life—here at home, in the places where it counts the most, our most far-reaching cultural products are yet held in deep derision and distrust. Our most significant fantasy products, among which popular literature, film and music must be included, are changing the contours of the globe on a daily basis; yet, these same forms of expressive culture are shunned in educational circles and declared anathema in high school and college curricula. Did anyone notice the outrageous script on the Berlin Wall was done in the style of comic book calligraphy, and also resembles the gaudy style of New York subway inscriptions? That handwriting is on the Wall, and everyone but we ourselves seems to recognize its semiology. Did anyone notice in the gush of CNN live reports in Poland in 1991 that Solidarity's campaign poster in the free elections portrayed the mythic image of Gary Cooper, alone in the street in *High Noon*, wielding not the old six-shooter but a holster that contained the word "vote"? Do any of us really understand the full meaning of watching the Denver Broncos play the Seattle Seahawks—in Tokyo? We may be buying the Hondas and the Nissans; but what we are exporting in return has far-flung consequences. Already in Japan, courtship and marriage customs have changed enough to spur an incipient generation gap because of the Americanization of those institutions. Lastly, did anyone notice thirteen years ago that the anti-American Iranians nevertheless demonstrated in the English language? In fact, they appeared to be protesting and marching with an American 1960s-type of atmosphere. Strange bedfellows made for the camcorder.

These continuities are the straws in the winds of change—the powerful storm is riding on the elements of electronic communication and its deep-seated capacity to move the supercultural audiences in this new hypertextual humanities.

All of this talk about the eclipse of American international power and prestige reveals a terrible ignorance of our own true vitality and strengths. We want to continue to define power within the old parameters of blocs, allies, and hemispheres. Both Mikhail Gorbachev and Saddam Hussein, for better or worse, have recently demonstrated the futility of enclave-building. The new American power lies in the ability of the American imagination to inspire the collective vision of peoples—both empowered and disenfranchised—to dream in a way that Americans have dreamed themselves, albeit mythopoetically, for more than two hundred years.

This ignorance of our own true nature is most blatantly revealed in the very persons and authorities who should know better. Those persons responsible for education in America must be willing to explore new methods of pedagogy and new definitions and materials of culture, literature, literacy: in short, we must re-define our notion of an educated person for the twenty-first century. The defenders of the Augustan Age will not readily surrender to the alleged barbarians; Rome was already sacked once, it will have been argued. The barricades to authentic relevance have been in place many decades. The battles will be waged from lowly department curriculum committees to the upper chambers of the Provost. The battleground will cover a wide territory: the art novel versus the best seller, epic poetry versus the dub poetry of the Caribbean, the composition of gender, sex, race, and age of the authors, the significance of Near Eastern or Far Eastern materials, along with a host of hazards endemic to such exploratory efforts.

Twenty years ago it was believed that every college student should read Melville's *Moby-Dick*. Furthermore, part of the education based on art novels like *Moby-Dick* unconsciously included a component of initiation which more or less informed students that they had most fortunately been transformed into a superior species—the college-educated person. Regretfully, the college graduate learned little from the academic process that would prepare him or her for the world that awaited. Looking ahead from 1993, we must take cognizance of the fact that we can, as a society that faces some severe social, political and economic problems, no longer afford to dally with four years of our young people's lives. It may be regrettable that *Moby-Dick, Great Expectations,* and *Look Homeward, Angel* may become materials for specialists; but, our student in introductory literature courses will be reading Alice Walker, Norman

Mailer, Erica Jong and Stephen King. If our loss will be the knowledge of Captain Ahab and his mythic descent into the maelstrom, the significant gain will be a knowledge of why Alice Walker ends *The Color Purple* on the 4th of July. Our students will learn of Juneteenth and its relationship to the graphic scene of reconciliation and harmony between the sexes and the races that underlies that novel's powerful conclusion. We all need to see and understand the continuity between Frederick Douglass' 1850's condemnation of the Fourth of July and the conclusion of the 1985 Walker novel. If we do not start recognizing, accepting and teaching the plenitude of the new American mythos, we shall all before long join Ahab in a long, mad descent. We must seize our greatest resource—a plenteous imagination that feeds both our culture and the larger global culture both through time and distance—and convert that rich plenitude into a viable pluralism that acknowledges and values those continuities.

Then we need to develop that knowledge of our rich microcosm into its inevitable extension. We must deepen and extend the Humanities in all cultures as the end result of the internationalizing of Popular Culture Studies. This will explain ourselves and our cultures and in so doing domesticate and control the giant forces that will be unleashed in the development of the future powerful electronic world and its resulting power in the human potential.

The transition to the developing potential of the international Humanities can be smooth or bumpy depending on our understanding. Incomplete comprehension will surely result in dysfunction and the probable dysgenic dislocation of the world's population with all the convulsions such chaos could bring.

Full comprehension, on the other hand, can serve as a radar screen, a lightning rod and a peace-maker. It can be a screen to tell us of the troubles and stop them before they erupt. With these three assistances it will still require the most artful brinkmanship to avoid catastrophe; without them the boiling cauldron is dangerous indeed, always with the potential to splash its fire over the edges or to spill itself entirely in a giant holocaust.

Popular culture is the *lingua franca* of the world, already, and its universality and acceptability is gaining credibility every day. For better or worse it is the culture, it is the Humanities; it is a language the people who are gaining power everyday understand. People in power ignore this given only at their peril.

The essays in this book represent only a fraction of the possible studies that are needed for a reasonable understanding of the way popular culture builds on the past and prepares for the future, on how the present stands on the shoulders of the past and provides the shoulders on which the future will stand. With the insights gained from these studies, however, considerable preparation can be gained for future examinations.

In the first essay, Nadine Brewer faces us with perhaps the most promising fact and potential of our present and future—the unleashing of female importance and power. The path has been narrow and unsure, but it seems now that the Genie has been freed from the kitchen and bedroom, and with unforeseeable consequences. In the second essay David Crouch develops the ever-growing realization of the importance of cultural geography, environment, land use, landscape and ecology through the raising of it to an iconic level in popular culture studies. In the third essay, Margaret King points out how the whole world is going a-theming and basing the movement on the vision of Walt Disney in foreseeing the importance of the theme part in mankind's serious leisure activity. More immediate in the everyday experience of all of us is popular music. The three essays on the subject demonstrate that though the world is beginning to flash on the magic of the microchip it still moves and will continue to move on the wings of song.

Continuing to be among the most important media Will Rockett and David Prindle, in the fifth and sixth essays, talk about the symbiotic relationship, between the movie screen and television, their distinctions and relationships, especially on American politics. One particular selection, that is the similarity between the Western and some Vietnam films, is the subject of the next paper. The medium, though somewhat different in subject matter, continues in the next paper, which develops one of the more persistent seeming aberration in Fundamentalist religious fervor, the handling of snakes.

The next series of papers touches on the ever-present power of the spoken and written word. The politics of language as exercised by Noah Webster reveals a side of America's first lexicographer most people ignore. In the next essay Ray Browne develops the thesis that crime and detection writing, since it deals with one of the most fundamental aspects of society—violence and apprehension of the perpetrators—the genre novel of crime fiction is developing into general fiction. The next paper demonstrates how through one particular kind of novel, girl scouts, society "constitutes itself through literary representation."

The final three papers develop several aspects of folk culture, the first having to do with one particular family in the oil business when wildcatters could operate on the small scale. The next dovetails folk, popular and fine arts traditions into a pluralistic national tapestry, and in the final we ride away on totems and fetishes in biker culture.

In short, here is a computer chip of essays which together and separately constitute a comprehensive probing into future developments in popular culture studies. The past is the base of a pyramid that will always reach skyward. The upward reach needs guidance. These essays suggest ways and means that guidance might take.

A New Pair of Spectacles

NADINE BREWER

In any study of the importance of the past on the present and future, it is perhaps most appropriate to begin with women's role in society, since it is through them, many people would insist, that there is a present or a future for humankind. Some people—women and men—insist that in Woman's constant battle for equality in opportunity and acknowledged achievement there is a need for new evaluations and claims: "Woman starts at an advanced point if she recognizes that she has always been closer to her goal of equality than some may have appreciated," urges Nadine Brewer in the following article. She presents convincing evidence to prove her thesis.

I am not tragically colored. There is no great sorrow damned up in my soul, nor lurking behind my eyes. I do not mind at all. I do not belong to the sobbing school of Negrohood who hold that nature somehow has given them a lowdown dirty deal and whose feelings are all hurt about it.... No, I do not weep at the world—I am too busy sharpening my oyster knife.

Zora Neale Hurston
How It Feels To Be Colored Me

The French poet Paul Valéry once described art—or literature—as "a pair of spectacles through which we see the world." That is probably as good an analogy as any and might also apply to the manner in which we utilize history and social analysis; but if those spectacles, fitted to one perspective (or era, or tribe, or school of thought, or gender), are passed from one to another without adjustment, the vision resists focus or deforms; in either instance, the image becomes distorted. Such distortion has too long persisted in most considerations of Woman's image in history and literature—and I use the singular of "woman," because her story, or "our story," is and must be collective (Sochen). I foresee no clearly focused feminine image, no portrait of Woman, until "we [all] have faces," to borrow C.S. Lewis' astute title, and until we "speak to the condition of every woman, whatever her main concerns," in order to lend fine distinction to all our faces (Castro 256). It may well be time to exchange the lenses that we have used since the sixties, for the most part, for new ones. Indeed, we were ready for new ones even then, as research has shown.

The current feminist movement, that which we have experienced over the past two-plus decades, was not born in 1963 with the publication of *The Feminine Mystique* (as crucial as that work may be), but the revolutionary approach to women's concerns was probably necessary at that time; that is, the first step in any successful revolution—"that the idea of freedom and the experience of a new beginning should coincide," in the words of Hannah Arendt—is to snag attention, usually by centering on the negative (Arendt 29). The 1960s' revolution underscored the inequity, the suppression, the abuse that women had suffered for too long (just as the American Revolution underscored the abuses of King George), then quickly moved from revolt—the bra-burning stage—to the "rights-of-man" stage. After that, the stages began to get a bit fuzzy, normal for most revolts: groups that had worked together for a united cause disbanded, and women went home to work singly or in smaller coalitions; some women involved themselves in other causes, such as the protest against the Vietnam War and/or support for Civil Rights; others fought for status in previously taboo roles, such as that of the clergy in many denominations; and still others for free day care and abortion. Any attendant cause seemed fuel for the major issue—equality for Woman.

It was during that period that Women's Studies were introduced on many campuses, *Ms.* magazine was founded, NOW was born, the Equal Employment Opportunity Act was enacted, *Roe vs. Wade* established precedent, Shirley Chisholm declared herself a candidate for the Democratic Party nomination for president, Ella Grasso became the first woman to be elected as a state governor without dependence on her husband's name, and women's history gained attention. It was also that period that saw a renewed push for an Equal Rights Amendment. Then, as ratification failed, anti-feminism gained and New Feminism seemed to lose impetus. Many feminists, worried by the seeming quiet, felt that the movement was dying; many still do, pointing out that the market place has lost glamour, struggles for equal pay and benefits are usually limited to single cases, Anita Hill's voice was ignored, and Women's Studies programs are being canceled. Some also note with horror increasing glances back to the fifties with Jane Fonda's recent decision to "spend time taking care of her man" and a resurgence of interest in writers such as Helen Gurley Brown. In many ways, New Feminism seems to be on hold.

Interestingly, these circumstances mirror those immediately

following the passing of the nineteenth amendment: historians and Suffragists thought that the "women's movement fell apart after 1920," but they were mistaken, as are many now: far from dying, the 1920s' movement "splintered into a variety of causes—pacifism, professional politics, business and professional interests," and a myriad of social objectives (Ware 88). However, as the lack of united fervor was reinforced bit by bit by the "New Woman," Brett Ashley, Daisy Buchanan, Jean Harlow, Blondie and Stella Dallas, dreams of ever securing ratification, equity and role modification diminished. Nevertheless, the goddess was not dead, just wounded, as Annis Pratt points out (Pratt 117). The groundswell that began long before Seneca Falls and provoked the movement early in this century had archetypal birthmarks that we are only now beginning to discover.

Those birthmarks have been carefully highlighted by the refocusing of women's history in recent years: well researched books have literally created publishing history, in both numbers of works and quality; essays have incited interest in previously forgotten writers; novels and poetry collections have been reissued. Yet, in most universities, American Literature course offerings are still dominated by the same few male writers, and Women's Studies are too often token courses. In other arenas, such as the Aspen Institute readings, the few works included by women are those such as "Women and the Law," which points out that in the Constitution women were and are refused the right to public speech, but totally ignores that *in fact* women were and are speaking out.

There are various reasons for such a state of affairs, but is it just possible that women have been reinforcing that state? Are we, as women—by refusing to look beyond the image, by focusing on the negative in women's history and on "protest writers"—falling to establish an image of our own? A clearly focused, creative, integrated force who does not need to prove her equality to anyone? Indeed, is it possible that, in our defensiveness and rush to prove that women are as "equal as men," we are still accepting the patriarchal definition of "hero?" And, in doing so, are we rejecting selected images, "faces," as being less heroic than others?

The search in America into women's history actually began early in this century and manifested itself in the various branches of popular media, where it may have gone unheeded because of its small but undying voice. Much as some would like to forget the occasion, Mother's Day, begun in 1907, seems to have set off the popular search. It was also about that time that many states began acknowledging heroic deeds by females, most of them Frontier heroes. By 1927, Brant Baker had completed his striking sculpture, *Pioneer Woman*, in Oklahoma City; and in 1935 a monument was erected to Jane Todd Crawford, "Heroine of the Wilderness," in Danville, Kentucky, an occasion enlightened by Dr. Stewart Roberts' address: "Perhaps she had something that we have lost for awhile and may well regain" (Stewart Roberts). (At the same time, women such as Edna St. Vincent Millay, Pearl S. Buck, Lillian Hellman, Georgia O'Keeffe, Patsy Montana and Mother Maybelle Carter were making great strides in art, literature and popular music.)

Even though much of that early recognition may have seemed token and did not right many wrongs, nor result in social/economic transformation as we might have wished, it signaled a beginning. Moreover, it is fitting that those first honored were from the Frontier because, with the penning of John Filson's sketch of Daniel Boone in 1784, a legend leaped to life that in time would take on the proportions and force of an Homeric epic, a legend that would become one of the most powerful myths in history—the myth of the American Frontier Hero.

Unfortunately, women, whom A.B. Guthrie calls the "unsung heroes of the great movement to the West," were not hailed as a part of that myth, though they certainly helped to create it (Guthrie 54). A few eighteenth-century captive narratives, some later dime-novel adventures of Annie Oakley and Calamity Jane, and some degrading tales from the Crockett Almanacs about one-eyed backwoods belles who wore buffalo skin petticoats and wrestled bears barehanded just about complete the nineteenth-century published lists of women's "Frontier lore." Frederick Jackson Turner added insult to injury in 1893 when he totally ignored the existence and influence of women on the Frontier. There were few stories portraying women as Woman, possessing the strength, daring, integrity and sense of destiny demonstrated by those long hunters, scouts, mountain men, wagon masters, cowboys and lawmen who have fashioned the yardsticks against which much of our behavior is measured. However, we know that women in the Western states were managing their own businesses and ranches, running their own newspapers and living self-directed lives long before Eastern women were able to vote (Myres 268).

Some of the statistics are truly amazing: in 1886, one-third of the land in the Dakotas was held by women—though it was technically against the law for women to own property; by the end of the nineteenth century, 1,238 women were engaged in publishing and printing and 1,127 were compository linotype operatives and typesetters in 11 Western states. "So diverse were Western women's interests, that the 1900 census revealed that in addition to the expected milliners, dressmakers, laundresses and teachers, Western women were employed as bank officials [some ran their own banks], wholesale merchants, butchers, blacksmiths, lighthouse keepers and 'boatmen' " (Myres 265-68). Many more owned and ran hotels and boarding houses, managed homesteads as did Polly McChesney in Winston Churchill's *The Crossing*, or worked as traders as did Debby in Constance Skinner's *Debby Barnes, Trader.*

On the original Western Frontier, Kentucky, women were earning college degrees—the University of Kentucky was one of the first state universities to open its doors to women—and by 1930, Census Records show that women outnumbered men in professional jobs. Indeed, the number of Kentucky women in professions was five times the national average and, despite the exodus set off by the Depression and the displacement by returning war heroes, 1950 records reveal that women retained 42 percent of those positions, though they represented only about 30 percent of the state's labor force (United States Census Records). Descendants of those early Frontier heroes, though "usually ignored in histories," twentieth-century Kentucky women simply demonstrated their hardy beginnings:

But to learn of a woman migrant on horseback fording a swift river, one child in her arms and one hanging on behind her, to find other women improvising a substitute for flax, defending a fort under siege, or fighting off Indian attackers, is to see women as active participants in the rough, precarious life of the settlements. Visible or not, "refined" or not, women helped settle the Kentucky frontier. And in doing so, many showed resourcefulness and courage that are seldom remembered. (Irvin 1)

But despite their demonstrated courage, the perceived *image* of Kentucky heroes does not match reality, because they were and are *ordinary women*, perhaps not as visible as Amelia Earhart, Eleanor Roosevelt, Jessie Lopez de la Cruz or Antonia Brico—those who could rival the male "hero"—but certainly as heroic.

For too long we failed to note that heroism. In our search into women's history we seemed to swing from one extreme to the other; that is, when not pointing out how abused women were, we searched for those few who ventured far beyond what had been women's roles, ignoring the heroism of those who stayed home, viewing them sunk in the "cult of domesticity." Thus, the heroism that remained in the every day, the expected, such as the holding together of a family by running a boarding house or managing an eggs-and-butter business, was seldom noted. Yet, those women shaped our schools, our churches and our businesses—indeed, our very lives, as recent research reveals.

Thanks to the works of Sandra Myres, Susan Ware, Anne Scott,

Shirley Abbott, Helen Deiss Irvin, Linda Kerber, Julie Roy Jeffrey, Judith Plaskow, and truly a host of others, we know that nineteenth-century "domesticity described the norms and not the actual conduct of women" (Jeffrey 10). "The *reality* of women's lives changed dramatically as a result of adaptation to frontier conditions while the public *image* remained static.... Most women simply could not afford the luxury of the pedestal" (Myres 7). As to history's failure to paint an honest picture of women, Julie Roy Jeffrey writes that "some [historians] noted in passing that the frontier produced the new democratic woman as it fostered the new democratic man (and pointed to victories for female suffrage there).... Few paid much attention to the records left by the women themselves" (Jeffrey xii). Indeed, few thought that women had left any records of import:

It is generally thought that...women are sunk forever in statistical anonymity, poor faceless creatures lost in columns of figures...there are rich lode's of original materials pertaining to women's history in the National Archives. (Purdy 41)

Those "rich lode's" counter the image of women during the Depression and World War II, also. Susan Ware claims that "women fared better than men during the Depression" and that they "played a critical role in holding families together against the disintegrating forces of the Depression" (17-21). Some will say that "holding families together" was in "woman's sphere" and does not count, therefore, as heroism. But as long as we refuse to recognize female heroes, no matter what sphere they choose to work in, we shall suffer from a distorted image, a fragmented sisterhood and confused role models from which to form a Selfhood. That is, the "naming of reality" must be "grounded in community," a community of acceptance (Welch 337). Judy Chicago's *Dinner Party* makes the same point:

Sadly most of the 1038 women included in the Dinner Party are unfamiliar, their lives and achievements unknown to most of us. To make people feel worthless, society robs them of their pride: this has happened to women. All the institutions of our culture tell us—through words, deeds and even worse silence—that we are insignificant. *But our heritage is our power* (emphasis mine). (241)

American women, no matter what frontier they worked on, have always been "many-faced" and, as well as factory laborers, journalists, cotton pickers and housemaids, *were* wives and mothers and cooks and laundresses—just as surely as Odysseus and Daniel Boone were husbands and fathers and hunters and carpenters. And, a look through new glasses at Woman's past, our past, may well reveal that by the time of the Great Depression, she had already clearly set down her definition of heroism through her literature.

In *Womanspirit Rising,* Carol Christ restates John Ruskin's observation concerning the symbiotic nature of society and literature: "Stories shape experience; experience shapes stories." Speaking to women of Appalachia, she goes on to declare that they need to hear the "stories of others, to reconnect with their own folk history, in order to free [themselves] from social, religious and conjugal bondage" (Christ 229). And indeed, she is pointing out what women writers have been doing for the past 80 years—writing the stories of women; women who were surely moving from an image created and defined by men and social dicta to being self-directed creators of their own lives and stories. Because, if historians and sociologists were misreading women's lives, women writers were not: writers such as Elizabeth Madox Roberts, Zora Neale Hurston, Olive Tilford Dargan, Zona Gale, Sarah Orne Jewett, Ellen Glasgow, Edna Ferber, Sheba Hargreaves, Vingie Roe, Harriette Arnow, Lillian Smith, Margaret Walker, Constance Skinner and, of course, Willa Cather, set down the stories of Woman who stood apart from the distortion of a "feminine mystique" or "cult of domesticity," who contrasted sharply with the image of women depicted by most male and some female writers. Stark and ugly at times, the stories of these authors portray women as capable, strong, risk-taking individuals in body, mind, spirit and emotion. And, curiously enough, it is through their very womanhood, the rituals of that womanhood, and an intense awareness of sisterhood, that they arrive at a sense of Selfhood, independence and power. In other words, they do not abandon their own identities, nor do they go outside everyday life to perform heroic acts—no more than did those early Frontier heroes.

With the exception of Cather, these authors did not find much welcome in literature classes, for various reasons: they were dubbed "regional" or "historical"—despite the fact that nothing was more regional than *Mainstreet* or *The Sound and the Fury,* and little more historical than *The Sun Also Rises* and *The Great Gatsby;* some, such as Giles, Ferber, Hargreaves, Skinner, Gale, Hurston and Roe were "popular," whereas others, such as Roberts, were too "literary"; some addressed questionable issues, such as Socialism and miscegenation, as did Dargan, Smith and Roberts; and some, such as Hurston and Margaret Walker, had as their heroes black women; and all their works were pejoratively labeled "love stories," though that theme predominated much more in the works of

Fitzgerald and Hemingway than in the works of these women. The principal misconception was that, since most of the works—"literary" or not—were widely read and popular, it was too easy to categorize them as "sentimental" novels written by "sentimental women." And that view persisted amongst academicians, despite the accolades and awards: even Book-of-the-Month-Club selections, Pulitzers and Pulitzer nominations did not win slots in courses.

The criticism that these works did not deal with great, earth-shaking, universal themes does not hold either. What they did not deal with were great scenes of war and destruction, "wastelands," bloody prohibition feuds, the New Deal, presidents, "flappers," expatriots or Christie's "American Girl." What they did deal with was the growth of consciousness, self-affirmation, the refusal to weaken before destiny and society's inequities, and the "soul's relationship to fate"—all on the individual level:

What was true in the world of literature was even more vindictively true in the world of actuality. There, even when the awareness of the desperate need for changing the economic and social arrangements was coupled with an awareness of the worth of the individual who was a victim of the existing order, the tendency was to accept the graph, the statistic, the report of a commission, the mystique of "collectivism," as the final reality. The result was that, in that then fashionable form of either-or thinking, the inner world of individual experience was as brutally ignored as by an overseer on a Delta cotton farm. (Warren 38)

Robert Penn Warren was writing of Elizabeth Madox Robert's first novel, *The Time of Man* (1926), a Book-of-the-Month-Club selection and hailed by Ford Maddox Ford as "the most beautiful piece of writing to come out of America." Sherwood Anderson declared that "no one in America [was] doing such writing," and many critics consider the book to be one of the ten finest American novels (Slavick viii). But despite its prestige and popularity, it soon went out of print. It and another of her novels, *The Great Meadow,* touted the best novel of the great drama of the Kentucky Wilderness and nominated for the 1930 Pulitzer, have recently been reissued. Another, *My Heart and My Flesh,* in J. Donald Adams' words, the book that "reduces Faulkner to melodramatic claptrap," and which approaches "Dostoyevsky in psychological intensity," is soon to be reissued (Adams 86). Both books, as do all of Roberts' works, concern the growth of a single consciousness—individual, spiritual and social evolution; and Warren is accurate in signaling such emphasis as provoking their brief printing history, but that is not the only reason: their heroes are *ordinary women,* and their heroics do not include "killing bears and Germans, rescuing women from other men, and scoring touchdowns" (Pearson and Pope 6). Instead, they include mothers, wives, protectors, rescuers and bread-winners.

Ellen Chesser, protagonist of *The Time of Man,* is the only surviving child of itinerant farmers. Her story is that of the growth of selfhood, of *beingness,* in a world that does not accord her any value. She is "the voice out of the soil" (Roberts' notes); and her only possession is an implacable belief in her own "I am" (*Time* 9, 73). Ellen is Woman on the edge of change; her world offers no promise and no certainties. She constantly seeks role models, women to "tell things to," to share dreams with, but as soon as one is found, she gets married and snaggle-toothed, kills herself over an unfaithful husband or gives up—"her broken hair hanging in oily strings around her forehead"—as has Ellen's mother (*Time* 27, 77). Nevertheless, via true Bakhtinian dialogism, Ellen integrates outer events with her inner strength until she is wholly integrated, body, mind and spirit; and finally, it is she who singlehandedly rescues her husband from an angry masked mob. Like Emily Dickinson's bee (and like Zora Neale Hurston), Ellen Chesser does not separate experience into acceptable and unacceptable—"a clover any time to [her] is aristocracy"—and her story ends on a note of transcendence, "The honey of life in her heart" (*Time* 379); one who does not need to ask another for her "turnings" (395).

Ellen's "twin," Theodosia (*My Heart and My Flesh*), begins as her opposite; that is, she has everything an old family of the Old South can offer. Then it is all taken away. She, as all of Roberts' heroes, must fully develop her own wholeness, her "I am," before she can enjoy any true worth.

The entirety of Roberts' *oeuvre* concerns the growth of Woman. Lewis P. Simpson observes that Roberts' heroes take on "classical, mythical proportions" and views her image of the spinning spider of the female mind as "God symbolized as feminine mind" (cited in Slavick xvii). Whether or not it is "God" who is symbolized, it is Woman who is Creator. In *He Sent Forth a Raven,* Roberts' last novel (1938), the protagonist Jocelle draws "life out of Wolflick [farm] where a lonely tomb closed over" (*Raven* 255). And Diony, hero of *The Great Meadow* and named for the Titan Dione, makes the long trek through the Gap and "creates a world out of chaos," beginning the saga in the Wilderness; Ellen poses the "bare breath in the throat" of the American Woman, and Roberts' subsequent heroes face the problems of history, tradition, the "voices" of society and patriarchal rigidity. Their successes are founded not on defensiveness and causes, but on a simple belief in themselves, their lives, their "sisters," and the ability to take control. Throughout it all, it is Woman who creates her own destiny, chooses her mate. And it is she who determines the direction of the future: in other words, "Men brag aroun' a power about subduin' o' a frontier, but after all, hit's the Marthies...that actually do the subduin' " (Hargreaves 341).

Vingie Roe, whose Sandra Dehault declares equality and recalls both *Jane Eyre* and *Daniel Deronda* —"a woman is a human, same as a man" (*The Splendid Road* 166)—wrote only "popular" fiction, as did Hargreaves and Janice Holt Giles. (Indeed, Giles, like Ferber, made a small fortune with her novels.) Giles' most famous hero, Hannah Fowler, is one of the first women on the early Frontier, a large, plain woman reared and trained by her father Samuel, whose story begins in 1778. Hannah is a true Frontier woman who can track and farm as "well as any man," who proposes to her choice of husband, who saves herself and unborn child from Indians, and who has as her dearest friend Jane Manifee, Frontier hero and crack shot. Hannah and Tice, her husband, share many jobs, even the care of the children. And Hannah is a woman in every sense of the word, one who, though totally self-sufficient, enjoys love-making as much as she enjoys farming and who is ashamed neither of her feelings nor of her difference:

She could walk all day on the track of game, and loved to. She could swing an axe and fell a tree as swiftly and as expertly as Samuel. She could wrestle a plow from sun-up to sun-down behind a team of oxen. She could lift and work and endure, alone or beside a man. But, she reckoned, for all a woman could do what a man could do, she was different inside. She, Hannah, loved a house-place, too, and a fire on a hearth, and the clack of a loom...(Giles 53)

...they's just times when I look at him an'...I could jist sink down from the weakness inside of me.... That's the way I feel sometimes, like my bones had turned to jelly, an' a shiver had run up my back and made me have cold-bumps all over my arms. That's what love makes you feel like, Janie Fowler. (Giles 220)

Hannah made that eloquent speech to her eldest daughter, Janie, then still in the cradle. Her sense of clarity and independence never leave her, qualities she passes on to all of her children. Her youngest daughter, Rebecca, hero of *The Believers,* becomes the first Kentuckian to avail herself of the new divorce law (1809), when her husband joins Mother Anne Lee's Shaker Movement. Deploring the fact that "a woman is bound...to whatever her man wants" (Giles 222), Rebecca announces her decision to divorce to her "traditional" mother who, upon hearing that Rebecca's husband Richard no longer makes love to his wife, declares that "the most unnaturalest thing I ever heard of" and supports her daughter's divorce (Giles 296).

Hannah may seem extraordinarily liberated for the early Frontier, but those early women were decidedly more so than those who came later. Harriette Arnow evinces regret for the American Woman's life in the nineteenth century in her declaration that she hated to "emerge from the Eighteenth Century," because "life was better for women way back then" (Eckley 124). That is why few realistic female heroes appear in literature before early in this century. Nicholas Karolides, in his study of the pioneer in the American novel, does not note a startling change until after 1920 in the portrayal of women as heroes (which would accord with public recognition of women). However, it is truly a notable change:

She has developed in the literature from a two-dimensional doll to a heroine who is full of life and a large enough figure to meet its challenges...It is she who is the builder, the creator, the vital strength.... Another variant in the presentation of the heroine is her attitude towards herself. Her concept of her role in the group, and her acceptance of herself change in the passing years. (Karolides 96-98)

Therefore, if Hannah seems "liberated," so do all heroes of the authors I have listed: Ellen Glasgow's Dorinda Oakley chooses not to marry at all, preferring to manage the farm, much as Willa Cather's Alexandra Bergson, who does finally decide to marry—after the farm is highly successful. Margaret Walker's Vyry, a freed slave who suffers with her family and is burned out twice in the white backlash following the Emancipation Proclamation, chooses between her two husbands and gives lessons to the one of her choice in just exactly how a farm is to be run.

Ishma Waycaster, Dargan's hero in both *Call Home the Heart* and *A Stone Came Rolling* leaves her husband and child, because she can no longer stand the combined pressure of annual crop failure and the painful awareness that she is unlearned. Moreover, she leaves with another man, bears his child, and works in the Labor Movement before going home again to her family. Her husband, Brent, also "liberated," understands her need to bring about change. They work together, alongside their son, in the famous Gastonia Strike that helped legitimize labor unions. These two major works of Dargan (Fielding Burke) stand out amongst the novels of the 1930s, and could indeed have been published simultaneously with *The Color Purple* and *Alice Doesn't Live Here Anymore*. (Fortunately, the earlier and better of the two was reissued by the Feminist Press in 1983.)

Ishma is a large enough hero to fill the space of two novels, as is Harriette Arnow's Gertie Nevels in *The Dollmaker.* Gertie seems a later edition of Millie Ballew, hero of Arnow's *Hunter's Horn,* much as all of

Roberts' heros seem developed versions of Ellen Chesser. Millie has no more choices than does Ellen; the wife of a mountaineer also trapped by his place in history, Millie represents what *is*, the static social and economic reality of the 1920s. And, she *endures*. Gertie, on the other hand, though the mainstay of the family as is Millie, is forced to adapt to a changing world when her husband, Clovis, takes a job and moves the family to Detroit. On a new "frontier," Gertie is lost; she longs for home where she had found peace in nature and was needed by her family. Her conflict is emblemed in her art: a native carver, Gertie has been for some time carving a figure—presumably a head of Christ—which has no features and for which she seeks a model. The figure is a metaphor for her search for meaning and, much as she rejects every face as being worthy, she rejects the possibility that a meaningful life can be found in the dirty, screeching city. Her frontier, then, is not only the city with its strange mix of people, but her own self-centeredness, her reluctance to let go of the past and its certainty. It is in listening to the stories and pain of others, in the *sharing of experiences,* that she finds a common bond by which she transcends her own feelings of alienation. As a final gesture, she rends in two the sculpture on which she has labored for so many years.

Carol Pearson and Katherine Pope see Gertie's gesture as an admission of defeat, as a denial of her own worth and dignity. However, Wilton Eckley, biographer and friend of Arnow, sees the reverse: that is that, in Gertie's daughter's words, she is "letting her out." No longer bound by an ideal and unrealistic hope, Gertie is free and realizes that even her very human, inelegant neighbors "would ha done" as models (*Dollmaker* 549). I agree with Eckley that Gertie, faced with a new "frontier" and change, must re-affirm Woman's power in society on that new frontier and, in doing so, must relinquish patterns of the past and learn to *accept all faces.* Gertie understands at last that her failure to find an acceptable face turns not on the inferiority of the models, but on *her own faulty vision.*

In her enlightening book, *The Psychic Grid,* philosopher Beatrice Bruteau writes that to change the image is to open up an "alternative state of consciousness. Self-images, group images, historical images deliberately are altered in this process, with a resulting shift, first of emotional stresses, then of behaviors, and finally of institutions" (207). Which is to say that a periodic readjustment of our spectacles can change our reality. Perhaps it is time to change the images we hold of our foremothers, to welcome—without stridency, defensiveness, or excuse—*all of their stories* and to reconnect to our own folk history, so that we may witness that resulting shift. One way to such accomplishment is to honor our sisters in all their endeavors, as have Judy Chicago, Marisol Escobar and Isabel Bishop in their art. Another way is to read and introduce the strong voices of historians and novelists. As Annis Pratt says, "[women novelists] have made of the women's novel a pathway to the authentic self, to the roots of ourselves beneath consciousness of self, and to our innermost being" (178).

Another manner of deliberately changing our own vision is to be a bit more flexible and curious in considering "popular" rituals and customs: at large family reunions—and often at church affairs—in the South, men have traditionally been served before women and children; "Take an Old Cold 'Tater and Wait," as Little Jimmie Dickens sings. That custom has often been hailed by feminists as an example of women's submission and oppression. However, according to my own years of research into both written and oral histories, it is more likely that the "tradition" grew directly out of a combination of two other formalities of Frontier life, the most familiar that of a scout or hunter returning to a fort or stopping by a cabin. No matter what hour of day or night he arrived, he was served something to eat while everyone gathered around to hear the latest news—he was a sort of Frontier MacNeil-Lehrer.

The second convention is probably the more influential, though many male and feminist writers, and many "outlanders," would fail to recognize it—that that grew out of women's deep need for the company of other females. Women suffered so terribly from isolation on the Frontier that when they gathered with their semblables they wanted only to engage in "woman talk." Feeding the men and getting them quickly out of the way served to lengthen time spent in like company and eventually established a ritual. Besides, women were probably as bored with talk of crops, hunting and war as men were of quilts, weaving and babies. Shirley Abbott puts it well:

...sisterhood was nothing new to me. It has been a zealously guarded secret among Southern women for years. Next to motherhood, sisterhood is what they value most, taking an endless pleasure in the daily, commonplace society of one another that they never experience in male company. (167)

Careful research often yields contradictory messages and, when dealing with women's history and literature, we must carefully search out those contradictions. Those women who may *to us* appear too traditional, powerless, and *obeisant* to the system, may have in reality been role models for young women longing to be liberated, as was young Sarah Perkins—born in 1909 to poor Kentucky sharecroppers (a true-to-life Ellen Chesser)—who went to the city in 1925 to work as a housemaid:

I looked around and saw women starting shops and running farms. Becoming strong. Owning property. Women had got tired of being pushed off into the background. I always looked up to people, especially women, who bettered theirselves. I thought, "If she can do it, so can I." Even the tea parties helped, because I saw women in pretty dresses talking about things I'd never even heard of. I saw women becoming people I never thought they could become. By *theirselves.* (Perkins)

Sarah echoes a common refrain in the appraisals of American female "senior citizens" that I have interviewed. That is, what has often been perceived by my generation as ordinary, popular, or even sexist history, they perceived as "liberating." It is like the import of the successes of Mother Maybelle Carter or Patsy Montana: Maybelle became important in the late 1920s not because of what she sang but because of what she signaled in the professional field—she was on national radio, and that is what some 15 million young women from across the South recognized; and few cared that Patsy Montana sang "I Want To Be A Cowboy's Sweetheart," since she won a gold record in 1935. The negative impact seems to be a result of our perceptions, not of the facts. Alice Walker points out the same situation: when she went "searching for her mother's garden," she found the poetry of Phillis Wheatley, the black slave whose "Goddess" of "golden hair" imaged the Liberty refused her, an image that has "held Phillis up to ridicule for more than a century":

But at last, Phillis, we understand. No more snickering when your stiff, struggling, ambivalent lines are forced on us. We know now that you were not an idiot or a traitor; only a sickly little black girl...a woman who still struggled to sing the song that was your gift, although in a land of barbarians who praised you for your bewildered tongue. It is not so much what you sang, as that you kept alive, in so many of our ancestors, *the notion of song.* (237)

Whether actualized in popular novels, "literature," poetry, art or folk songs, that "notion of song" is our legacy, handed down by throngs who, as Zora Neale Hurston did not have time to bemoan her Negrohood, did not have time to bemoan their Womanhood. They were too busy "sharpening [their] oyster kni[ves]." They knew something we must never forget: that, to paraphrase ever-so-slightly Joseph Campbell, "the hero is the champion of things becoming, not of things become, because [s]he *is*" (Campbell 258).

That notion is also our future. Woman *is* and is becoming. That the novels of Alice Walker, Toni Morrison, Marge Piercy and many others have received honors is a true gain; that Woman is fully accepted in all facets of the film industry is wonderful; that Woman is viewed as a fully developed sexual being is hopeful; that those like Judith Christ, Carol Gilligan and Starhawk have reaffirmed the status of Woman is necessary. However, that Woman is still treated as "other" in academic circles, the political arena and in the courts remains to be rectified, and it is probably up to her to do so by accepting her own history and lore—and by communicating that history and lore to her sisters.

In other words, Woman starts at an advanced point if she recognizes that she has always been closer to her goal of equality than some may have appreciated. As Anne Schaef says, "We are [and have been] all engaged in a long and difficult process of *growth* and evolution. It is time to describe, affirm, and *grow*," a statement that echoes closely the story lines of those early novelists (Schaef ix). The past of Woman's creative endeavors, like Woman, is; it provides a wealth of experience and knowledge; it establishes precedence and undercuts the sad endings to the Anita Hill cases. Indeed, the fact is that others may admit Woman's history and equality more readily when Woman recognizes and appreciates it herself— and readjusts her spectacles so that all faces are both equal and heroic. Toni Cade Bambara issues the invitation in *The Salt Eaters* :

Knock and be welcomed in and free to roam the back hall on the hunt for that particular closet with the particular hanging robe, coat, mantle, veil or whatever it was. And get into it. Sport it. Parade around the district in it so folks [will] remember themselves. [Will] hunt for their lost selves (266).

Works Cited

Abbott, Shirley. *Womenfolks*. New York: Ticknor & Fields, 1983.

Adams, J. Donald. "Elizabeth Madox Roberts." *The Virginia Quarterly Review*. XII. Jan.-Oct. 1936.

_____. *The Shape of Books to Come*. New York: Viking P, 1934.

Arendt, Hannah. *On Revolution*. New York: Pelican, 1977.

Arnow, Harriette Simpson. *The Dollmaker*. New York: Macmillan, 1952.

_____. *Hunter's Horn*. New York: Macmillan, 1949.

Bambara, Toni Cade. *The Salt Eaters*. New York: Random House, 1980.

Bruteau, Beatrice. *The Psychic Grid*. Wheaton: The Theosophical Publishing House, 1979.

Burke, Fielding (Olive Tilford Dargan). *A Stone Came Rolling*. London: Longmans, Green, 1935.

_____. *Call Home The Heart*. London: Longmans, Green, 1932.

Campbell, Joseph. *The Hero With A Thousand Faces*. Princeton: Princeton UP, 1949.

24 Continuities in Popular Culture

Castro, Ginette. *Radioscopie du Féminisme Américain.* Paris: Presses de la Fondation nationale des Sciences Politiques, 1984.

Cather, Willa. *O, Pioneers.* Boston: Houghton Mifflin Co., 1913.

Chicago, Judy. *The Dinner Party.* New York: Anchor P/Doubleday, 1979.

Christ, Carol and Judith Plaskow. *Womanspirit Rising.* San Francisco: Harper & Row, 1979.

Eckley, Wilton. *Harriette Arnow.* New York: Twayne Publishers, Inc. 1974.

Ferber, Edna. *Cimarron.* Garden City, New York: Doubleday, Doran and Company, 1930.

Giles, Janice Holt. *The Believers.* Boston: Houghton Mifflin Company, 1957.

_____. *Hannah Fowler.* Boston: Houghton Mifflin Company, 1956.

Glasgow, Ellen. *Barren Ground.* Garden City, New York: Doubleday, Inc., 1925.

Guthrie, A.B., Jr. "The Historical Novel." *Western Writing,* ed. Gerald W. Haslam. Albuquerque: U of New Mexico P, 1974.

Hargreaves, Sheba. *The Cabin At the Trail's End.* New York: Harper Brothers, 1928.

Hurston, Zora Neale. *Their Eyes Were Watching God.* New York: Harper & Row, 1937.

Irvin, Helen Deiss. *Women in Kentucky.* Lexington: The UP of Kentucky, 1979.

Jeffrey, Julie Roy. *Frontier Women.* New York: Hill and Wang, 1979.

Karolides, Nicholas. *The Pioneer in the American Novel 1900-1950.* Norman: U of Oklahoma P, 1967.

Kerber, Linda D. and Jane De Hart Mathews. *Women's America.* New York: Oxford UP, 1982.

Myres, Sandra. *Westering Woman and the Frontier Experience.* Albuquerque: U of New Mexico P, 1982.

Pearson, Carol and Katherine Pope. *The Female Hero in American and British Literature.* New York: R.R. Bowker Company, 1981.

Perkins, Sarah (Ledbetter). Personal Interview. 14 August 1984.

Purdy, Virginia C. and Deutrich, Mabel E. *Clio Was A Woman.* Washington, D.C.: Howard UP, 1980.

Roberts, Elizabeth Madox. *The Great Meadow.* New York: The Viking P, 1930.

_____. *He Sent Forth a Raven.* New York: The Viking P, 1935.

_____. *My Heart and My Flesh.* New York: The Viking P, 1935.

_____. *The Time of Man.* Lexington: The UP of Kentucky, 1982.

Roberts' notes, most of which are held in the Library of Congress and the Appalachian Archives at the University of Kentucky, are in the process of being edited by William H. Slavick.

Roberts, Stewart. "Memorial Address." *Supplement to Kentucky Medical Journal.* 30 May 1935.

Roe, Vingie. *The Splendid Road.* New York: Duffield and Company, 1925.

Schaef, Anne Wilson. *Women's Reality.* San Francisco: Harper & Row, Publishers, 1981.

Skinner, Constance L. *Debby Barnes, Trader.* New York: Macmillan, 1932.

Slavick, William H. Introduction to *The Time of Man*. Lexington: The UP of Kentucky, 1982.

Smith, Lillian. *Strange Fruit*. New York: Reynal & Hitchcock, 1944.

Sochen, June. *Her story: A Woman's View of American History*. New York: Alfred Publishing Co., 1974.

Walker, Alice. *In Search of Our Mother's Gardens*. San Diego: Harcourt Brace Jovanovich, 1983.

Walker, Margaret. *Jubilee*. Boston: Houghton Mifflin Co., 1966.

Ware, Susan. *Holding Their Own: Women in the 1930's*. Boston: Twayne Publishers, 1982.

Warren, Robert Penn. "Life Is from Within." *The Saturday Review of Literature* 2 March 1963.

Welch, Sharon. "Ideology and Social Change." *Weaving the Visions*. Eds. Judith Plaskow and Carol P. Christ. San Francisco: Harper & Row, Publishers, 1989.

United States Census Records in the Louisville Public Library: Louisville, Kentucky.

Representing Ourselves in the Landscape: Cultural Meanings in Everyday Landscape

DAVID CROUCH

People on the land and their relationship to it has always been integral to human existence. How they work that land can be shaped not only by their idiosyncrasy but by their relationships with other people. The result is that their voices are heard and read, through the everyday landscapes they themselves create.

Allotments are those small plots of ground, ten by 30 yards in the U.K., where people grow vegetables and flowers on rented land. In the U.S.A. they are of a similar size and are called Community Gardens or Vacant Lot gardens, earlier Victory Gardens, a term that persists in New England and has been given national currency through educational television.[1] What is fascinating about these plots is that they have become part of popular culture, and have a very distinctive appearance. They are significant as icons, and for half a million families in Britain, part of everyday life. In the U.S.A. there are three million of these plots.

The position they occupy in British popular culture may seem obscure and idiosyncratic, but provides insight into the way we view landscape and how it is constructed in popular culture. The way people use allotment plots is to construct a landscape through *their own* popular culture. They may rework and recycle, adapt and convert what is made by commercial culture. For the plotholder, it is almost all "their own"; but the media, national companies and writers have taken them into different spheres. That makes the study of allotments of particular interest.

The position of allotments and community gardens in popular culture was very different a hundred years ago. Most plotholders were poor, and worked a plot because they needed the cheap food to live. They emerge in contemporary society as something people do from choice, not through necessity. There are aspects today of an inherited culture that is reworked through contemporary values and practice, indicative of the dynamic of popular culture. The reasons people have allotments has changed over the last century, yet there is a continuity in the social relations and cultural practice within which the activity happens. The landscape is a central, and informative, part of this culture.

The landscape is constructed by the people who work the plots. The owners of the land have little impact upon the landscape that is produced, except for the overall layout of the plots—familiar in Britain as in the U.S.A., in rectilinear pattern. Beyond that, there is no outside control. Plotholders use their plots when they can fit it in between other everyday events, but the position of the plot in their everyday life transcends the mundane. There are distinctive characteristics in the connections between this everyday culture and the way the landscape is made, and their interpretation in wider popular culture, that provides a fascinating case for our attention.

Making Landscapes?

The idea of landscapes in western culture is centered around consumption rather than production. A landscape appears as constructed by someone else: a company, a designer, a government, a wealthy owner, or by Nature. It is read as an icon of what people stand for, but rarely of an ordinary everyday culture; rather of someone else's idea: an image of the countryside; of the past; of a nation; an idea of a region's identity and heritage.

Translating these ideas into private gardens, these gardens are 'read' as landscape if they are seen to embody these wider notions; to imitate landscaped estates or display idiosyncratic personality, rather like the untutored landscape designer. The implications are of conscious presentation, for private or public enjoyment and consumption. This set of approaches is further embodied in the landscapes of mass culture in art, in greeting cards and paintings, as Martin Lindauer unwrapped in a recent issue of the *Journal of Popular Culture*. They are a widely enjoyed, but we consume "other people's icons" that are presented as landscapes. They are consumed as though a vital part of our shared identity, although they in fact relate to a rather limited set of positions in contemporary culture, notably of the elite.[2]

Thereby landscape becomes part of the high culture-low culture debate, in so far as who gives value to landscape. "Good landscape" is interpreted through particular icons. In Britain this is especially in terms of legitimate owners of large rural estates and the aesthetic ownership of architects. Glossy magazines interpret "the important" to a wider public.[3] Other kinds of places are regarded as "folksy," deprecated as local, and amusingly trivial. This is becoming more critical today as the event of the Theme Park and the reification of Heritage becomes pervasive; people even begin to use their own suburbs as Heritage event, as John Dorst has recently described. These are formula-led according to particular ideas of "consumer landscapes," and use crude assumptions of what people want, but bear little empirical and ethnographic evidence as to their value. Landscapes have come to be associated with leisure, created by somebody else, rather than products of the culture of people who use them, giving Sharon Zukin the term "landscapes of power." Landscape has slipped from the elite to the leisure business, but remains largely unexplored in terms of its place in popular culture.

People *do* make diverse use of landscape. The experience of walking in the countryside or city is varied, undertaken with a diversity of images, ideologies and expectations (Crouch). To what extent do landscapes figure as a component of our material culture in the everyday experience of ordinary people? Moreover, what form of representation do they take? J.B. Jackson directed attention to the unsung landscapes that are built, unselfconsciously, from the everyday activities and events of ordinary people, particularly through the shape of their towns—the accumulation of unspectacular artifacts that are actually meaningful in the expression of a culture.[4]

How these "self built" landscapes may be positioned within the everyday life of people who make them is considered through the example of the allotment/community garden. This is based on an extensive ethnographic study of allotment holding that investigates the construction of landscape through everyday cultural practices; ideologies and values, and social worlds of over 100 plotholders, and the visual ethnography of their landscape. An important part of this paper is the evaluation of how this ordinary world has been reinterpreted by a wider popular culture.[5]

A Distinctive Material Culture[6]

The rows of parallel rectangular plots, spaced evenly across an open space provide merely the basic structure of allotment landscapes. The space may be divided by hedgerows, dotted with trees, leftovers from earlier fields, or laid by a landlord to demarcate boundaries. The inventive structures are beyond this outline; sheds, huts and glasshouses; sticks and other plant supports; often with bizarre origins and imaginative application; corrugated iron sheeting and doors recycled from somewhere else. These features have a practical purpose in protecting, supporting and separating what is being grown; provide a place for storage and provide shelter for the plotholder.

The details of this landscape are provided by the material used; women's tights and old pipes; zinc foil and cut plastic bottles; compost containers made out of recycled wood and iron bars. The sheds are likely to be home-made and exhibit the wide limits of this eccentric landscape: wooden panels, multi-coloured wood from grocery boxes, railway sleepers and window frames from refurbished houses. Some material will have come from waste skips. The way people plant and work their land adds further to this rich variety of visual texture.

Allotments assume a whole range of visual identities. This is partly a result of their location—in villages, suburbs, and the inner city in the U.K., in city centres and spread across diverse parts of town in the U.S. Moreover, people are an important part of this landscape: not only in the features they make and place in their plots, but by virtue of their direct visible presence in working the landscape.

For many people these landscapes become a favoured place; an escape from the tumult, and isolation, of everyday life. However, this is not a negative escape. It replaces one set of activities with another; a freedom and liberation *chosen,* and shared, suggested in this poem by Tomlinson:

> these closer comities
> of vegetable shade,
> glass-houses, rows
> and trellises of redly
> flowering beans.
> This is a paradise....
> *John Maydew, or The Allotment.* Charles Tomlinson 1972

The culture of the allotment is distinguished by its origins. In Britain, this means a working class culture where mutual aid was strong. Particular rituals came to link their lack of material possessions, human agency and initiative with working together, and a co-operative interdependency, with self provisioning rather than consumption. These origins were found typically in rural Britain and in mining areas, a culture that has survived and been translated into diverse contemporary cultures across Britain.

People who needed a plot a century ago relied on what they could grow or make, to enable them to have something to give to friends, a *gift relationship* that established mutual aid, a practical device that helped them cope with surpluses and scarcities. Although there was frequently great pride in the home, there was also an element of the 'take us as you find us' tradition that eschews display. This resembles Goffman's category of *back* regions, as opposed to the fronts of our homes and other more public activities dominated by concern for display. These back regions he

Fig. 1 Landscape at Ponty Pridd Wales, UK 1986, David Crouch.

Fig. 2 Men share time at Ponders End, North London, 1987, David Crouch.

Fig. 3 Pigeon Loft, Co. Durham, 1986 Dave Thomas, kind permission of photographer.

Fig. 4 The bike is replaced increasingly by the car. The project remains the same. St. Albans UK. 1987 Author.

Fig. 5 Individuality and idiosyncrasy in sign. 1991. Maggie Lambert, by kind permission of photographer.

Fig. 6. Material on an allotment path, 1991. Maggie Lambert, kind permission of photographer.

argues, are "relative to a given performance, where the impression fostered by the performance is knowingly contradicted as a matter of course" (Goffman). The allotment provides the ideal place to "let your hair down"; expectations of behaviour are different. As *back regions*, allotments are out of the way; but they are at the centre of a way of life, where "signs no longer are to do with affluence, but are connected with a more relaxed attitude of apparently not thinking and not caring" (Garner). Architect Ray Garner regards the allotment shed as 'the most prolific and vigorous' remaining example, in Britain, of the self builder's art.

Its landscape reflects practical purpose, but the particular detail of the landscape reflects its cultural context. The original layout by the owner was intended to be strictly utilitarian, simply making the best of little space, to minimise investment in "charity"; a moral landscape for hard work. The plot size was big enough to answer the political agitation for land on which to grow food and keep the holder from the alehouse, but small enough not to require time away from the landlord's work. Today there is still hard work, but the users have taken control.

Today the co-operation between people working on an allotment is strong, evidenced in sharing plants, swapping hints and working together in making and repairing buildings; organising shows and giving away produce to the elderly. The everyday culture is supported by ritual; in particular ways of working land, times of planting and harvesting; the events surrounding the annual show. The setting in which these rituals takes place is socially disarming; there are no demands of Style in the contemporary sense, yet there is a ritual of wearing clothes that acknowledge that liberation and anti-Style atmosphere that surrounds the activity. Despite the ongoing chores, there is a sense of celebration too, as evidenced in this autobiographical account in the novel by the English Culture critic Raymond Wiliams:

...his grandfather had started on the strip again, raking and raking at the earth until it seemed he was trying to change its nature. Already there was nothing larger than a marble, but still, endlessly, the raking and fining went on. Though he said nothing, Will doubted whether in the growing it would make any difference. It was less this, he thought, than some ritual of service.... already the damp valley was thickening, and evening was drawing along the valley.
Raymond Williams, *Border Country* Chatto and Windus 1960

These events play an important and continuing part in the lives of the holders and their families, and underpin the collective character of this culture. Ruth Finnegan observed, in her study of amateur music making in

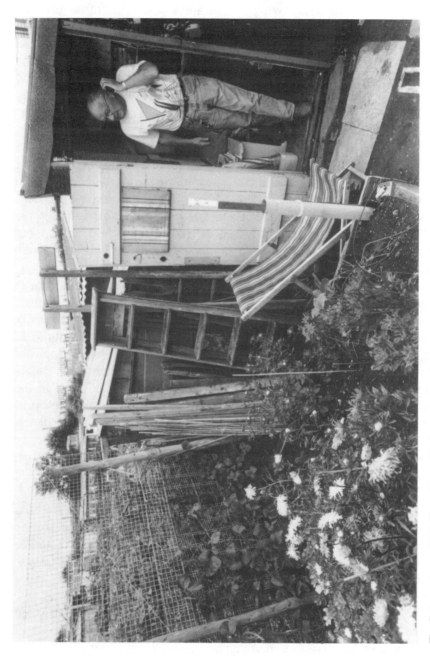

Fig. 7 A sanctuary. 1991. Peter Fryer. Kind permission of photographer. Newcastle, UK.

an English town, that leisure provides the setting for everyday life and culture in a way that often has been overlooked in the emphasis on *work* (Finnegan). And plotholding is fun, too, as one holder explained in these words: "I make an outing of going to my allotment; I take my lunch, and look forward to meeting friends": others said, "I spend half an hour working, half an hour talking when I am at my plot"; "it is the best way to catch up on local gossip"; "it's lovely just being there." These exchanges take place within a cultural context that is neither random nor ephemeral.

Co-operation and collective action were important in the political struggles that led to the provision of plots by landowners and charities, and remain significant in efforts to hold onto land when owners wish to sell, or in campaigning for more land. This has renewed their political radicalism. The significance of recycling is connected with a generally expressed weariness, even cynicism, for aspects of popular materialism. Holders often *prefer* to use material that has had another use; to invest energy and ingenuity rather than money. This is expressed clearly by people who are materially able to do without recycling: "The allotment is a great leveller: you all have the same sort of plot; you all pay the same rent." There are no barriers to participation [in some districts there are plots designed for the disabled too]. The allotment population today is diverse; still the majority is manual workers, but there are many professional and managerial people.

There is a shift from *need* to an ideology based on recycling, anti commercialism and a concern for the environment, health and particularly organic cultivation. The two sides, of need and ideology, are significant in one unusual example of *improvement* of an allotment site in the cathedral city of Durham, north east England. Located in a residential area that has been gentrified in recent years, with a growing population of middle income residents, the site is worked by a mix of social groups. They successfully campaigned, with widespread popular support, to avoid the owner, who happened to be the Church, selling the site for development in 1990. However, some of those leading this campaign sought to replace sheds they see as "tatty," because the site is prominent, is near the cathedral and city centre, and so argued to retain popular support with a more "attractive" site. People who have worked plots for years are bemused at this attitude, and sense the move to turn a working place [landscape] into a "pretty park." The middle class are of varied opinions on this, and as yet there is a dynamic stability between the two sides: some old sheds have been gentrified, other remain. Yet this example is more significant because it is unusual, and even here, there is a rapport amongst the members, and slow adaptation, rather than replacement. There is a strong continuity in the culture.

More widely across Britain, there is a frequently expressed pride in the landscape of these sites. People adorn their sheds with old couches and ornaments; materials are "arranged" with great care around the buildings, not thrown in a heap; flowers are encouraged. the plot itself provides a means of self expression and individualism. The growing of flowers traditionally underlined a gender stereotype: flowers, particular sweet peas and other scented or delicate varieties were grown for "the wife"; the men were really interested in the digging and in growing food. This underlay a wider gender division in allotment cultivation, where men left home on Sundays to spend the day at the plot, whilst the woman looked after the family. Men frequently came from a shared work environment, whose culture was extended, in a very different form, to the allotment. Whilst these patterns may have typified the earlier generations, today's plotholder is increasingly likely to be a woman. Especially but not exclusively from middle class homes, these women are championing their rights to grow food too; and to escape from the home. Their acceptance amongst men has been dramatic, and in places they have chosen to have their own competitive clubs for shows. In places, the gender roles have reversed. Amongst mining communities where redundancy has been significant in recent years, men work their plots whilst they "wait for the wife from work to bring home their pocket money to buy some more seed."

The allotment culture is increasingly multi-cultural, and this has introduced new sources of variation in the way land is worked, and has proven important in unselfconscious community development. Afro Carribean families visit their plot together, making huge changes in a short space of time; Chinese plotholders deploy their traditional skills in carefully terracing plots, making sophisticated structures to irrigate their land; people from Mediterranean countries bring their own skills of cultivation, using enormous amounts of compost on small spaces of land to produce high yields of beefsteak tomatoes and zucchini. Sam Bass Warner has traced seven distinctive cultures in growing crops from different groups of immigrants in the city of Boston, U.S.A. (Sam Bass Warner). In Eastern Europe since the war, allotments have been a popular form of cultural expression, a rare outlet for individuality and idiosyncrasy, expressed in the most extreme versions of shed construction.

Representation in other Popular Cultures

Other parts of popular culture have dealt with this phenomenon in a variety of ways. As may be expected, the peculiar cultural construction, often seen as radical or eccentric and wayward, is of curiosity. Alternatively, it may be ignored because it happens outside the familiar structures of cultural life; it may appear anachronistic. Surprisingly, it continues to reflect its powerful ideological position in society. More-over, there is a distinct change in its symbolism which demonstrates its dynamic power.[7] The distinctions between the symbolism used in America and in Great Britain are also instructive of how wider culture uses distinctive symbols from everyday life.

In Britain, allotments have passed through a period in the 1950s, a time of rising popular wealth, when a still familiar image was pervasive. This was an image seen through a grainy winter landscape, with straggling vegetables occupying the view. An old, unemployed labourer is seen wearing a cloth cap, pushing home his rusty bike, a bunch of carrots slung over the handlebars. Plots had come to be associated with the period of rationing and wartime need, seen on the margin, both visually and culturally; "behind the hoardings on the main street and on the edge of the permanent way" (Hoggart). This mirrors sketches on television in the 1960s, enjoyed by a self mocking working class getting used to identifying with consumer culture. One extremely popular TV comedy series of the 1980s, *The Two Ronnies*, figured down-at-heel old men sitting on a wheelbarrow, seemingly wasting their time on rundown patches of ground.

Sensing the negative image amidst a society that found itself rapidly "modernising," a Government Commission was set up in 1966 to explore ways to improve their image and thence viability for the future (Thorpe). With some surprise, it found over half a million people made plotholding part of their everyday life. The report argued for a renovation of their *landscape* as a means of becoming more socially respectable to the wider world. The sites would be consciously landscaped along design principles; curving pathways and shaped plots; designer sheds and be called *leisure gardens*, adopting an European term used for sites where people have grander sheds, chalets, where they are allowed to sleep. This new form never became popular in Britain. Away from the plots themselves, allotments continued to carry nostalgia. Even their depiction in comedy had become benign. Interviewing leisure managers today, however, reveals a corner of opinion that plotholding is anachronistic, failing to attract the young, lacking "panache."

More deeply, the allotment held a significant position in the British memory as an icon of the Second World War,. This took the form of the part played by the small plot in the war food effort—perhaps contributing up to ten percent of requirements in the U.K., 20 percent in the U.S.A. (Bassett). The media played an important part in the creation of this image. The poster "Dig for Victory" appeared in most towns and magazines in the U.K. at the time, urging people to do so, mirroring the epithet Victory Gardens in the U.S.A.

Fig. 8 Dig for Victory, UK World War Two Poster.

"Every Garden a Munition Plant"

Figs. 9 and 10 U.S.A. World War One and Two Posters, from Bassett R.

Many people in the U.K. recall the power of this image. As nearly two million families had plots at the time in the U.K., it is not surprising that they still occupy a respected place in the image of national as well as family identity. Official war artists found these interesting subjects, engaging ideas of the war effort, people pulling together. Allotments were dug in Royal Parks and so the image bore additional respectability and power.[9] For America, the *war gardens* of the first world war were given a more seductive image, mother earth enabling freedom; and in the second world war, an association with homeliness and fecundity.

Now the allotment has entered new reaches of popular culture, as a feature in advertising. Energy companies use them to draw attention to the lost cost of their fuel—an appeal to ideas of recycling, conservation, depicted in the popular association of plots with recycled waste, saving energy in using compost, cheap, homeliness; one of the these advertisements tells a story through a conversation between a brother and sister on their parent's plot, talking about saving *their* energy.[10] The London Dockland Development Corporation spearheads development of the London docks, with huge investment projects for city commerce, and has an image of being out of touch with the remaining local and mainly low income population of the area. One of its brochures features a smiling plotholder; a reassuring image of humanity; the small scale, local; care for the environment and individualism in control of everyday life.[11]

More recently, the humble plots featured in a British Conservative Party TV election broadcast in 1991; filmed in warm glowing late afternoon colour, an old man sits in a deckchair resting from his labours on his allotment. He is in control of his own destiny; a warm scene of humanity, individuality, once again; an icon of a caring political party.[12] In the popular contemporary British TV soap opera about an old working class community of London's East End undergoing great changes, *East Enders*, one of the central characters has an allotment, which serves as an escape, retreat and sanctuary; a place to disappear to when stress engulfs him; a place to meet friends who console him.

There have been other images of the allotment in popular culture. During the 1970s, in both U.S.A. and U.K., allotments have been linked with the promotion of health and exercise. In the U.K. the Friends of the Earth, a campaigning environment organisation, led a practical campaign for more sites, engaging popular ideas about recycling, organic food and challenging waste in the land market. This approach has been even more effective in the U.S.A., where the Community Garden has been promoted as an exercise in Good Citizenship, the virtues of economy, and an appreciation of the environment. This echoes the similar "environment"

Fig. 12 San Francisco League of Urban Gardeners, event poster. 1990, by kind permission of SLUG.

Fig. 11 Railtrain behind shed, 1990, Frank Watson, kind permission of photographer.

and "health" movements of Europe, even in the nineteenth century, that gave rise, for example, to the allotment movement in Germany. In America, the upsurge of interest in Community Gardens came in the form of community development, allied to the city beautiful idea and the rescue of vacant city space.[13]

Artists and poets are fascinated by allotments. The young English artist Emma Lindsay painted allotments and their holders in a suburban area in the north east of England. Her paintings show a vigorous, colourful image, where ordinary vegetables take on unexpected exuberance. She says that this developed from her close involvement with the depth of community and friendship she found amongst the people who have plots. She uses a wide range of colors linked with the decoration of sheds and glasshouses that fill the frame and that appear to tumble down the valley. As she paints, the plotholders bring her gifts of their produce; her paintings contain this sense of humanity. Miriam McGregor translates her fascination with allotment landscapes through her amusing and whimsical engravings of events, and the Japanese wood engraver Kaouri produces a consistently English interpretation of allotments in the U.K., but with a distinctly Japanese line.[8]

An American artist living in Scotland, Gwynneth Leach, made a series of paintings in Tuscany during 1986. These capture both the Mediterranean competence in using all available space and a rich surface texture of a peopled landscape. Her most exciting work depicts the plots just over the wall from the famous landscape of the Boboli Gardens in Florence. An interesting alternative cultural heritage.

These images of cultural and visual richness have been used in two TV programs shown in the U.K. in 1992.[14] These demonstrate the combination of cultural diversity and self constructed landscape, and recognise the popular value accorded to this kind of alternative culture in contemporary Britain, a perhaps welcomingly different landscape, whose attractions include its symbol of freedom, and of environmental concern.

Popular Landscapes in Material Culture

It sometimes seems that our popular culture in the West demands commercial landscapes, prepared places that simply require consumption. The experience of the allotment suggests that this is at least an incomplete reading. There, we observe a varied landscape that is constructed from a social and political predicament converted through cultural practices that have changed over more than a century but retained central elements of ideology and forms of representation. This continuity amidst change is reflected in the survival of its landscape. It would appear that in other

Fig. 13 Engraving by Miriam McGregor. 1985, kind permission of artist.

ways popular culture understands this appeal; the values of the allotment
are benignly contradictory to those of the market place, that has in any
case more profitable interests in land.[15]

The settings of everyday life are important in the construction of
identity. In the allotment, its own aesthetic is produced from the social
relations and cultural practices that happen both inside and outside its
space, connecting as it does activities at home and at the workplace. The
site itself is a focus of shared ideology and aspiration. The aesthetic is
unselfconscious, and results from hard work, ritual and fun. Amongst
those who participate, the landscape is an image of their labours; to those
outside it is a very complex icon, translated and appropriated in diverse
ways by aspects of popular culture and its consumers each with their own
purpose. Despite its lack of intended overt display, it is thereby both a very
public and private landscape, which reflects its visibility and shared
culture, yet also the very intimate character of the places themselves. They
peculiarly combine individuality with neighbourliness, in the forms of
behaviour translated into often secret gardens hedged or closely fenced
with old doors and high corrugated iron sheeting; but despite the enormous

Fig. 14 Untitled woodcut by Kaouri. 1989, kind permission of artist.

Fig. 15 Goat, from Secret Gardens, Alec Leggatt. 1984, kind permission of photographer.

internal variety, the dozens of plots together merge into a whole landscape. The allotment is curiously neither urban nor rural; neither city nor country in terms of contemporary Western culture (Crouch). Superficially, it reminds of both a once more leafy city and of traditional small fields. However, the site is akin to neither twentieth century agriculture nor an urban park.[16] Its cultural origins make its landscape distinctive from both of these.

The language of allotments in popular culture is significant and revealing, notably in the distinctions between the American and European words. *Allotment* implies deference and allocation, qualities that indicate a relationship between powerful and powerless that have survived since that relationship was important in how plots became available. The *leisure garden* represented an attempt to replace that history with something that proved to be alien to British culture, and replaced the tradition of self help and a close community with a word more akin to consumer culture. The American term *vacant lot gardens* is brutally precise, like the factual European words *petits jardins* and *kleine gartens*. *Community garden* comes close to expressing the shared experience that typifies allotment holding.

The case studied is, typically, a dynamic culture, reflecting its changing position in popular culture. The relationship between landscape and culture is a liberating one that the argued overarching Postmodern culture cannot adequately contain, as Zukin has adeptly described. This is an ironic aspect of a dynamic material culture which started, in Britain and the U.S.A., from landowners' often grudging measures to provide land. It is now shared by diverse people who have made it their own.

Notes

The author thanks the Leverhulme Trust for the generosity of their support for the research background to this chapter in the form of a Research Fellowship.

[1]The author was interviewed about allotments in mid 1992 for ABC News.

[2]This issue has been considered by Graham Cox in Reading Nature, *Landscape Research* 13 [3] 1988.

[3]The interest in the influence of glossy popular magazines on domestic gardens was discussed by Pierce Lewis *The Making of Vernacular Taste;* the case of sunset and Southern Living paper to Dumbarton Oaks, Conference, The Vernacular Garden, 1990 (to be published 1993).

[4]Contributions in this vein include Anthony King, *The Bungalow*, RKP 1980; Colin Ward and Denis Hardy, *Goodnight Campers!* Mansell 1984; Hardy

and Ward *Arcadia for all*, Mansell 1986; Anthony Synott, Pink Flamingoes: Symbols and Symbolism in Yard Art in Ray Browne et al eds, *Dominant Symbols in Popular Culture* and Paul Groth, Lot, Yard and Garden, *Landscape* 1990; Richard Westmacott, *Patterns and Practice in Traditional Black Back Gardens in Rural Georgia*, University of Georgia 1991, and historically by John Stillgoe *Common Landscapes of America 1580-1845* Yale University Press 1982. Raymond Williams' novel *The Fight for Manod* Chatto and Windus 1979 explores meanings and the cultural relationship between landscape and the lives of different characters.

[5]The research used in this article is drawn from the author's work during his tenure as Leverhulme Research Fellow, 1986-8, and subsequent research to 1991.

[6]The material in this section is detailed in David Crouch and Colin Ward, *The Allotment*; its landscape and culture.

[7]The power of symbols in contemporary culture is explored extensively in Ray Browne et al ed, *Dominant Symbols in Popular Culture*.

[8]This is considered further in David Crouch, The Allotment; Symbol of Culture and ordinary surroundings in the1950s? *Ideas and Production*, IX-X, 1989.

[9]These illustrations are included in *Recording Britain*, David Mellor and Patrick Wright, accompanying the exhibition of the same name at the Victoria and Albert Museum, U.K. 1989.

[10]Advertisement by the Eastern Electricity Board. U.K. 1986.

[11]Promotion by the London Docklands Development Corporation. 1986.

[12]Conservative Party Political Broadcast. U.K. TV 1991.

[13]This is brilliantly illustrated by the San Francisco League of Urban Gardeners [SLUG] and in the Journal of the Community Gardening Association *America Green Community*.

[14]David Crouch is Consultant for the TV programs, "Vegetable Plots," Channel Four U.K. TV and "The Ballad of the Ten Rod Plot" [humorously echoing the old land measure, *rods*], ITV. He wrote the TV book: Allotments; a viewer's guide, Channel Four TV 1992.

[15]John Urry has argued this compellingly in *The Tourist Gaze*, Sage 1990.

[16]Mark Francis, *The Park and the Garden in the City*, Centre for Design Research, University of California, 1986.

Works Cited

Bassett R. "Reaping on the Margins." *Landscape* 25 [2] 1981.
Browne R., M. Fishwick and K. Browne, eds. *Dominant Symbols in Popular Culture*. Bowling Green State University Popular Press, 1990.
Crouch D. "The Cultural Experience of Landscape." *Landscape Research* 15 [1], 1990.
_____. "Popular Culture and what we make of the Rural." *Journal of Rural*

48 Continuities in Popular Culture

Studies Vol. 8 [3] Fall 1992.

Crouch D. and C. Ward *The Allotment; its Cultural and Landscape*. Faber and Faber, 1988.

Dorst J. *"The Written Suburb."* U of Pennsylvania P, 1989.

Finnegan R. *"The Hidden Musicians."* Cambridge UP, 1989.

Fiske J. *"Understanding Popular Culture."* Unwin Hayman, 1989.

Garner R. *"After the Coal Rush; attitudes and aesthetics of the allotment garden shed."* Diss. Humberside Polytechnic U.K., 1984.

Goffman E. *"The Presentation of Self in Everyday Life."* Pelican, 1959.

Hoggart R. *"The Uses of Literacy."* Penguin, 1958.

Jackson J.B. *"Discovering the Vernacular Landscape."* Yale UP, 1984.

Lindauer M. "Mass-Produced Art: Towards a Popular Aesthetic." *Journal of Popular Culture* 25, [2] 1991.

Tomlinson C. "John Maydew, or The Allotment." *Collected Poems*. Oxford, 1976

Warner S.B. *"To Dwell is to Garden."* Yale UP, 1987.

Zukin S. *"Landscapes of Power."* U of California P, 1991.

The American Theme Park:
A Curious Amalgam

MARGARET J. KING

Few people have changed the world of intellectually-stimulated leisure as much as Walt Disney. We live in a Disney World, as Michael Sorkin says, whether we know it or not. Disney was a driven man. He knew what he wanted in the way of entertainment and he was determined to accomplish it regardless of whether he had financial backing and artistic cooperation. He was the master of animation as well as theme-parking. He was America but he was more. In his understanding of human needs and his ability to execute them, Disney was the Michelangelo of entertainment.

Who doesn't live in Disney World?
　　　　　—Michael Sorkin, *Variations on a Theme Park*, 1992

[Duplication of history] dominates the relations with the self, with the past, not infrequently with the present, always with history, and even with the European tradition.
　　　　　—Umberto Eco, *Travels in Hyperreality*

Over the past four decades it has become progressively impossible to conjure up the American cultural landscape without a theme park. It is truly an exercise of the most vivid imagination to envision a California or a Florida without the emblematic Strasbourg cathedrals of Sleeping Beauty and Cinderella. The world's most recognizable European castles are no longer in Germany or Austria. They are planted in American soil. More ironically, the best-known castle in Europe might easily be identified as "Le Chateau de La Belle au Bois Dormant," architectural emblem of EuroDisneyland. This imposing structure, cartoon-like in profile, is an America-to-Europe import crowning the largest building project in Europe's history (Walt Disney Company 9).

The more natural exercise would be to evoke American civilization by traveling among the "lands" Disney built, the leading themes that

49

constitute a new concept in entertainment, in imagination, and in the concept of history and the collective historical imagination. At mid-century no one but Walt Disney and a handful of his right-hand designers had even heard of a theme park or could describe one effectively to the American public, or for that matter to the financial community which was given, and refused, its chance at making Disney's lifetime dream come true. Although theme parks are most often thought of as novel creations, forcing their "amusement park" ancestor into quaint or unfashionable obscurity, "themeing" was also born of a centuries-old lineage of older and more familiar forms.

The paradigm of a total world of the imagination, like that of the novel drawn in three dimensions had, as Richard Schickel put it in his profile of the creator, "...pointed Disney toward an ancient entertainment form that had fallen on dreary, even evil, days, a form that was ripe for fresh imaginings and venturings—the amusement park, which in the variation on it Disney worked has been properly named 'the atmospheric park' "(Schickel 22).

The theme park, as it now properly called, was born in Disney's distracted mind as he sat on a park bench eating peanuts and watching his two young daughters spin on the carousel, his idleness sparking the inspiration that there had to be a better way: a park the whole family could enjoy together. In typical midwestern style, not finding what he needed at hand, he decided to invent it himself.

In response to Disney's 1948 drawing-board concept under the "amusement park" rubric and called "Mickey Mouse Park," the industry experts offered this critique:

You don't want to do that...to waste money making sure the place is spic and span all the time. And how can you possibly think of a park without a midway filled with games of chance? Don't make a special effort to hire cleancut young kids: after all carnivals have been run by seasoned veterans for years, and they are best able to drag every last penny out of the patrons. (Smith 19)

It was just this conception of amusement park that Disney and his designers were working so hard to transcend, and they did so by breaking most of the rules. "Walt and his staff did not need this advice. Walt knew what he wanted to do, and he knew what the public wanted," comments the Disney archivist (Smith 19). By so doing the old-world carnival mold was transformed forever by wedding the three-dimensional fair to the two-dimensional, thus spinning off dozens of new park lifeforms with "themeing," the core of this incredibly productive centrifuge of innovation.

Through this ability to combine by harmonious synergy every artform, both at high and low taste and technology levels, theme parks are a magic amalgam, something new under the sun in concept but deceptively familiar in content. Drawn from the storehouse of history, they are nonetheless quite ahistorical. When Disney opened the prototype in Anaheim on July 17, 1955, a paradigm shift rocked the arts. Within an arresting aesthetic "prism" American popular culture came into its own, a culture which Disney was always so adept at both reading and creating throughout his career. In Disneyland, for this first time anywhere, began a strange genetic interplay: between bread and circuses, the art of film, set design, costuming, parades, vaudeville, painting, photorealism, animation, architecture, sculpture, and electronic engineering (most notably audioanimatronics), the computer-assisted arts, fiber optics, merchandising, and marketing. No other artform can showcase the interplay of ancient and modern, static and kinetic, tradition and futurism with the such mastery and bravura as seen on the unfolding stage set of theme-park history.

So successful have the results proven that the parks have become an international standard for profitability and progress. Walt Disney World has for some years been the world's most popular destination resort, and the Disney Company is the third most profitable on earth (Walt Disney Company 4-6). These institutions, with all their trouble attracting investors in the early 1950s, whose feasibility studies predicted doom, are in large part responsible for Disney's present enviable economic position.

What Disney had was that most American of talents, the national genius for marketing that assured U.S. preeminence in the global economy. He used the sensibility of the arts to set the sights and guide the stratagem of an enormously successful new business frontier. By using his television series *Disneyland* to pump the parks' purpose and progress, first in construction, then as the park attractions evolved—and setting films and character merchandise at the service of park development, an ideal integrated marketing system was born. This frontier has yielded the Sea Worlds, Six Flags, Busch Gardens, et al that dominate the increasingly sophisticated leisure landscape and its growing hold over our national habits of the mind and heart. These habits, led by Disney parks in Tokyo (1983) and Paris (1992), are bellwethers of the emerging "international style" of travel based on the jet, multiculturalism, and the universal symbol and sign design of theme park color, graphics, and representation. While the American intelligentsia has decried popular culture for this very system, it is one the rest of the world has meanwhile been learning to read with great relish and success. U. S. popular culture has been laying the groundwork through such systems for an international language encoded by the theme park and its installations.

If contemporary marketing theory was the method, theme parks, originally transformed by modern technology and planning, have roots readily traced to the history of trade, sociability, and the world map of the religious and trading calendar. Dominant blood lines extend to trade fair, expositions, carnival, midway, but also to that all-important grandparent, the World's Fair, beginning with London's Crystal Palace in 1851 and the first American fair, Philadelphia's Centennial of 1876. The World's Fair was itself an amalgam: a competitive trade show of nation or trade pavilions, each in effect "themed" with its own costumes, food, faces, and flags—a national exhibit "prism" of design and artifact display, often extended by live performance, food, music, and narration as well. World's Fairs "ringed the world," and "influenced almost every facet of life," including art and architecture, technology applications, consumerism, public policy, popular opinion, and futurism ("World's Fairs" 1).

At the 1964 New York World's Fair, Disney creations were commissioned for the event, proved to be among the Fair's highlights, then imported, covered with glory, to Disneyland. Audioanimatroics, pioneered in 1963 with the Enchanted Tiki Room, were market tested the following year in New York with "It's a Small World" and "Great Moments with Mr. Lincoln."

Aside from such "test marketing" exercises, the theme park is a stay-put installation, fixed, like World's Fairs or Expositions, but unlike these forms, permanent. Instead of the moveable feast of carnival or traveling fair, Disneyland is modeled on the town rather than the circus, periodic market, or religious feast. The opportunities for refinement of design as complemented by the technologies of power, lighting, computers, and the use of natural elements like waterways, fountains, trees and plantings, make these far different places (landscaping having been noted as the most instantly-identifiable of theme park features) (Trigg).

The many animation techniques innovated by Disney studios, together with those of live-action filmmaking starring the historical costume drama, set the technical and imagistic stage for the unanticipated offspring—the theme park. The first impulse for Disney's brainchild was educational, not entertainment: Disney's desire to take something from the studios to share directly with the schools was "Disneylandia," a traveling exhibit of dioramas animating great moments in American history and folklore. "I don't want to just entertain kids with pony rides and slides and swings," Disney explained. "I want them to learn something about their heritage" (Bright 39). As concepts snowballed, it became clear that the goal of what was then called "Walt Disney's America" was really something more monumental, a showcase (but not a *museum*) for the Disney outpouring of the arts. It was the studio's mastery of all the major artforms, and their pushing the envelope of these forms, that served so well in laying the groundwork for these "concept" places. Along the way and in the process of honing the techniques and knowledge to build upon the original Disneyland models, other artforms based on computer technology were added, notably audioanimatronics, fiber optics, laser lighting, and the monorail.

The interbreeding of traditional features within theme park design poses some arresting prototypes while raising broad questions about the current uniqueness of themeing as against the backdrop of other more traditional genres: the midway, the small town or county fair, the museum exhibit, the living history museum such as Sturbridge Village, live musical and reenactment performance, and the industrial or process park such as Hershey Park and Astroworld.[1] Add to these the culture park (Polynesian Culture Center, Dollywood, Opryland, Six Flags, Knott's Berry Farm, Fiesta Texas), and the nature park, (Safari and Sea Worlds) and most recently, the movie parks by Universal Studios and Disney/MGM. Answers are best sought in the theme park format, mapping the genotypes for each of these forms.

But there is something about the parks that can't be quite duplicated by other entertainment formats: their sense of place, or "placemaking' and the creation of that feeling through all the senses. These range from the aroma of French coffee roasting in Market Square, New Orleans at Disneyland to the look and feel of overhead sun and cactus in the southwest as found in Frontierland, or the geometry of topiary and mirrored surfaces in Tomorrowland or Future World/EPCOT.

But it was the Disney knack for taking older forms and improving upon them to his own tune, converting them to Disney creations, that make theme parks cultural watersheds. In *Travels in Hyperrealilty*, Umberto Eco counts them on his list of "Fake cities," adding that "The pleasure of imitation, as the ancients knew, is one of the most innate in the human spirit" (Eco 46).

Clearly the craft of themeing, as formulated in the Disney studios, is far more than imitation. It is the recreation of the world—not as it is, was, or ever shall be, but as something far more compelling—the way we see that world in the collective mind's "compound" eye. For the thinking visitor, it is an appreciation of the various lenses and how they work in concert to produce this image of the world that is the essence of the magic at these stylized new "places." Every conventional venue, from baseball stadium to cocktail lounge, from boardroom to bedroom, from museum lobby to drive-in diner, now bears the mark of themeing, including the re-creation of history (Main Street, Adventureland, Frontierland, New Orleans and Liberty Squares); the realm of childhood fantasy (Fantasyland), and the future (Tomorrowland).

As diversity and creativity continue to raise demands within the leisure and travel industry, theme parks hold the built-in key to answering (and in fact to feeding) these demands.

With his corps of think-tank developers, Disney began to integrate the elements of Worlds Fair, trade show, and amusement park to arrive at a new synthesis, a new environmental aesthetic. He draws heavily on the concept of "managed celebration," a style of leisure social engineering seen earlier at Coney Island (Kasson). From the concept of themeing—by motif, era, industry, or style—Disney arrived at the various "lands," based on the spoke-and-wheel radiating plaza, the Disney designers' term, of Disneyland in the original conception.[2]

Affection for Denmark's Tivoli gardens has been noted as a key source of inspiration for Disney's own park vision (Reeves 12)[3] but Tivoli is not the place Disney ended up designing. The Disneyland plan was neither derivative nor any analogical extension of concepts already in operation across the landscape in cities, beach resorts, and at the ends of trolley and subway lines. What he did was the typical thing for his repertoire and reputation. As an animator accustomed to playing Primal Cause with sound and image, he simply extended that role into the third dimension.

The concept of total control is the key to the theme park. Where else would it be possible to create the total universe brought into being by the Disney Imagineers? Like an animated feature film, the palette, graphics, landscaping, and architecture are all keyed to the main theme, with all theme areas orchestrated to fit the "Disney Deco" style. Unlike a World's Fair or trade show, with their various pavilions keyed to diverse subjects and design schemes, the theme park appears to have sprung full-blown from a single imagination. Designer John Hench summarized the World's Fair problem: "One of the worst things about, for instance, a World's Fair is that every facility is trying to outshout the others. People are subject to the pressure from the Russian Pavilion, as opposed to the French, as against the Italian—and it does make for a curious kind of mental fatigue"(Finch 414). And while the amusement park might feature rides keyed to themes such as "Lovers' Lane," "Carousel," etc., there was no particular effort to bill the attraction as any specific period or place, or to blend such settings into a harmonious message system of color, symbol, or scale. An aesthetics of unity, as much as anything else, set the theme park apart from its predecessors.

Free play of all the senses is built into the theme park ethos. Far from the "velvet rope" ethic of the museum or exposition, theme parks have done much to narrow the traditional distance between arts and audience, calling into play what Arnold Berleant has called "the profound process of art ....to evoke memories, knowledge, and human awareness as integral to our perceptual awareness"(Berleant).

The exhibitions of the World's Fairs, the thrill-and-chill mechanics of amusement park rides, are outstripped by the creation of a world Ray Bradbury described in his vision of an African veldt that could be entered simply by walking through a screen. There is limited value in comparing Disneyland et al to the conventions of a Switchback Railway, Loop the Loop, or Chute the Chutes. Within theme parks, the "ride" concept is muted. The Swiss Family Robinson Treehouse in Adventureland, for example, recreates the walk-through multi-level home as constructed from the contents of a wrecked cargo ship, one creative act upon another as drawn from fictional history. Only steps away, the atmospherics and visuals of the most popular ride, Pirates of the Caribbean, far outweigh the interest of the "ride" per se, which is simply a boat on tracks to move riders along the loop of the story of the pillage and burning of an eighteenth-century port.

As one travel writer put it, "You don't go to the Disney parks to ride the rides. You go for a journey of the mind" (Steers). Instead a journey of the mind through time and space was favored over the body—the kinetics of risk-taking, tests of skill, gravity games, and plays on the world of industry, motion, the physics of fun ("Coney Island").[4]

Disney's rides, "attractions," were predictably Disney originals, custom-built for fit with the Disney network of production and with the landscape of the park itself. Not restricted to the young adult audience as were the earlier parks, these catered across the board to every age group taste and temper. High-velocity rides like the Matterhorn Bobsleds roller coaster, and later Space and Big Thunder Mountains, fit the standard amusement profile, but are actually the minority case. "Visual" rides, including the "dark" rides like Snow White's Scary Adventure, Mr. Toad's Wild Ride, and Peter Pan's Flight (all in Fantasyland), stretched the ride form to "riding the movies." "Guests" run on high or low tracks, either to fly or motor or sail through an elaborate set of mechanized actors and customized settings with their own characters, plot, and mise-en-scene. Each "car," carrying one or two couples, swivels to focus attention ahead or to the side or behind, the way the moviemaker's camera commands the attention of the audience just where it is wanted and nowhere else. In contrast, carney rides relate to the older forms of steam train, factory belt, and mining railroad—older "production" forms recalling life in the turn-of-the-century industrial landscape before the late twentieth-century suburban consumer universe of "video cult."

Even the Matterhorn, among the original Disneyland attractions and the most distinctive landmark after the castle, scaled 1/1100 to the real thing in Switzerland, is far more than the roller-coaster ride it first appears to be, and exceeds theme or ornament for the ride contained within its steep walls and extreme caverns. In effect it is a giant artwork of symbolic architecture—at once a monument, icon, symbol, and recreation. By day it dominates the park landscape from its Fantasyland elevation. By night it becomes a doubly "dark ride," one of the most favorite and formidable in the park, by banishing the customary margins dividing inside from outside as nighttime engulfs the interior in a black hole. Thereby the Matterhorn becomes a strange topological negative space. Of course the idea of riding inside the mountain, rather than along the outside surface, is yet another instance of the "Imagineer" shift of perspective that makes theme parks intriguing galleries of space.

Another aspect, borrowing from the museum, trade show, and retail emporium, are the arts of exhibit at theme parks. Visitors see far more than they ride. The installations make extensive use of the expectations of animation, then carry those conventions into the round. Thus Disney's studio staff brought the static exhibit or mural frieze to life as Rome burns in AT&T's Communications ride, dinosaurs battle in Primeval World, the world's longest diorama; the Illuminations light show spotlights the world nations, the Country Bear Jamboree performs in Bear Country, President Lincoln delivers his address with full range of face and body language in the Hall of Presidents, ghosts waltz in the Haunted Mansion, and Goofy and friends play out a day's ritual in the "To Your Health" theater in MetLife's Wonders of Life pavilion in Future World/EPCOT. Public response to these shows of art wedded to technology is as much an appreciation of invention as the love of theater (Reeves 8).[5]

Harking back to Victorian concepts of refinement and education, another source for the theme park, art galleries can be found scattered strategically throughout the Disney empire. Although his mastery of popular forms is far better recognized, Disney related consciously to the formal academic world of the arts from the outset of his production, and this relation is evident in his conception and planning of theme park content. At his instigation, his artists were tutored by Jean Charlot, a French-trained artist imported for this purpose. When it came time to apply these lessons to the parks, a richly puzzling meld of high and low, art treasure and reject, were interbred and finally interlocked, to be inextricably fused in nearly every square foot. At the heart of theme parks' charm is this fusion, so suspect to intellectual taste but at the same time so appealing, that is finally the disturbingly provocative spell cast by the first theme parks and their progeny scattered across the cultural map.

For the past decade, an arts manager has been appointed and served as an important link to the "establishment" art world through museum borrowings and showcases at Disneyland (Disney Gallery) and EPCOT Center (at the Mexico, China, Japan, and Morocco pavilions of World Showcase). "The traffic between textbook and museum art on the one hand and popular and commercial on the other has become a central fact of twentieth-century life," writes Reuel Denney in his Introduction to the collected Charlot lectures (Denney). Exchange of exhibit ideas and artifacts between museums and theme parks is increasing every year, making the interchange and recycling between high and low styles a prime pursuit for popular culture studies (King 60-62).

Corporate support, always one of the stickier points of theme park foundation and reputation, can be usefully considered within the museum/arts connection. The transnational company names adorning pavilions across the Magic Kingdom, EPCOT, and Disney/MGM Studios can be compared alongside high-profile corporate support for a museum or a special exhibit, or for cultural events on public television. Should arts efforts, like the current "underfunded" Picasso still-life exhibition, be funded solely by patron admissions in the belief that anything else comes from an impure commercial motive? A prevalent criticisms of Disney's lands is their "commercial" flavor, in contradistinction to the commercial direction of the carnival and trade fair. In this telling sense the theme park is actually grouped with but above the museum as created for some higher or nonprofit purpose under a separate and elevated code.

Further, our perceptions and expectations of just what commercial space is have been greatly tempered by the theme park. We now shop, dine, play, and do business in malls, train stations, readapted factories, historic buildings, museums, refurbished churches and banks. Modifying the traditional notions of which activity matched what structure by playing with their histories and futures is another hallmark of the theme park sensibility.

Outside park limits, the arrival of Disney Stores in malls moves theme park merchandising into mainstream American retail space—which has itself been heavily inspired by the theme parks in the creation of automobile-free, themed storefronts along themed "avenues" under private control (Underground Atlanta and Caesar's Palace Forum Shops are examples). "Malls are really theme parks, aren't they?" posed a stockbroker researching this market. By a curious sleight of hand, transposing conventions of form and function, this is what has been achieved (Disney Co., Third Quarterly Report 6).[6]

Questions of "cultural exchange" are heating up at both ends of the cultural spectrum as travel and tourism continue as the leading U.S. industry, whose national and international economic flavor will be heavily involved with total destination resorts such as Disney's (Crandall 4).[7] In accord with these trends, leisure travel continues as the number-one status symbol among Americans as reported by the U.S. Travel Data Center ("Theme Parks of the Future" 43). As the theme park landscape expands to cross national boundaries, a new complex of formats and motifs drawn up from regional and national roots will combine with the basic themeing concept.

The value of thinking about theme parks in terms of studios, think-tanks, or laboratories rather than mere amusement centers has become ever more clear, first to the cultural analyst and design professional of the 70s, and lately to the mainstream public whose mission is one of sport and not study. As designer Marvin Davis has related, "Walt planned on having another Disneyland, but that was incidental. The really exciting part was putting together a city of tomorrow" (Reeves 10). As new techniques are showcased (Mission to Mars, hologram films, flight simulation), theme parks continue to play the role of what Alvin Toffler has called "enclaves of the future" (Toffler 347-8). Walt's famous pronouncement was that "Disneyland will continue to grow, to add new things, as long as there is imagination left in the world."

Critical response to the parks as an invention is, as ever, mixed. There are those who appreciate the Disney touch as an innate American talent for building on existing forms, the Edison of American entertainment and, like the inventor, hard-driving, civic-minded, and unapologetic about the long-range influences that might be loosed on the country. Other critics see in the parks a rampant privatism along the lines of the gentleman scientist turning out privately-financed cures and curiosities without public conscience or restraint. But neither contingent has been able to approach the theme park in the spirit of studying a creative stylist who carried his culture in some intriguing directions without seeming to diverge from the way it was already headed. This is surely the crux of Disney's genius: both the most intriguing and also the least susceptible of unclouded analysis.

Theme parks are a new artform. They depart radically from amusement parks, carnivals, fairs, and related historical forms, proposing new models for the way people enjoy themselves in public, relate to art and history, spend time, energy, and money, and think about and experience other popular forms. The tone has been set, the standard laid down, and public expectations raised: in short, a new cultural imperative has been created, one from which there is no turning back.

Our ability to stretch ourselves and our psyches between the imagined past and fantasies of the future is of critical moment in a world shattered, if not exploded, by the forces of technology, change, and future shock. As agents of change management, theme parks have filled gaps in sociability and the arts. At the same time, others have opened: our ability to perceive, evaluate, discourse upon, and make sense of, this new form and those following in its wake, has been severely strained. It is at least clear that history is being inscribed here, a nonlinear, post-literary understanding of the past. Historian Mike Wallace calls Disney the "premier interpreter of the American experience" (Wallace 33). In a single century we have accelerated at warp speed beyond the 1893 Columbia Exposition—and simultaneously exceeded any natural ability to understand this leap and how it has mediated what we learn about the world through the ways we consume and construe the products of the theme park package.

Notes

The author wishes to note use of the term "amalgam" by David Strole, Vice President of The Works, Long Beach, California.

[1] These "industrial" themes are often used to justify school trips to these parks as educational ventures.

[2] The original oil mock-up of the Disneyland schematic is on display at the Disney Gallery in Anaheim after its chance discovery and rescue from obscurity in a storage shed on the studio grounds. (Source: Van Romans, Director, Arts Management)

[3] "Walt Disney came back from Denmark in 1952, talking and talking about the Tivoli Gardens in Copenhagen, and wanting to build something like it here in the U.S."

[4] Coney Island was called a "showcase of the machine age."

[5] Ken Dresser, art director at Walt Disney World, describes SpectroMagic as "the most technically elaborate parade in the history of mankind."

[6] The 100th Disney store opened July 1991 in Daytona Beach, while the highest per-square-foot earnings are abroad at the Regent Street, London store.

[7] Six percent of the world's total gross national product is travel related, and in the U.S., it is by far the largest industry.

Works Cited

Berleant, Arnold. "The Museum of Art as Participatory Environment." manuscript, 1987.
Bright, Randy. *Disneyland: Inside Story*. NY: Harry Abrams 1987.
"Coney Island." *The American Experience*. WGBH Boston and WNET.
Crandall, Robert. "The World's Largest Industry" *American Way* (June 15, 1992).
Denney, Reuel. "A Tale of Two Studios: Artist John Charlot in Walt Disney's Atelier," Introduction to Charlot's 1938 lectures to the studios. manuscript, 1991.
Disney Co., Third Quarterly Report. 1991.
Eco, Umberto. *Travels in Hyperreality*. NY: Harcourt Brace Jovanovich, 1986.
Finch, Christopher. *The Art of Walt Disney*. NY: Harry Abrams, 1973.
Kasson, John. *Amusing the Millions: Coney Island at the Turn of the Century*. NY: Hill and Wang, 1978.
King, Margaret J. "Disneyfication: Some Pros and Cons of Theme Parks." *Museum* (Paris, UNESCO, Winter 1991), 4-6;"Theme Park Thesis." *Museum News* (Sept/Oct 1990), 60-62.
Reeves, Richard. "Worlds of Wonder," *Disney World: 20 Years of Magic. Newsweek* (Fall/Winter 1991).
Schickel, Richard. *The Disney Version*. NY: Simon & Schuster, 1968.
Smith, Dave. "Disneyland After 35 Years." *The Disney Channel Magazine* (Jan/Feb 1990).
Sorkin, Michael. Editor, *Variations on a Theme Park*. NY: Hill and Wang, 1992. Introduction.
Steers, Michael. telecom, Spring.
Toffler, Alvin. *Future Shock*. NY: Random House 1970.
"Theme Parks of the Future." *TWA Ambassador* (June 1992).
Trigg, Lois B. "Disney World: The Magic Behind the Plants." *Southern Living* June 1987.
Wallace, Mike "Mickey Mouse History: Portraying the Past at Disney World." *Radical History Review*: 32 (1985).
Walt Disney Company. *Annual Report*. 1991.
"World's Fairs, 1851-1940." Exhibit text, Smithsonian Institution Libraries, National Museum of American History. Washington, D.C., 12 Feb.-26 Aug. 1992.

Bringing it all Back Home: Uses of the Past in the Present (and the Future) of American Popular Music

GEORGE H. LEWIS

Music and song are the engines that drive most human activity and apparently are as old as humankind. The companions of Homer's Ulysses were lured from his ship by the singing of the sirens. Nowadays NASA comforts its astronauts with music on the radio. Undoubtedly the first contact Earth has with some intelligence out in space will be musical not mathematical formulas. Bartlett's Familiar Quotations *has nearly 400 references to song and music. It is the Mother's-Milk of life. Until recently "serious" scholars were disinclined to take popular music seriously. Now, however, as George H. Lewis demonstrates, popular music is becoming so important a part of the lives of us all that everyone concerned with culture must take it as very important.*

> Ring around a rosie
> Pocket full o posies
> Ashes, ashes, all fall down
> > > Children's Game Song
> > > circa 1350

> The kids dance and shake their bones...
> Singin' ashes, ashes, all fall down
> > > "Throwing Stones"
> > > The Greatful Dead
> > > circa 1987

Caught fast in the grip of the Black Plague, the folk consciousness of fourteenth Century England created a bright sounding ditty—a chant of "ring around a rosie" that, ironically, referred to the victims of that plague. Once beloved mothers, husbands, sisters and friends, these sudden

61

corpses—their pockets hastily stuffed with flowers of farewell—were collected by cart at night to be tossed into great pits and burned with lime. Ashes, ashes, all fall down.

The trauma of a century in which over fifty percent of the population died in this horrible manner was etched into the lines of this simple children's song, which has been sung in English speaking countries of the world for nearly six and one half centuries since that dark time of death. For most, the song has lost its original meaning over the centuries and is thought of as a light melody of children at play. Yet beneath its innocent surface, the dark shadow of the past has hidden, to be tapped and loosened by (fittingly) the Greatful Dead in 1987. "Throwing Stones," a song warning of the infection of human kind by a virus of violence that has pious politicians throwing stones and the desperate underclass cutting throats in the night shadows of urban ghettos, was included on their multimillion selling collection *In The Dark*, in which the refrain "ashes, ashes, all fall down" regains something close to its chilling original meaning. In this song, the past is returned to the present in the form of a dire warning concerning the future. If the past, with its infectious sicknesses of violence and death, cannot be conquered, the Dead warn, the planet is doomed. As they sing, "the future's here…we are it. We are on our own." Otherwise, as in 1350, ashes, ashes, all fall down.

In examining the influence of past culture upon the present, and in speculating on the future, there is no better form to focus on than popular music. One of the things that has frustrated popular music scholars is the fact that this form of culture contains—actually is predicated upon, emotional connections and chords it strikes in the listener (or performer, for that matter), and that this critical dimension has so far been found to be well nigh impossible to quantify and empirically assess. And yet it is this very characteristic of music—the way the best of it burrows deep into the soul and won't let go—that ties the present so strongly to its (and our) past.

When Mexican Americans, for example, hear the popular song "La Bamba" they are, in most cases knowingly, connecting to their heritage and their past. This song, created in Mexico (most likely the Veracruz area) around 1700, mixes West African cross rhythms (there were more West African slaves in Mexico in that century than there were Spanish) with Spanish/Amerindian-derived lyrics and music, and is one of the few truly authentic folk/popular songs that connects the Mexican past to its present. In addition to its nearly 300 years of popularity, "La Bamba" also is important to the Mexican-American community because of the fact that Ritchie Valens recorded it in Los Angeles in the mid-1950s and made it a popular song all across American. "La Bamba" became hitched to the young singer's personal mystique—a Mexican-American who had "made it" in America on his own terms. With his death in the 1959 plane crash that also killed Buddy Holly and the Big Bopper, Valens became the stuff of romantic myth in the Mexican-American barrio—the elusive one who, once heard, is already lost in the past—a theme that is strong in this culture, most especially in the romantic lyrics of its highly popular ranchera songs.

The past, then, as encoded in popular music, is always with us in the present, waiting quietly to be loosed on the wings of some half forgotten song. Black Americans, hearing B.B. King's signature song, "Sweet Little Angel," are connected to their past by the single string blues runs King coaxes from Lucille (his guitar), which are, in turn, tied to the blues structures pioneered by T-Bone Walker and Lonnie Johnson in the late 1940s and early 1950s. For white country audiences, hearing Emmylou Harris and her Nash Ramblers play Bill Monroe's "Scotland" in their 1991 live performance at the Ryman Auditorium in Nashville (original home of the Grand Ol' Opry) brings back multiple layers of the past (the days of the original Opry, Monroe's early 1950s recording of the song, the earlier "roots" of the audience as suggested by the song's title and musical form). Even today's heavy metal fans can wax nostalgic when they hear Led Zepplin's classic "Stairway To Heaven," recorded by the band in 1970 and still popular today. (This song, with its mix of delicate Celtic-inspired acoustic music and the swaggering bluster of electric blues, has, perhaps more than any other single song, defined the development of both the "power ballad" and the raw bombastic mainstream heavy metal song— musical references to "Stairway" are in evidence all over the heavy metal map, and have been for the past decade, at the very least.)

The Past In The Present

My past is present in an hour glass
Rodney Crowell
1989

There are many reasons why popular music is used to summon the past and recreate it in the present. In the remainder of this essay, I wish to note several of these I see as the most important—whether they are used by the audience for the music, its musical creators, or the larger social institutions of the society—groupings that are constantly seeking ways to symbolically authenticate themselves in the eyes of their constituencies.

The Audience

People use music to selectively remember their past. In general, the music that is listened to during the formative years—from, say, 12 to 25, is the music people always remember fondly, and to which many return during later years of their lives. This fact can be seen reflected in the buying patterns charted by the popular music industry over the years. In general, the largest amount of popular music is consumed by the 12-25 age group—the group that has been, historically, targeted by the industry as the ones to pitch their product to. When people move beyond 25 in age, although they still will listen to some popular music, they typically tend to buy much less of it, and to continue to prefer the musical styles of their youth to others that may have evolved since that time.

On the other hand, the focus of the popular music industry is on defining "new" sounds for the current 12-25 year olds to adopt as "their" sound. These two facts have created an interesting situation, with respect to the ways music is used to pull the past into the present.

To the extent that musical styles shift over generations, they are likely to be seen as "a-historical" by each crop of 12-25 year olds—a "new" style that is embraced as *their* sound. Rap music is a good and current example of this. At the same time, for those over 25, their earlier style gives them identity, as individuals and as a generation, to which they can (and do) turn to recreate their own pasts in the present. Thus one gets, in addition to individual nostalgia and idiosyncratic meaning, the use of popular music to define the collective nostalgia of an entire generation, whether this be the flappers of the 1920s, the big band dancers of the 1940s, or the social experimenters of the late 1960s Woodstock generation.

With this latter generation—that of the baby boomers—there has been an added twist, with respect to the appearance of the past in the present. As the generation moves into its 40s in age, many of its members have become relatively affluent members of society—a fact dramatized effectively in films such as "The Big Chill" and "Grand Canyon." At the same time, the record industry has introduced the digital based compact disc audio format. This technology creates a clearer, brighter sound which has been used to enhance older recordings of popular music. The result has been an unprecedented demand on the part of the over-25 audience for digital versions of "their" generational music. Compact disc plants are in operation 24 hours a day, attempting to keep up with the demand.

In 1990, the Recording Industry Association of America reported that consumers over the age of 35 accounted for 29 per cent of the total dollars spend on prerecorded music. (Those under 19, in 1990, accounted for 28 per cent of the total dollars, in comparison.) Much of this baby boomer music is what the industry calls "catalog sales," or compact disc versions of past music, in addition to "boxed sets" of (many times) unreleased versions and out-takes of earlier artists' materials. Many of these artist of the past are also enjoying a renewal of their careers, from Dick Dale (1960s surfing music), Roy Orbison (who, until his fatal heart attack in the late 1980s, was recording new material with Tom Petty, Bob Dylan and others), and Natalie Cole (who won 5 Grammies in 1992 for her album reprisal of her father's most well known songs). Recognizing the popularity of this past music in the present, radio has created a new format, classic rock radio, which targets the aging baby boomers and their generationally based music.

So, at present, the recording industry is serving two generational publics—the current younger generation (as they always have done), and the baby boomers who are consuming huge amounts of their past music in the new digital format of the present.

But not all popular forms of music change so dramatically that they can be used to define a generation. When musical styles change much more gradually—as they do in American country music—current stars and hits can be defined as *extensions* of the past, and current artists can call on this past to validate themselves and their music—something that George Strait, to give just one example, has done effectively through his career. Under these conditions, the older generation (over 25) is more apt to listen to (and purchase) current popular music, seeing it as a link to their personal past and a heritage, or tradition, that extends backwards in time to a "roots" situation, rather than seeing music as unique to their specific generation. The over-25s have their personal favorites from the past, yet they are more apt to locate them, as individuals, in the stream of history, rather than to define their generation as unique—a point underscored by the tremendous commercial success of the Nitty Gritty Dirt Band's 1972 *Will The Circle Be Unbroken* album that brought together musicians of all of country's generations (from Mother Maybelle Carter and Roy Acuff to Norman Blake and John McEuan) to play collectively the timeless classics of the genre—songs such as "Wildwood Flower" and "The Wabash Cannonball."

Artists

When one turns to the musical artists themselves, as opposed to their audiences, the past can also be seen to be strongly represented in the present. Past hit songs are re-recorded by new artists for a new generation, as Michael Bolton did in 1991 with "When A Man Loves A Woman," (first made a hit by Percy Sledge in the mid-1960s), or as the Beatles did with Chuck Berry's 1950s "Roll Over Beethoven" in the mid-1960s—or as Emmylou Harris has done in 1992 with Stephen Foster's "Hard Times," to cite a more extreme example.

Artists will also mine the past for songs that connect them to this past and thus authenticate them by the association. Eric Clapton, Johnny Winter and Stevie Ray Vaughn, for example, have recorded songs of the blues legend Robert Johnson (such as "Crossroads") and, in the country field, everyone (including his own son) has recorded at least one Hank Williams song.

Some artists try, deliberately, to bring the past to the present in their reworking of songs from a particular musical tradition. Schooner Fare, a regionally popular group from Maine, for example, has taken a song, "Mary L. McKay" that goes back at least a century in Maritime tradition and reworked it as a popular song for the 1990s. The group feels that songs of the past, if not updated, will not appeal to today's audience. They will add the sort of harmony the present audience expects and likely change the key and/or the time signature, as they did with "Mary L. McKay." In this song they also use the ninth original verse as their introduction and the first line of the fourth original verse as the first line of their chorus. The rest of the chorus is new, written by Schooner Fare. As they remarked to me in an interview, "we're trying to bring these songs back and give them to people, because they're their songs."

Schooner Fare also writes songs explicitly about the past, such as "Salt Water Farm," about the singer's grandfather, who always wanted to own a farm, but had to keep a factory job all his life in order to feed his family. As the group says in introducing this song; "Tom wrote about his grandaddy who had a dream. Not just having a place, but time to return to it. I think it's something we all do..." Once again the past—in this case a romantically reworked past—is called up to the present for the ties it can renew and the lessons it can teach.

The past can also be used to make statements about the present condition of things. For example, Judy Collins recorded the old ballad "Farewell To Tarwathie," which is about going to sea to hunt the whale. However, she added the recorded singing of humpback whales to her version, appealing to a present day eco-consciousness by bringing the past, in which it was perfectly honorable to hunt whales, into a present in which they are seen as an intelligent and endangered species.

The use of popular themes from the past to carry modern lyrics is a time-honored tradition in popular music, from the Lone Ranger theme (William Tell Overture) to the Elegents "Little Star" (Mozart), Procol Harum's "Whiter Shade of Pale" (Bach) and Bob Dylan's "The Times They Are A-Changin" (the Scottish ballad "Come All Ye Tender Hearted Maidens"). In the folk movement of the 1960s, of course, tunes from the past served not only to carry the words, but also to authenticate the singer and the song as connected to a tradition and rooted in a heritage common to the audience—something that is also true in the blues, a music that can be traced through its musical structure and rhythmic patterns all the way to West Africa.

There also seems to be, in the development of popular music, various periods of getting back to the basics, in which artists study the music of the past and attempt a "revival" of the earlier form—usually in protest against the contemporary music scene. Such attempts to "get back" to authentic music are likely to involve some melding of the traditional form with an innovation from the present. For example, the English groups the Beatles, the Animals and the Rolling Stones, in their first years of popularity, recorded the rock and blues music of Black Americans, but presented this cultural heritage to America (and the world) in a "white English wrapper." The punk movement, in its attempt to get back to authentic rock and roll, wrapped it in a visual and theatrical pastiche that early rock never had. The American folk revival of the mid-1960s quickly moved from the roots music of Guthrie, Leadbelly and the Weavers into the electric arena of rock, led by Bob Dylan and Eric Anderson. And the new traditionalists in contemporary American country music, like Garth Brooks, are mixing the sexual suggestiveness of rock into their stage shows, even as their music is freshly honed, past oriented and "down home" in sound.

A last example of the artistic use of the past in the present lies in the practice of sampling, by use of computer technology, musical phrases from earlier recordings of significance. the works of James Brown, in hip hop and rap, and Led Zepplin have been especially popular for this purpose. The sampled phrase can then be manipulated through use of a digital computer, to change its tempo, sequence and timbre in whatever manner the present artist wishes. The manipulated phrase than may become a frame for the total song (via some type of "looping"), or merely an introduction, hook phrase or interlude. This technique has now moved beyond rap and the musical avant garde and into the mainstream of popular music, with Madonna's 1990 sampling of the music of Public Enemy on her "Justify My Love" single. Sampling thus acts as a connector between past and present—the past becomes the present in a computer-altered form and, for those in the know, acts as a touchstone and reference of musical roots and debts.

Societal Institutions

Finally, in focusing on the larger institutions of society, it is evident that, in seeking acceptance and validation, they attempt to use popular music's ability to connect the past to the present in many ways. Perhaps the most obvious of these is religion's use of popular song not only to celebrate the sacred, but also to tie audiences to a secular past. Popular hymns are passed down through the generations, and are a reminder of the religious heritage they represent. Such songs can also pass from the sacred to the secular realm, becoming, for example, anthems of social movements—such as "We Shall Overcome"—or the gospel-pop of groups such as the Dixie Hummingbirds. Television evangelists also use such songs in their broadcasts to validate their organizations and to tie them to the traditions of more legitimate and established religious institutions.

Politicians also use popular music to legitimate themselves and tie them to tradition. William Bennett, Bill Clinton and Pat Buchanan have all publically declared their allegiance to the baby boom's early rock and roll music (even claiming to be able to recite many lyrics by heart), while George Bush not only has attended Nashville's Grand Ol' Opry, he has actually played country music on stage with historical figures such as Roy Acuff and Bill Monroe.

Popular music of the past is now being used, increasingly, to sell more than just preachers and politicians. Smokey Robinson's 1965 hit "The Tracks Of My Tears" has been played by Budweiser as a part of their beer commercials, while Ray Charles and his soul sound have been used to sell Pepsi Cola. The Doors' "Riders On The Storm" has been used to sell Pirelli tires, Ben E. King's "Stand By Me" to sell Levi's 501 jeans, and the Beatles' "Revolution" to sell Nike athletic shoes. What is new in all of this is not the use of stars to sell products—that has been going on for a long time. It is, rather, the use of the actual music of the past (the baby boom generation, mostly) to authenticate the product in the present (so baby boomers will accept and buy it). To the extent that we feel the music of our past is authentic, honest, and that it helps define us, then the advertisers hope such feelings and emotions will connect to the product they're pitching. That this new connection of the past to the present works can be seen in the increasing number of past hit songs that are being used to sell commercial products today.

So, from the perspectives of the audience, the artists and the social institutions of the society, the popular music of the past is very much alive in the social fabric of today. The Cowboy Junkies record an album alone, overnight, in Trinity Cathedral in Toronto in 1989. Included are hit versions of past songs by Patsy Cline ("Walkin' After Midnight") and Elvis Presley ("Blue Moon") that softly echo in the cavernous acoustics of the church, giving the group an immediately recognizable style—ghosts of pops past softly floating through the still darkness of night in this huge sacred space. Simon and Garfunkel, recognizing the information-giving function of the classical ballad, in 1965 record the ancient "Scarborough Fair," and overlay it with a "contemporary" radio news report of crime, violence and the Vietnam War. The Beatles, in ending their final studio album together in 1969, record "Golden Slumbers," a song derived from a sixteenth century poem by Thomas Dekker. General Motors, in order to convince Americans of the honest strength of their 1992 Chevrolet pickup truck, uses Bob Seeger's 1970's classic "Like A Rock" as the theme of a series of television commercials. In all these examples, and many more like them that could be mentioned, the past is alive and doing very well, thank you, in the present.

Using The Past: How It Works

Get back to where you once belonged
The Beatles
1964

The musical past plays several types of tunes in our musical present, as I've attempted to point out in a general way. Here I would like to present three further examples which highlight the interaction among the audience, musicians and the social institutions of the society, as they combine to define the past in the present.

The Deck Of Cards

In early February of 1991, as Operation Desert Storm loosed American military might in the Middle East, country singer Whisperin' Bill Anderson chatted with host Ralph Emory on his "Nashville Now" television show. Anderson spoke of his latest song, adapted from an older one, about a boy in the military who is disciplined for bringing a pack of playing cards with him to war—and in a Muslim country, at that. But the young soldier shows how, since he could not afford a bible, these cards—read one by one—reveal a deeply comforting religious message.

Although Anderson did say he had adapted his song from an older one, he did not say how much he owed to the tradition of the past. When America was in Vietnam, Red Sovine released "The Vietnam Deck of Cards." When the Korean conflict was at its height, Red River Dave cut "Red Deck of Cards." And all during World War II, T. Texas Tyler sang his version (in which the soldier is disciplined for having his cards in chapel).

Tyler ran across the lyric concept for "The Deck of Cards" in a nearly identical recitation he found in a book. This recitation was originally used as a church sermon in the 1800s, and was, in turn, adapted from a British folk tale variously called "The Soldier's Bible" or "The Religious Card Player," and which traces its origin back to medieval times. Thus, the song Whisperin' Bill Anderson wrote and sang on "Nashville Now" in February of 1991 was a military update of a popular song that has accompanied Americans to war since, at least, the outbreak of World War II—a song with direct connections through time to medieval Europe and that suggests that God's purpose can be read into everything—even a gambler's deck of cards, if they are interpreted correctly. Or, by implication, war itself—if we, on God's side, just read the cards right.

Calling Elvis

In 1991, Mark Knopfler reformed his group Dire Straits to record a come-back album. The first cut on that disc was "Calling Elvis," a song that took Elvis' early 1950s song "Mystery Train" as its musical backbone, then mixed melodic (and lyric) bits and pieces of several of The King's biggest hits with his own clever lyrics: "Did he leave the building...can he come to the phone...calling Elvis...I'm here all alone."

Elvis has been called on—or called up from the past—increasingly in American popular culture since his death on August 16, 1977. For his fans, many of whom refuse to believe he is dead, Elvis has become a spiritual icon. He (and his music) connects them to their own pasts, as well as to a cultural tradition that seems increasingly under attack in the multi-cultural maelstrom of popular culture in the 1990s. Elvis has sold more records dead than he did alive. His stage show continues, in the form of several Elvis impersonators across the country—many of whom have been doing this for ten years or more, including appearing on a Float at President Clinton's January 1993 Inaugural Day Parade. Fans still, nearly 15 years after his funeral, make the pilgrimage to Graceland, his Memphis home. Elvis souvenirs, from bourbon bottles shaped in the singer's likeness to white cotton underpants with the names of his greatest hits stitched on them, are brisk sellers. His image now appears on a U.S. postage stamp. Musicians and artists, from Paul Simon (who entitled his landmark African/American fusion pop album "Graceland"), to Elvis Costello (who took his name), to Elvis Herselvis (female post-punk band) continue to be influenced by The King, as he lives on in the American imagination.

Elvis has not only served as a talisman of connection to the romantically stable and more simple past, he has also served as a springboard of critique and rejection of that past. The punk bands of the 1980s, adept at holding the icons of the larger culture up to gleefully savage ridicule, have certainly not spared Elvis and his music. The singer's

"Last 10 Days" were cynically chanted in song by the Nightengales as "previously unreleased diary entries" over an increasingly weak and tired sounding rhythm track. The Butthole Surfers blasted his image with feedback and raw guitars in "The Revenge of Anus Presley." And, in 1984, a bootleg recording on the "Dog Vomit" label was released. Entitled "Elvis' Greatest Shit," the album reproduced on its front cover the infamous National Enquirer photo of Presley in his coffin, and advertised "22 (count 'em) dumb songs on one long playing record album," including an out-take of his trademark ballad, "Can't Help Falling In Love," in which Elvis loses the beat and stops the song with a drawn-out and annoyed "awww, shiiiit."

Hawaiian Awakening
Beginning in the mid-1970s, there developed a cultural awakening in Hawaii. Young people, disgusted at the greed of the tourist industry and the way it was not only taking over their land, but also how it was creating a false culture and music to sell as "authentic" in the supper clubs of Waikiki, turned to their own past and traditions in order to forge a cultural and social protest. Young song writers and singers such as Peter Moon and George Helm connected with the few traditional musicians left, people like Gabby Pahinui (who, in order to eke out a living, had abandoned performing and was working on a garbage collection truck in Honolulu).

From such connections to the past, a new music was formed. The lyrics of this new music—many times sung in old Hawaiian—focus on the voraciousness of the tourist industry, the insensivity of the American military in their choices of sacred Hawaiian sites for bombing test ranges, problems of increased real estate development, and the bastardization and cooptation of traditional Hawaiian culture. The musical base of the movement fuses the contemporary sounds of rock, jazz and reggae with traditional Hawaiian chants and melodies. Hawaiian musical instruments from the past, such as gourds and stone rattles, are also used, along with modern electric guitars and keyboards. Traditional slack key Hawaiian guitar styles have also been revived and incorporated into the music of the "Hawaiian Renaissance."

These songs—in their messages and in the traditional instruments that are many times used in playing them—consciously attempt to connect themselves to that thin and fragile line of native Hawaiian music that had, until recently, been kept alive mainly in the rural areas by a handful of respected artists, such as Gabby Pahinui. George Helm, a singer and an activist, began his concerts with an Hawaiian line that translates as; "You are the favorite of the generation before." Helm (who was lost at sea during a protest against the American military) relied heavily on songs written in the first half of this century by native Hawaiians—songs that, in their fragile, rural voices, spoke out against the destruction of Hawaiian culture. Helm called these songs Hawaiian soul and brought them, in his performances, to the present generation—many of whom had never heard them, and were not even aware that they had ever existed.

This music—and its message of social and cultural protest—has become the most popular music of native Hawaiians today, outselling all other forms of music on the Islands, and—by its popularity—commenting upon the emptiness and artificiality of the pseudo-Hawaiian music being played for the tourists downtown. By bringing the past to the present, this music has linked the generations in a common cause of defending their culture and their land, authenticating this cause by tying it to the past. When the Makaha Sons of Ni' i' hau sing their "Waimanalo Blues" at an outdoor rally, or the Peter Moon Band plays in the dim smokey air of a local Honolulu club, the past is alive in their music and potent as an agent of cultural awareness and Hawaiian social change.

The Past In The Future

> The future's not what it used to be
> Mickey Newbury
> 1971

How is popular music's past likely to be used in the future? As far as audiences go, there will always be a time of identification with the music, and a recalling of that specific music as collective identity and nostalgia as one gets older. The baby boom effect that is with us now, I suspect, will recede to become just succeeding (and weakening) demographic echoes of its currently strong self. The amazing longevity of "classic rock and roll" as a central musical form will be recognized as more a function of its ties to the unique baby boom generation and its consumption patterns while this generation was growing older, than as an overall shift in the way generations following the baby boomers will relate to popular music. The focus will shift back to a youthful emphasis, and not be bifurcated as it is today. The 12-25 year olds will retake popular music, with each generation creating its own musical past as it moves into the future.

There will be, however, a strong need for people to seek out roots in the fast changing, multi-cultural world of the future. Consequently, there will be an increase in the revivals of traditional roots music in America—country, blues, Amerindian and hispanic forms—and their incorporation into various portions of the pop market, as well as their linkages to social movements that emphasize cultural pride and social rights.

This means that, from an artist's point of view, there may be more seeking out of past traditional forms on which to build. What the new music will sound like is hard to imagine. Some will be very traditional in nature (and some of this will be protest oriented) while other forms will likely use sophisticated digital computer interfaces and sampling to create whole musics of the future from the sounds of the past. A pop song created entirely from sampling randomly selected bits of a song by Robert Johnson, the blues great ("Hell Hound On My Trail" perhaps), and grafting those sampled and processed sounds onto the musical structure of the Rolling Stones "Sympathy For The Devil" (played backwards) might constitute a future pop hit built upon the music of the past.

The music industry, in its search for new sounds, will mine the traditional musics of the world's cultures to create sounds that are syntheses of past and present—American hip hop, say, combined with traditional chants from the highlands of New Guinea. This new world pop (which has already begun happening—listen to Paul Simon's "Graceland" or "Rhythm of the Saints" or some of the Hawaiian/reggae combinations popular in the Islands today) will be exciting stuff, musically. But one needs to wonder how much of the past, collected and used this way, will make it *as the past*, into the future?

The post modernists see this indiscriminate borrowing and combining of elements in a fearful light. We may be creating a new music, they warn, but we are also tearing pieces of the past out of their cultural contexts in order to do it. By using the past to build the future in this way, we run the risk of severing the ties of significance we hold—torn from its cultural context, the past is not the past at all.

In a very real way, then, given the direction popular music is headed, one must take seriously a comment made recently, and only half in jest, by recording artist and producer T-Bone Burnett; "In popular music, science fiction and nostalgia are becoming the same thing." The circle, past and future, continues to close upon itself. Elvis lives. James Brown shows up in a rap by Public Enemy. And in the streets of America, the children still dance, and shake their bones.

On the New Nostalgia:
"These Foolish Things"
and Echoes of the Dear Departed Past[1]

MORRIS B. HOLBROOK

An airline ticket to romantic places-
O, how my heart has wings-
These foolish things
Remind me of you....

> —Strachey, Link, and Marvell,
> "These Foolish Things"

Yesteryear, yesterday, the life we have left behind has always created a longing, a nostalgia, for "the good old days" that is best fueled on the wings of song, especially popular songs:

> *You call it a waste of time, this taste*
> *For popular tunes, and yet*
> *Good-bye to care when you whistle the air*
> *Of the song you can't forget.*
>
> (The Organ Man. *Stanza 3. Guy Wetmore Carryl)*

America's air is filled with music as we turn our ear to the past and its fond memories.

Introduction

"These Foolish Things"

When the author was a boy, just about to become an adolescent, he first discovered the joys of popular music in general and jazz in particular. He would sit for long hours and listen to his father's old 78 r.p.m. recordings of great musicians like Teddy Wilson and Benny Goodman or singers like Billie Holiday and Nat "King" Cole. One of the tunes that these masters liked to perform is a piece that the author stills loves today, one that perfectly captures the theme of this essay.

Like many other facets of popular culture, this song reflects a close

74

link between the consumer and the artist. Both consumer behavior and artistic activity call upon the imaginative investment of creative energy. Both move, in fun, past barriers toward joy. And both engage an involvement with the role of products and other objects of popular culture in our daily lives as human beings.

Hence, it should surprise no one that everyday consumption experiences tend to permeate the imagery, metaphors, and symbolic language created by artists. The aforementioned song, recalled from childhood, provides a good example. I refer to the great composition by Jack Strachey, Harry Link, and Holt Marvell from the mid-1930s called "These Foolish Things."

Offhand, I cannot think of a clearer case or a more striking illustration of capitalizing on the use of consumption symbolism to evoke the most profound meanings that can be captured by the American popular song. Published in 1935, "These Foolish Things" serves as a veritable compendium for instances of deep significance found in the objects of ordinary consumer behavior. It contains, just to name a few, such rich consumption-related images as a "cigarette that bears a lipstick's traces," "an airline ticket to romantic places," "a tinkling piano," "silk stockings," "dance invitations," "gardenia perfume lingering on a pillow," and "wild strawberries, only seven francs a kilo" — not to mention vivid allusions to flowers, parks, playgrounds, tourist attractions, restaurants ("candlelight on little corner tables"), transportation (trains and steamers), entertainers (Garbo and Crosby), and telecommunications ("a telephone that rings" or "long, excited cables"). It features memorable lyric lines: "A tinkling piano in the next apartment,/Those stumbling words that told you what my heart meant." It is, of course, a passionate love song that celebrates the romantic implications associated with these "foolish" things from the daily life of our mundane existence. But it is also a work of considerable harmonic complexity, especially in the "B" part of its AABA form, otherwise known as the "bridge." This bridge or B-section challenges the powers of almost any singer—almost any singer, that is, except one of those old masters fondly recalled from childhood, Nat "King" Cole.

Nat "King" Cole

As a musician and vocalist, Nat Cole had everything to offer. His piano style shaped the approaches of such latter-day greats as Oscar Peterson (whose early recordings derive directly from work by the "King" Cole Trio). His singing style served as the original model for Ray Charles (whose enormous subsequent influence on pop and rock singers belies the fact that he began as a virtual "King" Cole copy cat). Charles (the singer) plays pretty fair piano, and Peterson (the pianist) can muster a decent singing voice. But Nat Cole, the pioneer, could do and *did* do it *all*.

Nat Cole does it all, for example, in his version of "These Foolish Things," recorded in 1957 by Capitol (W-903, Mx 17346) and reissued on Time-Life (SLGD 15) and on a Capitol compact disc (CDP-7-46649-2), in which Cole builds from a near whisper (accompanied only by guitar) to a stunning show of strength (backed by Billy May's swinging arrangement for big band). This development progresses toward the song's verbal and musical peak in the second repetition of the bridge. Here, drawing on lessons learned from the rhapsodic rubatos of Billie Holiday (who set the norms for this sort of singing in such performances as "When You're Smiling" with Teddy Wilson and Lester Young), Nat Cole lengthens his phrasing to hold it back, to build tension, and thus to give the moment exquisite emphasis as he sings the words, "these...things...are...*dear*...to...me...." Listeners who respond to this expressive musical climax cannot fail to sense the power and to feel the force of nostalgia in people's lives.[2]

The Force Of Nostalgia

"These Foolish Things" in general and the version by Nat Cole in particular are, of course, paeans to the power of the past in the present wherein we conduct our daily lives. Even the most ordinary objects attain meaning by virtue of their ability to arouse memory-laden images and emotion-enriched recollections from days of yore. Even so simple an object as a piece of clothing, a clock, or a coin can serve as the focus for this stirring of sacred associations with the past.

This sort of phenomenon surfaced recently when a touching evocation of cherished remembrances appeared in an otherwise unremarkable movie written by Stu Silver and entitled *Throw Momma from the Train*. In this film, Owen (played by Danny DeVito) tries to persuade Larry (Billy Crystal) to murder his unbearably harridan-like mother (Anne Ramsey). The resulting black comedy (heavy with satiric overtones that parody Hitchcock's *Strangers on a Train*) eventually takes Crystal to DeVito's house, where he meets the shrew herself and where Owen shows Larry his prized collection of coins.

> Owen: You want to see my coin collection?
> Larry: No!
> Owen: I collect coins. I got a dandy collection.
> Larry: I don't want to see it, Owen.
> Owen: But it's my *collection*.
> Larry: I don't care. Look, Owen; I'm just not in the mood.

OK?

Owen: [Removing a box from under the floor boards, lying on his belly like a small child at play, and beginning to extract the coins from their envelopes] I never showed it to anyone before.

Larry: [Impatiently] All *right*, I'll look at it.

Owen: No, it's OK.

Larry: Show me the collection.

Owen: No, you don't mean it.

Larry: [With exasperation] Show me the damned *coins*!

Owen: [Happily] All right. This is a nickel. And this one, *also*, is a nickel. And here's a quarter. And *another* quarter. And a *penny*. See? Nickel, nickel, quarter, quarter, penny.... And *here* is another nickel.

Larry: [Bewildered] Why do you *have* them?

Owen: What do you mean?

Larry: Well, the purpose of a coin collection is that the coins are *worth* something, Owen.

Owen: Oh, but they *are*. This one, here, I got in change when my Dad took me to see Peter, Paul, and Mary. And this one I got in change when I bought a hot dog at the Circus. My Daddy let me keep the change. He *always* let me keep the change. Uh, this one is my *favorite*. This is Martin and Lewis at the Hollywood Palladium. Look at that. See the way it shines, that little eagle? I loved my Dad a lot.

Larry: [Realizing...] So this whole collection is, uh....?

Owen: Change my Daddy let me keep.

Larry: [Tenderly] What was his name?

Owen: Ned..... I really miss him.

Larry: [Gently] That's a real nice collection, Owen.

Owen: Thank you, Larry.

The scene with Owen's coin collection strikes one as a minor masterpiece of cinematic compactness. Its ultimate moral is articulated by Larry: "The purpose of a coin collection is that the coins are *worth* something.... That's a real nice collection, Owen." In sum, the point that should not be missed—in the present essay as well as in the scene with Larry and Owen—is that collections of objects from the past involve one type of nostalgic consumer behavior that draws forth powerful feelings of tremendous significance (in this case, loving memory of a lost father).

Such consumption experiences engender and reflect the deepest and most profound meanings in people's lives.

An Illustration:
The Songs Of David Frishberg

But where—the impatient reader might ask—where are the spirit of Nat Cole and the essence of "These Foolish Things" today when we need them most? One answer is that the romantic fusion of consumption symbolism with the deep meaning of products from the past endures in the songs of David Frishberg. Though hardly a household name,[3] David Frishberg ranks as one of the greatest composers of songs currently active—that is, living and working today. In particular, with reference to our present concerns, no other active composer has even begun to compete with Frishberg's uncanny ability to capture the intricacies and delicacies of the nostalgic consumption experience.

According to such sources as the enthusiastic article by Whitney Balliett (1988) in the *New Yorker* (reprinted in his book on *American Singers*), Frishberg has acquired this ability via a background almost perfectly suited to produce a master of songs about consumption. Born in 1935 (and, thus, coeval with "These Foolish Things"), raised in Minneapolis/St. Paul, and educated in journalism at the University of Minnesota, Frishberg first paid his dues as a publicist and advertising copywriter before gigging around New York as a jazz pianist in the 1960s, moving to Los Angeles to work as a composer during the 1970s, and more recently adopting Portland as the home base for his performing career of the 1980s and 1990s. This performing career has settled into the self-accompanied rendering of his own brilliant songs. These songs embody the unexampled fusion of an advertising-acclaimed sensibility, a literate sensitivity to the nuances of consumption symbolism, a musical sense deeply imbued with the ethos of jazz, and a sensuous awareness of nostalgic memories associated with objects from the past.

Frishberg's best material has appeared in two mostly instrumental albums (Concord Jazz CJ-37 and CJ-74), in two volumes of *The David Frishberg Songbook* (Omnisound N-1040 and N-1051; partially reissued on Concord CCD-4462), in two live singing performances at Vine Street and at the Great American Music Hall (Fantasy F-9638 and Fantasy F-9651 or FCD-9651-2), in a recent session of studio recordings (Concord Jazz CCD-4402), and in a concert from Rochester, New York (recently broadcast over WBGO in Newark and taped off the air, with appreciation, by the author).[4] All these offerings are almost impossible to find in the record stores (though the compact disc on Fantasy called "Can't Take You Nowhere" and the newer Concord recording entitled "Let's Eat Home" sometimes show up in the CD racks). Those interested should leave no stone unturned in their quest to find Frishberg recordings before they go irretrievably out of print in the manner typical of the greatest jazz offerings.[5]

In the broadcast of his Rochester concert, Frishberg jokingly suggests that his songs are all about names, humiliation, and food. One can put it even more simply than that. His songs are all about *consumer behavior*. They are loaded with business references, marketing imagery, and consumption symbolism. And they are works of genius.

The songs of David Frishberg have addressed numerous themes of concern to observers of contemporary society. These include the potential venality or mendacity of the modern materialistic and capitalistic culture ("Blizzard of Lies," "Wheelers and Dealers,"), the corruption of political leaders (a tune dedicated to J. Danforth Quayle and called "Long As You're Lookin' Good"), the elusive but insidious allure of financial wealth ("Long Daddy Green," subtitled "The Almighty Dollar"), dangers of the advertising hype and communicational clutter that saturate our electronic society ("The Sports Page"), and the character flaws and human foibles that afflict civilization ("Can't Take You Nowhere," "You Would Rather Have the Blues," "I'm Hip," "My Attorney Bernie"). But it is in his songs evoking remembrances of things past that Frishberg undertakes his most sustained thematic development.

Thus, often, Frishberg's songs reveal a deeply wistful sense of nostalgia. Later, I shall return to three conspicuous examples concerned with conveying three "orders" of nostalgic experience ("Do You Miss New York?," "The Dear Departed Past," and "Matty"). Here, I shall pause to dwell only briefly on this general aspect of Frishberg's oeuvre.

Fondness for great sports figures and reverence for other heroes or heroines from the past fill Frishberg's songs and lend them some of their most poignant moments. For example, "Van Lingle Mungo" and "Dodger Blue" consist almost entirely of ballplayers' names artfully strung together to make ingenious rhymes.[6] Legend has it that the premiere of the latter song—at a Dodgers Oldtimers Banquet—reduced the otherwise stoic Walt Alston to tears.[7] Even more tender is Frishberg's loving portrait of a favorite film actress in "Marilyn Monroe." Similarly deep sentiments, mixed with unalloyed admiration for the originality of his heroes, enrich Frishberg's songs in honor of such great jazz artists as Bix Beiderbecke and Zoot Sims. In "Dear Bix," he adopts a conversational style, chiding the pioneering cornettist (who drank himself into an early grave) even while commemorating the fierce independence of his music. On a more upbeat note, "Zoot Walks In" offers a virtually complete definition of creative innovation and a rousing celebration of musical creativity in honor of a great jazz figure who recently passed away.

Other songs pursue the more materialistic side of the thematic longing for days of yore that permeates Frishberg's work. For example, one especially pensive piece, entitled "Sweet Kentucky Ham," conveys the loneliness of a traveling musician, on the road, far from family, friends, and even acceptable food:

> It's ten p.m.
> They're rolling up the sidewalks in Milwaukee.
>
> * * *
>
> And you turn the pages of your magazine,
> And you feel you ought to quit while you're behind
> 'Cause you've got sweet Kentucky ham on your mind....

Such songs convey a profound but nonetheless relatively conventional recollection of home and a bittersweet longing for familiar places and surroundings.[8]

A far more challenging premise for a song motivates Frishberg's amazing exercise in environmental consciousness. Given the nearly impossible task of writing a plausible piece of music on the subject of ecology, Frishberg adopts a kind of retrospective postmodernism to compose an anthem sung by our own descendants—traveling, homeless, through the galaxy and looking back on "The Green Hills of Earth" that we, their ancestors, have destroyed:

> But wander we will, for wander we must;
> Remembering still, we're only children, children of the dust;
> And wherever we wander, wherever we roam,
> We'll never forget the world we called our own;
> The green hills of Earth..., Our home.

This theme of nostalgia combines with consumption symbolism and marketing imagery concerning products long past the decline phases of their life cycles, activities long out of fashion, and ancient heroes long since gone to produce David Frishberg's masterpiece, "The Dear Departed Past."[9] From the perspective of those interested in consumer behavior, "The Dear Departed Past" is a song without equal. It portrays the lifestyle associated with a reverence for the consumption experiences of a bygone era with a richness of imagery that makes it an unqualified masterpiece. Just as, today, we look back on "These Foolish Things" to praise it as a durable achievement of the songwriting art, citizens of the Twenty-First Century will surely single out Frishberg's "Departed Past" as among the most literate, most musical, and most enduring of artworks—glorious in its complexity and internal rhymes, fascinating in its perspicacity and turns of phrase[10]:

> That's when basketballs had laces,
> And halfbacks played safety on defense;
> That's when there were parking places -
> A hotdog for a dime; White Castles, seven cents.

For reasons deeply embedded in lines like these, pervasively distributed throughout the melodies and harmonic progressions to which they are set, and solidly embodied by the relatively few performances that have found their way to records, tapes, and discs, it has been David Frishberg's gift to place and forever to fix the role of business references, marketing imagery, and consumption symbolism within the context of the American popular song. In this, he has combined the material of popular music with the concerns of consumer research so as to draw upon and to sustain a tradition of including consumption symbolism in pop songs that harks back to a development in the 1930s of which "These Foolish Things" remains a shining example. Frishberg's tunes have revealed, again and again, how the nouns (people, places, and things) of daily life produce verbs (uses, activities, and events) rich in consumption experiences that accumulate to build lived worlds embracing memories of the significant consumer behaviors that form our cherished links with the Dear Departed Past. In such a world, we recall the heroes, the homes, and the happenings—Zoot Sims and Marilyn Monroe, Kentucky and the green hills of Earth, watching baseball and eating hamburgers—whose consumption has brought meaning to our lives. In such a world, these things—truly—are dear to us.[11]

Indeed, they have given me the theme for this essay.

Preview

In the sections to follow, I shall survey the role of nostalgia in the lives of consumers from the viewpoint of historians, social scientists, critics of pop culture, artists, and others who have occasionally chosen to devote their attention to this neglected topic. This survey will cover a broad range of consumer products involving many different kinds of consumption experiences. These include popular music from the past sixty years, examples of entertainment and everyday household items from various periods of time, films, movie stars, television programs, fashion designs, and advertising. Herein, I shall traverse a fairly broad spectrum of consumer tastes associated with products from the past and with experiences linked to the days of yore. I shall, in short, give plenty of scope for the emergence of phenomena related to the effects of nostalgia on the events of today. In this, I shall remain true to both my heart and my head. My head leads me toward the conceptual background reported in what follows. My heart takes me back to the memory of that first exposure to "These Foolish Things" and to the impact of a continuing nostalgic infatuation with "The Dear Departed Past."

Nostalgia And Consumer Behavior

In "These Foolish Things," Strachey, Link, and Marvell draw on symbolic consumer behavior associated with a variety of consumption experiences and with deep meanings in possessions to capture the fleeting memory-drenched moments that depend for their evocation on the imagery suggested by the common things—the consumer products and their usage—found in ordinary life. Thus, the songwriters call upon such everyday objects of consumption as cigarettes, lipstick, airplanes, pianos, stockings, dances, gardenias, strawberries, bed linens, candles, restaurants, and pop singers to suggest the experience-deepening force of consumption symbolism inextricably linked with the human condition—or, at least, with the human condition that stems from living in the current Western consumer-oriented society of the "material world." As the song states so explicitly at its climax in the B-section of the second chorus, "These things are *dear* to me...."

It seems fair to assert that much consumer behavior involves similar phenomena based on emotionally-charged associations with product-related experiences from the past. Thus, in his magisterial volume entitled *The Past Is a Foreign Country*, David Lowenthal has chronicled the countless ways in which consumers—increasingly, it seems—depend upon objects from the past to develop a sense of their own identity:

Nowadays, the past is...pervasive in its abundance of deliberate, tangible evocations.... the trappings of history now festoon the whole country. All memorabilia are cherished.... Long uprooted and newly unsure of the future, Americans *en masse* find comfort in looking back (xv).... the past seems to matter more and more; innumerable facets of modern life reflect its heightened import. Physical relics are treasured national talismans.... For individuals as for nations, things salvaged from the past have come to embody greater value—and are preserved in greater quantity and variety—than ever before (365).... More than any previous generation, we cram our houses with furnishings that deliberately evoke the past, adorn walls with family photos and mantels with memorabilia, and convert streets into 'Memory Lanes'.... Dreams of re-experiencing dominate much of what we read, see, and hear: beyond mere curiosity lies a deep fascination with how things used to be, an eagerness for lifelike insights into the past, near or remote, familiar or arcane. (367)

In general, these echoes of the past form part of the cultural fabric of contemporary society. In particular, they exert an irresistible effect on consumer behavior. Indeed, their role in the consumption experience serves as the main theme of the present essay.

Consumer researchers have recently begun to turn their attention to issues related to the effects of nostalgia. Thus, in the early 1990s, an awakening to the phenomena of nostalgia has appeared in reviews by Belk ("Role of Possesssions"), by Havlena and Holak, by Holbrook and Schindler ("Echoes"), and by contributors to the volume edited by Belk (*Highways*). In this, the consumer researchers echo the observations found in the news media and in other reflections of the society around us.

The News Media

Quite conspicuously, the phenomena of nostalgia have commanded widespread attention in the major news media. For example, a story in the *New York Times* (Rothenberg, "The Past") proclaims in its title that "The Past Is Now the Latest Craze" and asserts that a "new wave of nostalgia"—involving a "passion for the past"—has swept over us (D19). According to Rothenberg,

A booming market in nostalgia is turning yesterday—when all our troubles seemed so far away—into the latest craze in the communications and consumer products industries. (D1)

Thus, articles on interior design and home furnishings now assert the virtues of "Decorating With Nostalgia, Emotion and Other Intangibles" (Slesin, "Decorating" C1) and celebrate the nostalgia-drenched meanings to be found in "touching tableaux of a bygone era" (Slesin, "Lasting" C1). The business press views the behavior of vintage car collectors as illustrating a "market truism" that "people love the wheels of their youth":

baby boomers...are redefining classic cars as those with fins, four-speed shifts and 400-horsepower engines: in short, the muscle cars they loved in high school. (Johnson A1)

Music critics suggest that "slower than sunspot cycles and as inexorable as the tides, pop-music nostalgia trails the present by about 20 years" (Pareles, "70's" 28). And those concerned with the arts in general contend that "In the Arts, Tomorrow Begins With Yesterday" (Braudy):

now that we've reached the 1990's, it's nostalgia that's news.... nostalgia for a community with closer relations to nature and innocence has been potently intensified.... the image-merchants have appropriated many things—among them the arts—to make capital of this nostalgic longing.... Ever since there have been people, there has been someone to say the past was better.... But...the nostalgia of today...certainly seems to be a lot more pervasive (1).... At the heart of all nostalgias is a desire to recapture innocence, to open the door to an ideal past, an Eden of time where great things are happening forever (16).... The merchandising of that nostalgia...plays on the hope that there is somewhere a real connection, a golden bough to ease the path back to what has been lost. (17)

Marketing Responses to Nostalgia

Not surprisingly, advertisers have reacted quickly to such swings in nostalgia. In this connection, Moriarty and McGann found that—historically—nostalgic themes, art, and typography in print ads tended to increase during the 1960s and 1970s. Meyers updates this focus on the use of nostalgic advertising appeals in a column for the *Minneapolis Star Tribune* entitled "Ads Seek Loudest Blasts from the Past." He quotes Rebecca Holman from D'Arcy Masius Benton & Bowles as saying that "people are studying nostalgia today the way they studied sex in advertising...years ago" (1D).

For example, evidence of this trend includes the resurrection of old ads for such products as Campbell's Soups ("M'm! M'm! Good!"), Timex Watches ("it takes a licking and keeps on ticking"), Maypo Hot Cereal ("I want my Maypo"), Camel Cigarettes ("I'd walk a mile for a Camel"), Clairol ("does she or doesn't she?"), and Coca-Cola ("I'd like to teach the World to sing in perfect harmony").[12] (For further discussion of past- and nostalgia-related advertising themes, see Havlena and Holak; Stern.)

Musical Consumption and the "Big Chill" Syndrome

A comparable perspective, focused more narrowly on the market for music, informs a recent article in *7 Days* by John Leland on "Adult Musical Taste." Leland discusses the manner in which consumers return for solace and sustenance to the consumption habits of their younger days in general and to those connected with music in particular. Thus, he pictures today's baby boomers as "children of the '60s slipping begrudgingly into adulthood..., singing along with old R&B records...songs that are now 25 years old" (10).

With respect to this focus on "musical demographics," Stipp adds that "the most important factor determining people's musical tastes is their age":

The music of our adolescence can have a profound impact on our musical tastes for the rest of our lives, because these are the formative years for music preferences.... The connection between age and popular music preferences is so strong that a fan's age can be predicted from his or her favorite oldies. (48-49)

According to Leland, the ability of quarter-century-old music to appeal strongly to "a 35-year-old...audience whose tastes never changed—and who never identified with anything as deeply as the music of their teens" (13) depends on the strongly emotional, memory-recalling, nostalgic power of songs from one's youth:

Songs are powerful mnemonic devices—especially songs that once played an important part in our lives. The most dippy or banal song...can tell an emotionally rich story, a story in which we cavort in a supermarket of possibility that is no longer open to our adult selves. They can instantly recall images of what we wore, whom we were with, what was in the emotional offing the first time we heard them. More importantly, they recall how we *felt*—a certain tittery excitement, maybe a footloose dread or optimism, the tingle of sexual wonder. Diaries of our private fantasies as well as our social lives, songs bring back emotional states that are no longer part of our lives. Even heard through adult ears, they aren't insipid—they're shorthand for experience. (11)

At times, such temporal retreats are portrayed with understated acceptance as part of the normal backdrop to the ongoing lives of consumers. For example—in the movie *Big Chill*—when college classmates from the University of Michigan in the late 1960s reconvene to attend the funeral of a friend, they spend their time eating the same foods, wearing the same clothes, telling the same stories, thinking the same thoughts, and listening to the same music that they shared during their college years. Indeed, in honor of this film, Leland (1990) coins a telling phrase to describe his central focus as "the big-chill-soundtrack syndrome writ large" (13).

At other times, this preoccupation with consumption-centered habits from the past can provoke responses bordering on hostility—as in Leland's crafty putdown of "Lite FM" (14) or Gorman's mock warning that

"Nostalgia Can Choke the Ongoing Stream of Your Life" (16). Thus, Buhle ("Intro.") reacted to the Big-Chill phenomenon with some disdain:

As later dramatized by the...somnambulant Yuppie confusion in the hit film *The Big Chill*, key symbolic cultural tastes almost froze in time so as to maintain the illusions of a vanished authenticity. Subsequent social life, for millions among the largest and most prosperous generation in U.S. history, became a commodified meditation on an unforgettable past.... The proliferation of flea markets, the salvaging and sales of every remotely defined "collectible," offered a particularly manic expression of the impulse to recover something lost in the junkyards and attics of American consciousness. (xviii-xix)

Comparable sentiments surfaced in a recent *New Yorker* cartoon. A man with shoulder-length hair and bulging eyes sits in a barren room decorated only by "Love & Peace" posters on the wall—strumming a guitar and singing "Love, Love, Love, All you need is Love" while his exasperated significant other screams at him from the doorway: "The sixties are over, Ralph. The seventies and the eighties, for God's sake, are over. Give it a rest!" (*New Yorker*, Jan. 15, 1990, 33).

The Baby Boomers

These and other comments found in the popular press have tended to link such trends with the aging of the baby-boom generation and their reverence for objects encountered during the days of their youth in the 1950s and 1960s (Johnson; Leland; *The Economist*). On this theme, Miller suggests that "nostalgia makes boomers buy": "Baby boomers...are taking a little trip down memory lane, and marketers are merrily following after them" (1).

In a similar vein, the sociologist Fred Davis has argued that nostalgia is a general phenomenon endemic to the current epoch and amounting to nothing less than a "nostalgia boom" (x) in which members of contemporary society are engaged in a "nostalgia orgy" (105) through which they seek to resolve their "*collective* identity crisis" (106) by means of a "collective search for identity" (107) that "looks backward rather than forward, for the familiar rather than the novel, for certainty rather than discovery" (108). Currently, Davis sees the nostalgic impulse that he documented in 1979 as recycling a decade later:

Nostalgia waxes and wanes, and it's certainly waxing now, as the baby-boom generation passes into phases of life that create conditions that can elicit nostalgic responses. (quoted by Rothenberg, "The Past" D1)

Meanwhile, Lowenthal agrees that our society has entered an era of "rampant nostalgia":

Fashions for old films, old clothes, old music, old recipes are ubiquitous, and nostalgia markets every product (xvi).... our rampant nostalgia, our obsessive search for roots, our endemic concern with preservation, the potent appeal of national heritage show how intensely the past is still felt (xxiv).... Nostalgia...fills the popular press, serves as advertising bait, merits sociological study; no term better expresses modern malaise.... If the past is a foreign country, nostalgia has made it 'the foreign country with the healthiest tourist trade of all' (4).... The present alone is inadequate to our desires.... Disenchantment with today impels us to try to recover yesterday. That discontent takes many forms: a devotion to relics, the treasuring of antiques and souvenirs, a tendency to value what is old simply because it is old, the rejection of change. These reactions...reflect the same yearning for times gone by (33).... the cult of nostalgia, the yearning for roots, the demand for heritage, the passion for preservation show that the spell of the past remains potent.... The past remains integral to us all, individually and collectively.... it is assimilated in ourselves, and resurrected into an ever-changing present. (412)

The Anecdotal Evidence

The symptoms signaling this wave of collective nostalgia surround us everywhere in our everyday experience and familiar lives as consumers. These signals include the devotion to memorabilia (Hughes) that characterizes an aficionado of flea markets and swap meets (Belk, Sherry, and Wallendorf, "Collectors"). They encompass the potentially fanatic activities of serious collectors (Johnston and Beddow), who very often focus on objects that evoke memory-laden associations to provide meaning in their current reminiscences (Belk, Wallendorf, Sherry, and Holbrook; Belk, Wallendorf, Sherry, Holbrook, and Roberts). On a grand scale, they embrace the idolization of past heroes and heroines who have played roles as ideal models for emulation and adoration (O'Guinn). On a more mundane level, they surround the continual revival of fads, fashions, and other quaint foibles or follies that constantly cycle and recycle through our lives as consumers: Teddy Bears, Ouija boards, zoot suits, canasta, hula hoops, the twist, pet rocks, mood rings, flat tops, duck tails, beehives, afros, chrome, fins, miniskirts, midiskirts, Beatlemania, and Batman (Carr, Case, and Dellar; Marum and Parise; Sann).

Possessions and the Sense of Past

As noted repeatedly in the work of Belk ("Role of Possessions;"

"Possessions and the Sense"), our possessions evoke meanings that convey a "sense of past":

Photographs, souvenirs, trophies, and more humble everyday objects act, in part, as repositories for memories and meanings in our lives.... such objects aid in creating and perpetuating a sense of past. ("Role of Possessions" 1)

Thus, in part via possessions, "remembrance is in very large measure a reconstruction of the past achieved with data borrowed from the present" (Halbwachs 69):

Our home—furniture and its arrangement, room decor—recalls family and friends.... furniture, ornaments, pictures, utensils, and knick-knacks...recall for us older customs and social distinctions. (129)

For example, old photographs "share a tendency to make of the past a possession that can be savored, handled, treasured, and kept safe from loss...so that these photographs can produce and reproduce the bittersweet emotion of nostalgia" (Belk, "Possessions and the Sense" 3). Souvenirs and mementos remind us of special moments and events, help us to remember, and thereby serve a "concretizing function" (Gordon 135). Various "debris" such as "grave goods, mason's marks, sinopie, the contents of rubbish-tips" may serve as "bridges that provide backward-turning links that help us to seize the past" (Cherry 78). Antiques serve as "the reassuring, tangible fragments of the past" that convince us "it wasn't just a dream" (Hillier 71):

This brings us straight back to the idea of the antique as a fetish-object which has soaked up some of the history to which it is a witness, and can help us to evoke that past.... Here again is the idea that a particular antique has absorbed something of an earlier time, something which we may be able to distil from it.... While some...think that antiques help one to recover the past, others see them as poignant relics of a past which can never be restored, reminding us of past ideals superior to those of the present. (77-79)

Further, as Lowenthal documents in great detail, relics from the past may play a major role in determining our current sense of identity (197):

relics remain essential bridges between then and now. They...provide archeological metaphors that illumine the processes of history and memory.... We respond to relics as objects of interest or beauty, as evidence of past events, and as talismans of continuity (xxiii).... Possession of valued relics...enhances life.... To have a piece of tangible history links one with its original maker and with intervening owners, augmenting one's own worth (43).... we treasure the old things in our homes for the pastness inherent in them; they reflect ancestral inheritance, recall former friends and occasions, and link past with future generations (52).... The popularity of ruined castles, the price of patinated bronzes, the market for 'distressed' furniture attest the continuing appeal of marks of age.... The worn and tattered state of treasured mementoes—battered jugs, old cigarette packets, dog-eared theatre programmes—is integral to their companionable value (149).... How do we come to know about the past?... The simple answer is that we...live among relics from previous times (185).... To gain assurance that yesterday was as substantial as today we saturate ourselves with bygone reliquary details, reaffirming memory and history in tangible form (191).... Tangible relics survive in the form of natural features and human artifacts. Awareness of such relics enhances knowledge gained through memory and history (238).... For most people, relics render the past more important.... a table that has been in the family for generations...brings...a "sense of past".... that tangible sense persuades us that the past we recall and chronicle is a living part of the present (249)..... Every relic is a testament not only to its initiators but to its inheritors, not only to the spirit of the past but to the perspectives of the present. (412)

Collections As Organized Embodiments of Nostalgia

A more organized manifestation of such nostalgic consumption— also treated at length by Belk and his colleagues (Belk, Wallendorf, Sherry, and Holbrook; Belk, Wallendorf, Sherry, Holbrook, and Roberts)— involves the phenomenon in which nostalgic consumption gets embodied by formal or informal collections. As documented extensively in the aforementioned references, such collections may acquire supercharged emotional attachments based on the most profound product meanings associated with earlier times. A collection (e.g., old cars) may "serve as a kind of religious object" (Dannefer 392) that provides "a point of contact for treasured memories of the past" (392-393) so that "it is difficult to disentangle the enthusiast's nostalgia for an experienced but now bygone era from his nostalgia for his own childhood" (407): "For the car enthusiast...the past...is experienced through the car" (411).

As noted by Belk, et al. ("Collecting"):

Contemporary collecting is unevenly but broadly distributed across age, gender, and socioeconomic categories. It seems to reflect a heightened acquisitive and possessive orientation that epitomizes the modern consumer culture. The considerable inputs of time, money, skill, and energy devoted to collecting also help to make it a consumption activity eminently worthy of study. *But most importantly, collecting is a passionate sphere of consumption from which collectors seem to derive significant meaning and fulfillment in their lives.* (190, italics added)

In other words, collecting calls forth the highest levels of customer involvement and evokes the most profound depths of consumption experience.

This point appears clearly in a recent play by Terrence McNally entitled *The Lisbon Traviata*. McNally's work offers what must be the first full-length theatrical production that takes record collecting as its central theme. On its surface, the play depicts a love quadrangle involving four homosexual men, two of whom (Mendy and Stephen) are held together emotionally by their shared devotion to opera in general and to the performances of Maria Callas in particular. Thus, much of the action and most of the humor in Act I revolve around Mendy's desperation to hear a new bootleg recording of Callas singing *La Traviata* in Lisbon. This scene contains lines guaranteed to move any compassionate record collector to the deepest commiseration. In this, it reflects the playwright's own avowed musical fanaticism and obsession with opera recordings and performances:

In the first act of McNally's play, audiences are treated to an encounter between two rabid fans of Maria Callas.... Mendy goes into a frenzy when Stephen mentions a pirated recording he owns of a performance of *La Traviata* sung by Callas in Lisbon in 1958.... Most of the first act dwells on the two men's Callas obsession and their disdain for other great singers.... McNally, himself, admits to having been an ardent Callas fan during the Golden Age of Opera. (Botto 66)

In Act II, we find that Stephen's apartment features row upon row of vertical shelves that house literally thousands of lps and CDs carefully arranged in a well-organized order that permits him to pluck examples of interest from the filing system with barely a glance. In a touching comic thrust, Stephen recounts how he had to explain to his father why anyone would want more than one recording of the same piece of music. "For the same reason," he says, "that *you* need to watch the Super Bowl again every year." Thus does the collector notice subtle distinctions, even those among performances of the same composition by the same artists recorded on different occasions.[13] The extent to which such subtle differences *matter* is the *essence* of the true collecting spirit.

The Collecting Cycle: Dimensions for a Typology of Collectors and Collections. Certain key dimensions of collecting might serve as the bases for a general typology or a classification scheme suitable for characterizing collectors and collections. In constructing such a set of dimensions, I have drawn heavily on materials collected by the Consumer-Behavior Odyssey (Belk, *Highways*; especially the chapter by Holbrook "Log"), on supplementary observations (Holbrook "Audiovisual," "Psychoanalytic," "Steps"), and on additional interviews (Wimmer). Further, I have benefited from Wimmer's systematic validation of the dimensional scheme against corroborative depth-interviews with two new informants.[14]

In general, collecting behavior can be conceptualized according to the familiar consumption cycle of acquisition-usage-and-disposition. However, of particular importance in the case of collecting is the problem of maintenance—that is, storing or housing the collection (comparable to keeping an inventory of any other consumer product). Further—cutting across the distinctions among *acquiring, maintaining, using,* and *disposing*—virtually every aspect of every collection reflects certain facets of its *theme.* Hence, taking the theme as central, the collecting cycle appears as shown in Figure 1.

Each of the major stages of the cycle (shown in CAPITAL LETTERS) raises certain questions of the type sometimes referred to as "who?, what?, where?, when?, how?, and why?" These issues appear in small letters (with parenthetical explanations) in the diagram. In particular, *acquiring* implies some *motivation* (Why?) and some *mode* of collecting (How?). *Maintaining* raises issues concerning *space* and spatial relations (Where?). *Using* involves various aspects of the *social situation* surrounding the collection (Who?). *Disposing* suggests questions concerning factors related to *time* (When?). And, as previously noted, the *theme* introduces considerations of *substance* that permeate all the other aspects of the cycle (What?).

Given these questions raised by the collecting cycle, each aspect of the scheme suggests distinctions or continua that might serve as the key bases or dimensions for a typology of collectors and collections. Here, I shall list these proposed bases or dimensions in skeletal form, with a brief discussion and example of each.

Motivation for Acquiring (Why?). The reasons for collecting appear to be arrayed along four primary continua.

(1) Hobby/Profession: One informant collects Christmas ornaments as a hobby but takes pictures of collections of objects as part of her profession as a

photographer; another raises orchids for *both* purposes (with a special tagging system to keep the two separate).

(2) Aesthetics/Utility: Some collections contain objects that are appreciated for their beauty alone and never used (e.g., silver spoons on the wall), whereas other collections comprise objects prized for their functional utility (e.g., dishes in daily use, with constant fear of accidental breakage).

(3) Monetary/Emotional Value: At one extreme, a man who saves old clothes and letters keeps these objects primarily for their emotional value; by contrast, those who invest in the art market may expect some sort of monetary reward.

(4) Type A/Type B: Danet and Katriel distinguish between collectors of Type A (motivated primarily by the desire to acquire knowledge and to reach completion) and Type B (motivated primarily by the pursuit of beauty manifested by individual items of high quality); for example, a Type A record collector would buy a poor performance of a musical piece for the sake of completing the series; a Type B collector would purchase or keep only performances of high artistic merit.

Mode of Acquiring (How?). The manner in which collections accrue suggests five key distinctions.

(1) Single/Multiple: At one extreme, a woman collects a number of different kinds of items (marbles, urns, stones, gems, rubber stamps, etc.); at the other, one man focuses on just a single type of object (his automobiles—where financial considerations pose formidable constraints).

(2) Simultaneous/Sequential: Some collections depend on being possessed simultaneously (e.g., a complete set of china or baseball cards), whereas others may permit sequential ownership (e.g., house restorations, thoroughbred horses, or customized cars).

(3) Purposive/Haphazard: One woman collects her dreams purposively (by awakening three times a night to enter them in a diary that she keeps by her bedside) but collects other objects in a more haphazard manner (buying marbles or gems only when she happens to run across something that appeals to her).

(4) Impermeable/Permeable: Many collectors create collections that are impermeable in the sense that they do not mix gifts from friends with their

other collected possessions; others own permeable collections that easily absorb gifts or donations (a public museum being an obvious example).

(5) Completable/Uncompletable: One who collects dishes, baseball cards, or recordings by a particular singer could conceivably reach completion and achieve closure by acquiring the full set; by contrast, a collection of dreams, sea shells, or heart-shaped objects is inherently uncompletable and can never be finished.

Maintaining the Space (Where?). The spatial aspects of maintaining a collection appear to vary on at least four dimensions.

(1) Vertical/Horizontal: Many collections are housed "vertically" in a central location (as when displayed in a special cabinet or on custom-built shelving); others are spread "horizontally" throughout the living area (as in the case of a heart, bunny, or duck collection scattered around the house).

(2) Inaccessible/Accessible: All or part of a collection may be stored away from easy access (a trunk full of Barbie Dolls or Xmas ornaments buried deep on closet shelves), whereas others remain readily accessible at all times (CDs stored in a cabinet next to the stereo system or spoons permanently displayed on the dining-room wall); also, some collectors rotate parts of their collections between long-term storage (inaccessible) and short-term display (accessible)—a practice that appears to be especially common among art collectors who live in small apartments.

(3) Structured/Unstructured: Collections with high degrees of structure may reside in specially-built display cases or in other highly symmetrical arrays (one woman's entire house being organized as a conspicuous example of such pervasive symmetry); at the other extreme, when complete lack of structure prevails, a collection may actually escape recognition (as in the case of some children's stuffed animals, strewn around their rooms in total disarray).

(4) Cared For/Ignored: Some collections require or evoke energetic efforts to take care of them (e.g., growing orchids or polishing a car); by contrast, others require little upkeep (e.g., a shelf of rare books or a head-to-foot tattoo job).

Social Aspects of Using the Collection (Who?). Some collections are intended to be used solely by the collector, whereas others serve as a vehicle for social interaction between the collector and others. Within these aspects of the social situation, four distinctions apply.

(1) Personal/Impersonal: (Im)personal collections are (not) closely related to the private history of the owner; photos or tattoos with special significance would typically exemplify the personal side (as in a carefully preserved album of

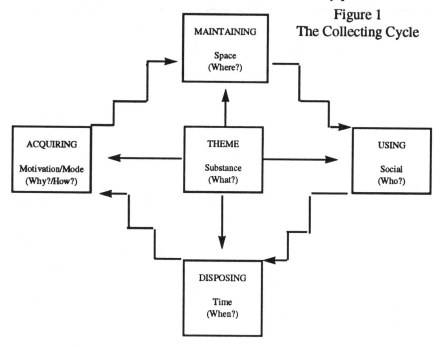

Figure 1
The Collecting Cycle

family snapshots); stamps or books might be more impersonal (as in a set of stamps commemorating heroes from the American Revolution); needless to say, if one acquires an album of family photos from a pawn shop or if one's great grandfather thrice removed was George Washington, the positions of these two examples would be reversed.

(2) Social Substitute/Supplement: A collector might treat a collection as a substitute for interactions with other people (e.g., developing a "serious" relationship with one's Barbie Dolls); other collections might actually enhance social interactions (e.g., a fancy automobile used for courting members of the opposite sex).

(3) Private/Communal: On a closely related point, some collections are enjoyed in private (one's secret stock of porno magazines), whereas others almost demand communal sharing (one's investment in a fine wine cellar).

(4) Extroverted/Introverted: On another closely related point, some collections intentionally reveal aspects of an extroverted personal identity to others

(tattoos, cars, household decorations, Xmas ornaments), whereas others protect an introverted need for distancing (old letters, secret diaries, sex toys).

The Time for Disposing (When?). Collections either do or do not come to an end in three important ways.

(1) Open or Perpetual/Closed or Self-Contained: Some collections contain seeds or starter items that spawn second-generation collections (as for a bell collector who gives one bell to each grandchild in hopes of encouraging new collections to spring up); others remain self-contained and do not aspire to generating new ones (as when a woman resisted buying marble-shaped gems because she did not want to connect her marble collection to her gem collection but preferred to keep them separate).

(2) Retained/Divested: Once a collection is complete, the owner may choose to retain it (old stamp books in the basement or a sequestered set of owls) or to divest it (photography collections sold to a museum or an architect's plans donated to a school library).

(3) Mortal/Immortal: Collections may be dismantled or "deaccessed" intact after the owner's death; the former suggests mortality (as when the tattoo collection dies with its owner); the latter confers a type of immortality (as when future generations can appreciate a family's bequest to the local art museum for purposes of constructing a wing named in their honor and used to house their collection of paintings by Degas).

Thematic Substance (What?). Finally, collectors may or may not be aware of various themes that characterize their collections. These aspects of thematic substance suggest seven additional bases for classification.

(1) Conscious/Unconscious: A collector may consciously amass a set of possessions (snapshots in a book, letters in a drawer, entries in a diary) or may unconsciously assemble objects with a common theme (artworks that all happen, without awareness, to represent animals).

(2) Intended/Unintended: On a similar distinction, the "collector" may or may not intend some group of objects to constitute a "collection"; the owner does intend his Barbie Dolls as a collection; by contrast, a mother and her children do not appear to view themselves as intentional collectors of stuffed animals (though they are certainly conscious of owning a lot of them).

(3) Tangible/Intangible: The objects in question may be tangible (e.g., marbles and gems) or intangible (e.g., dreams).

(4) Unisensory/Multisensory: The objects may appeal primarily to one sensory mode (visual responses to snapshots, auditory responses to recordings) or to multiple modalities (the visual and auditory aspects of bells, music boxes, or videotapes); on the latter point, Danet and Katriel note the importance of olfactory sensations in collecting such objects as erasers or soaps; as usual, mixed cases or changes often occur; for example, in collecting musical recordings, the shift from lps to CDs entails a (literal) loss in the visual component associated with album graphics and cover art.

(5) Active/Reactive: The items collected may or may not require physical or mental manipulation for their full appreciation; on the active side, books must be read and cars driven; on the reactive side, music must be heard and paintings admired; however, one seldom encounters a pure case; most real-world examples involve some blend of active and reactive responses on the part of the collector—as when attending to the beautiful pattern on one's new "retro" necktie even while laboring to construct an impeccable Windsor knot.

(6) Animate/Inanimate: As emphasized earlier, the objects collected may or may not be alive (though we stop short of considering people as suitable items for collecting, pace Zsa Zsa and Henry VIII); thus, collections of parrots, ferrets, and rubber plants are living things; marbles, automobiles, and spoons are clearly insentient; some representations of people, animals, or plants occupy a position in between—such as Barbie dolls, animal sculptures, fake ficus trees, or figurines.

(7) Real/Artificial: In a related distinction, collectibles range widely in their degree of reality versus artificiality; for example, one mother and daughter collect authentic and fake potted plants, respectively; one woman fills her home with real houseplants but, on her stove, features a phony berry pie that looks good enough to eat (valued because it fits with her collection of heart-shaped objects); another has real living pets, but her friend settles for a stuffed dog.

Home

As emphasized by Davis, the word *nostalgia* comes from the Greek *nostos* (to return home) and *algia* (a painful yearning) so as to be virtually synonymous in its derivation with *homesickness* (1). Its original usage, by a Swiss physician named Johannes Hofer in 1688, referred to the extreme homesickness experienced by mercenary soldiers fighting far from their native lands. As such, nostalgia was originally viewed as a disease. (For further historical details on this nosological role of nostalgia, see Starobinski; for a review of its clinical psychoanalytic aspects, see Fodor.)

Over time, however, the term "nostalgia" has undergone considerable "semantic drift" (Davis 4) in the direction of the sense commonly accepted today (with reference to a longing for the past).[15] Today, we no longer necessarily associate "nost*algia*" with "sickness." Nevertheless, we can still detect a strong affinity between simple "*nost*algia" and a reverence for *home*.

This connection appeared as early as Homer's *Odyssey*—the quintessential masterpiece on the struggle to return home. It echoes through such works as Milton's *Paradise Lost*, right down to its more contemporary manifestations in novels like Joyce's *Ulysses* and Wolfe's *You Can't Go Home Again* (to name only two among many). Indeed, the basic story of *Genesis* begins the *Bible* with an emphasis on the predicament of Adam and Eve—cast out of their blissful Eden and forever condemned to struggle back toward Elysium.

Metaphorically, when God banished Adam and Eve from their Bower of Bliss, they very soon had reason to look back with longing to how nice things had been in the good old days. Since then, a wistful desire to recapture the dear departed past has haunted humankind.

Many agree with M.H. Abrams that this impulse to regain Paradise—to achieve a reconciliation with Lost Innocence and a reunification with the Prelapsarian Beauty of the World—is the essence of romanticism. Thus, Homer's Odysseus strives toward home, and the hero of Joyce's *Ulysses* repeats a comparable journey. Poets like Milton in *Paradise Lost*, novelists like Proust in *Remembrance of Things Past*, songwriters like Lennon and McCartney in "Golden Slumbers," and screenwriters like George Lucas in "American Graffiti" have constantly reiterated similar themes. In sum, it seems fair to say that this homeward-looking sense of nostalgia infuses our consciousness of the basic human condition.

As the erstwhile classics scholar and former Commissioner of Baseball—the late A. Bartlett Giamatti—never tired of pointing out, the ethos of our national pastime hinges on the essence of this nostalgic impulse: The intense desire to get back *home*. Sensitive to its literary roots, Giamatti makes the connection with baseball explicit:

If baseball is a Narrative,...what is the nature of the tale oft-told that recommences with every pitch, with every game, with every season?... It is the story...of going home after having left home, the story of how difficult it is to find the origins one so deeply needs to find. It is the literary mode called Romance.... Why is home plate not called fourth base?... Meditate upon the name. *Home* is an English word virtually impossible to translate into other tongues. No translation catches the associations, the mixture of memory and longing.... *Home* is a concept, not a place.... So home drew Odysseus.... So home is the goal—rarely glimpsed, almost never attained—of all heroes descended from Odysseus. All literary romance derives from the *Odyssey*. (90-92)

Not surprisingly, then, baseball is the nostalgic sport par excellence (a fact that will emerge more clearly when we reconsider three songs by David Frishberg).[16]

   Also not surprisingly, the spirit of home and the meanings embodied by the possessions contained therein pervade much of the recent research on symbolic consumption by such social scientists as Campbell, Csikszentmihalyi and Rochberg-Halton, Kron, and McCracken (*Culture and Consumption*, "Homeyness"). In connection with consumer fanaticism and the collecting impulse, Holbrook ("Audiovisual") endeavored to capture this leaning toward *nostos* in an audiovisual essay subtitled "The 25-Cent Tour of a Jazz Collector's Home":

I conclude with an analogy: Ordinary consumer behavior is to fanatic consumption as a house is to a home. In the maudlin poem by Edgar Guest..., "it takes a heap o' livin' in a house t' make it home." Similarly, fanatic consumption takes us through a massive amount of lived experience that, in time, comes to form the boundaries wherein we reside, where we are centered, where we find our home—our place of comfort, rest, and sustenance. Our houses contain furniture, food, clothing, and other material objects. But, if we are lucky, they also contain the central core of our consumption experience—the deeply involved appreciative responses, the passionately committed activities, the emotionally charged reactions that inform our truest, most profound consumer behavior and that provide a niche in time and space where we can reside.... So I end on a serious note. I may have been giving you the 25-cent Tour; but, in my heart, this space that I've been describing is a 24-karat place to reside.... Besides the people in my life, because I am a fanatic, certain objects come alive for me. They fill our house. They make our house my home. (148)

Popular Culture

   The message of nostalgia appears ubiquitously in our works of popular culture and high art alike (Skretvedt and Young). Here, I shall discuss only a few especially salient illustrations.

Magazines. A recent example of nostalgia in popular culture involves the birth of magazines intended to cater to the nostalgic impulse. Specifically, in this connection, Rothenberg ("The Past" D19) mentions *Memories* ("which...trafficks in articles about events of the last 50 years"), *Victoria* (which "celebrates old traditions and pastimes and whose name derives from the Victorian era"), and Joe Franklin's *Nostalgia* (which wistfully recalls "American values and the small towns from which they derive"). Indeed, the December 1989/January 1990 issue of *Memories* contained articles featuring a retrospective on Gregory Peck, a rehash of the Brink's robbery, a review of TV westerns from the 1950s, a reminiscence on Winston Churchill, and a recollection of Willie Shoemaker—all supported by revivals of old advertising for Clairol ("Does She...or Doesn't She?"), Osterizer ("Give the Gift you'd like to Get"), Hunt ("Oh, Mamma Mia!..wait till you taste Rollettes...made with Hunt's Tomato Paste"), Purina Dog Chow ("Makes dogs eager eaters"), General Motors ("Shake Hands with Mr. Goodwrench"), Revlon ("She's Very Charlie"), and Land O Lakes Butter ("The Taste That Brings You Back").[17] Perhaps a contemporary ad for Kodak, in the same issue of *Memories*, says it best: "Why trust your memories to anything less?" To cite another example, the March 1991 issue of *Joe Franklin's Nostalgia* featured stories on "the authentic, unreconstructed diner," "Nashville's Grand Ole Opry" as "a Saturday night ritual," "big reptiles" (as in "dinosaur mania"), how "nickelodeon singers turned moviola screens into music halls," the historic "advertising giants from Betty Crocker to Chiquita Banana," and the era of "the Harlem Globetrotters' magic circle."

Movies. To these examples from the print media, one might add those of the movies. A minimal list of nostalgia-drenched films would include the following:

Since You Went Away 1944	*It's a Wonderful Life* 1946
The Best Years of Our Lives 1946	*Life With Father* 1947
I Remember Mama 1948	*The Last Time I Saw Paris* 1954
An Affair to Remember 1957	*Wild Strawberries* 1957
Carnal Knowledge 1971	*The Last Picture Show* 1971
Summer of '42 1971	*Amarcord* 1973
American Graffiti 1973	*The Way We Were* 1973
Class of '44 1973	*If Ever I See You Again* 1978
Somewhere In Time 1980	*Back to the Future* 1985
Peggy Sue Got Married 1986	*Stealing Home* 1988

to mention only a few (Halliwell).

Television. Similar examples abound in the television revivals or reruns that fill the airways:

I Love Lucy	*George Burns and Gracie Allen*
Groucho Marx	*Jack Benny*
Donna Reed	*Dennis the Menace*
My Three Sons	*Leave It to Beaver*
The Brady Bunch	*The Honeymooners*

especially the latter, which has produced a veritable cottage industry for nostalgia freaks (McCrohan).[18] Noting this tendency toward "nostalgia for the glory days," O'Connor suggests that "network television has evidently decided to rush headlong into the past" (C1). Thus, NBC recently announced plans to produce a weekly syndicated program called *Memories...Then and Now*: "Regular features will include a 'Where Are They Now?' segment, nostalgia quizzes and a repeat of celebrity blunders—'Oops'" (Rothenberg, "NBC" D17). Further, Ira Gallen has captured underground status as a media hero with his public access program known as *Biograph Days, Biograph Nights* (Alexander):

A cult favorite, the program...is an affectionate glance at the television programs and commercials of the 50's and 60's, a time the 39-year-old Mr. Gallen calls "the age of innocence," an era he looks back on with fondness (C1).... it is his collection of 50's and 60's toys that causes guests to gasp in delight. "I've seen the smell of a Lionel train transformer drive someone absolutely wild with nostalgia," he said. (C10)

Music. But—above all—nostalgic themes have achieved a pervasive influence on American popular music (Jacobs).[19] With respect to these musical moments—since before the turn of the century in songs like "Old Folks at Home" (Stephen Foster 1851), "My Old Kentucky Home" (Stephen Foster 1853), "Dixie" (Daniel Decatur Emmett 1860), "Old Black Joe" (Stephen Foster 1860), and "Carry Me Back to Old Virginny" (James Bland 1878)—each era appears to have elicited its own characteristic paeans to the play of memories:

1920s: "Remember" (Irving Berlin 1925); "Where or When" (Rodgers and Hart 1927); "I'll See You Again" (Noel Coward 1929); "Stardust" (Parish and Carmichael 1929)

1930s: "Memories of You" (Razaf and Blake 1930); "Something to Remember

You By" (Dietz and Schwartz 1930); "As Time Goes By" (Herman Hupfeld 1931); "If I Forget You" (Irving Caesar 1933); "Yesterdays" (Harbach and Kern 1933); "My Old Flame" (Coslow and Johnston 1934); "Last Night When We Were Young" (Harburg and Arlen 1936); "These Foolish Things" (Marvell, Strachey, and Link 1936); "It Seems Like Old Times" (Tobias and Stept 1937); "September In the Rain" (Dubin and Warren 1937); "They Can't Take That Away from Me" (George and Ira Gershwin 1937); "Old Folks" (Hill and Robison 1938); "That Old Feeling" (Brown and Fain 1937); "I'll Be Seeing You" (Kahal and Fain 1938); "September Song" (Anderson and Weill 1938); "I Thought About You" (Mercer and Van Heusen 1939)

1940s: "The Last Time I Saw Paris" (Hammerstein and Kern 1940); "A Million Dreams Ago" (Quadling, Howard, and Jurgens 1940); "A Nightingale Sang in Berkeley Square" (Maschwitz and Manning 1940); "Remind Me" (Fields and Kern 1940); "I'll Remember April" (Raye, de Paul, and Johnston 1941); "I'm Old Fashioned" (Mercer and Kern 1942); "I Remember You" (Mercer and Schertzinger 1942); "I've Heard That Song Before" (Cahn and Styne 1942); "White Christmas" (Irving Berlin 1942); "Yesterday's Gardenias" (Robertson, Cogane, and Mysels 1942); "I'll Be Home For Christmas" (Kent, Gannon, and Ram 1943); "Long Ago and Far Away" (Gershwin and Kern 1944); "Some Other Time" (Comden, Green, and Bernstein 1944); "The Things We Did Last Summer" (Cahn and Styne 1946); "Time After Time" (Cahn and Styne 1947)

1950s: "Unforgettable" (Irving Gordon 1951);[20] "Somewhere Along the Way" (Gallop and Adams 1952); "Oh! My Pa-Pa" (Turner, Parsons, and Burkhard 1953); "I Left My Heart in San Francisco" (Cross and Cory 1954); "Memories Are Made of This" (Gilkyson, Dehr, and Miller 1955); "Moments to Remember" (Stillman and Allen 1955); "Graduation Day" (Sherman and Sherman 1956); "I've Grown Accustomed to Her Face" (Lerner and Loewe 1956); "I Remember It Well" (Lerner and Loewe 1958)

1960s: "Try To Remember" (Jones and Schmidt 1960);[21] "It Was a Very Good Year" (Ervin Drake 1961); "The First Time Ever I Saw Your Face" (Ewan MacColl 1962); "Once Upon a Time" (Adams and Strouse 1962); "Those Lazy-Hazy-Crazy-Days of Summer" (Tobias and Carste 1964); "The September of My Years" (Cahn and Van Heusen 1965); "Yesterday" (Lennon and McCartney 1965); "Homeward Bound" (Paul Simon 1966); "Old Friends" (Paul Simon 1967); "Penny Lane" (Lennon and McCartney 1967); "The Night They Drove Old Dixie Down" (Robbie Robertson 1969); "Yester-Me Yester-You Yesterday" (Stevie Wonder 1969); "Yesterday When I Was Young" (Aznavour and Kretzmer 1969)

1970s: "I'll Be Home" (Randy Newman 1970); "Always on My Mind" (Christopher, Thompson, and James 1971); "American Pie" (Don McLean 1971); "Old Fashioned Love Song" (Paul Williams 1971); "Souvenirs" (John Prine 1972); "The Way We Were" (Bergman, Bergman, and Hamlisch 1973); "My Little Town" (Paul Simon 1974); "Grandma's Hands" (Bill Withers 1975); "September Morn" (Diamond and Becaud 1979)

1980s: "The Old Songs" (Pomeranz and Kaye 1980); "Memory" (Nunn, Eliot, and Webber 1982); "Old Boyfriends" (Tom Waits 1982); "Old Time Rock and Roll" (Jackson and Jones 1983); "My Hometown" (Bruce Springsteen 1984); "Graceland" (Paul Simon 1986); "Homeless" (Simon and Shabalala 1986); "The Girl Who Used to Be Me" (Marvin Hamlisch 1989)

(For help in dating these and other familiar tunes, see Jacobs 1988.) Only the Rolling Stones (as usual) appear to have dissented in the form of their sneering question, "Who Wants Yesterday's Papers?" (Jagger and Richard 1967). Otherwise, all the songs just listed make essentially the same point, though they make it across a wide range of compositional styles and musical sensibilities. The point, of course, concerns the nostalgic role that memories and their links to consumption experiences play in people's lives. As if to stamp this theme forever indelibly on our minds, Frank Sinatra (1961) recorded his classic concept album with Alex Stordahl featuring a whole series of nostalgic tunes such as "When The World Was Young," "I'll Remember April," "September Song," "A Million Dreams Ago," "I'll See You Again," "There Will Never Be Another You," "Somewhere Along the Way," "As Time Goes By," "I'll Be Seeing You," "Memories of You," and—of course—"These Foolish Things." A few years later, Sinatra (1965) returned to this theme in an album with Gordon Jenkins that included such songs as "The September of My Years," "Last Night When We Were Young," "It Was a Very Good Year," "When the Wind Was Green," "I See It Now," "Once Upon a Time," and (again) "September Song." More recently, songwriter Carole King (1989) has expressed the deep resonance with the past evoked by music:

I have experienced—with other people's songs, hearing them on the radio—and I'm instantly transported back in time. I see the place I was when I first heard the song. I smell the smells I smelled. I can almost sense the people around me that I was with.... We all do have our own visuals and our memories and all the sense-memory things that we created or that were there for us. And I love that my songs...have that effect on people. I love being the instrument through whom those songs were written.

Gendron agrees that "the music industry seems constantly to be reinterpreting or reinventing the musical past, goading the consumer...toward...nostalgia" (32).

A Definition Of Nostalgia

Davis defines simple *nostalgia*[22] as "a positively toned evocation of a lived past in the context of some negative feeling toward present or impending circumstances" involving a "subjective state which harbors the largely unexamined belief that THINGS WERE BETTER (MORE BEAUTIFUL) (HEALTHIER) (HAPPIER) (MORE CIVILIZED) (MORE EXCITING) *THEN* THAN *NOW*" (18). Lowenthal agrees that "nostalgia is today the universal catchword for looking back" (4). However, some controversy exists concerning whether nostalgia pertains only to *one's own* store of remembered events from a "personally experienced past" (Davis 8) or reaches back *historically* so that it "engulfs the whole past" (Lowenthal 6).

In what follows, I shall favor the side of this debate espoused by Lowenthal. Briefly, it does seem plausible that one could identify nostalgically with people, places, or things from a bygone era that one has experienced only vicariously through books, films, or other narratives. True, as argued by Davis, nostalgia *might* attach itself to experiences recalled from *one's own* youth. But, as noted by Fodor, it might *also* focus on *the womb* via "a yearning for our prenatal home" (30). And, as contended by Lowenthal, it might *even* affix itself to objects "recalled" via collective memory from an era *before one's own birth*:

The remembered past is both individual and collective (194).... we need other people's memories both to confirm our own and to give them endurance (196).... Remembering the past is crucial for our sense of identity (197).... We synthesize identity not simply by calling up a sequence of reminiscences, but by being enveloped...in a unifying web of retrospection. Groups too mobilize collective memories to sustain enduring corporate identities (198).... historical knowledge is by its very nature collectively produced and shared; historical awareness implies group activity.... Just as memory validates personal identity, history perpetuates collective self-awareness (213).... Indeed, the enterprise of history is crucial to...the feeling of belonging to coherent, stable, and durable institutions. (213-214)

Indeed, nostalgia might even involve "the use of ancient materials to construct invented traditions" that serve the needs of the present (Hobsbawm 6). Apropos of such *historical revisions*, for example, consider the amazing revelation by Trevor-Roper that the distinctive clan tartans, the plaid kilts, the poems of Ossian, and even the bagpipe itself are only recent incorporations into the invention of Scottish tradition and *not* part of Scotland's early Highland culture.[23]

An acceptance of the viewpoint that nostalgia *might* attach to vicariously experienced objects common *before one's own birth* underlies much of the discussion that follows. In this vein, I shall pursue the definition of nostalgia proposed by Holbrook and Schindler ("Echoes"). Specifically—building on the work of Davis, Lowenthal, and others— Holbrook and Schindler ("Echoes") extend and expand their views of nostalgia to offer the following more general definition:

nostalgia [is] *a preference* (general liking, positive attitude, or favorable affect) *toward objects* (people, places, or things) *that were more common* (popular, fashionable, or widely circulated) *when one was younger* (in early adulthood, in adolescence, in childhood, or even before birth).

In this light, the present essay focuses on the trichotomy that Davis characterizes as the "three orders" of nostalgia in general and on what he calls "simple" or "first order" nostalgia in particular.

The Three Orders Of Nostalgia

Davis proposes a conceptually important three-fold distinction among what he calls First, Second, and Third Order Nostalgia. Because the present work focuses primarily on the most basic type of first order nostalgia, I shall proceed by progressing from third to second to first so as to end with the perspective on nostalgia that I wish to emphasize.[24]

Given the importance of pop culture and especially popular music in reflecting and illuminating the role of nostalgia in the consumption experience, we might again note that probably no contemporary artist and surely no songwriter has more fully captured the essence of the nostalgic spirit than has the singer/composer David Frishberg. I referred to Frishberg's songs in an earlier section, where they illustrated the role of consumption symbolism in conveying the nostalgic experiences of consumers. Here, Frishberg's oeuvre again commands our attention because it vividly portrays and thereby clarifies the distinctions among the three orders of nostalgia as they occur in the consumption experience.[25]

Third Order or Interpreted Nostalgia

In the scheme proposed by Davis, the third "order" of nostalgia— *interpreted nostalgia*—bears some resemblance to "the epoché or formal bracketing operation of phenomenological analysis" in that "the actor seeks in some fashion to objectify the nostalgia he feels" by raising *"analytically oriented* questions concerning its sources, typical character, significance, and psychological purpose" (24). Such an analytic "framing of the nostalgic response" involves a "stepping outside...of its givenness" (25) in ways that raise searching *questions* and reveal possible *choices* associated with the struggle to gain *authenticity* (Baugh).

In the illustrative work of David Frishberg, we frequently find such profound questioning, often laced with humor or tinged with a deep sense of ambivalence. Examples occur in "Sweet Kentucky Ham" and "The Green Hills of Earth," but perhaps the clearest case of interpreted nostalgia appears in Frishberg's song called "Do You Miss New York?" that offers a penetrating examination of his own ambivalent yearning for The City after moving from The Big Apple to Los Angeles (Frishberg, "New York"; "Live Concert"). As reflected by its title, this song pursues a series of probing questions such as

> When you're back in town for a quick look around, how is it?
> Does it feel like home or just another nice place to visit?

In these lyrics, the speaker conveys a deep sense of uncertainty and conflict concerning how he feels about the move West, first conjuring up unflattering images of N.Y.C., then trivializing L.A.:

> If you had the choice, would you still choose to do it all again?
> Do you find yourself in line to see *Annie Hall* again?

Indeed, at some point Frishberg must have felt that the balance weighed too clearly in favor of New York because, between the time he first recorded this tune (Frishberg, "New York") and the time he performed it at the live concert broadcast from Rochester (Frishberg, "Live Concert"), he introduced certain "improvements" that included the line: "Do you miss the thrill, the subways, the schlepping?/And is it second nature, still, to watch where you are stepping?" Thus, the tone oscillates between affection for and revulsion from the city he has left behind, so much so that it moves toward confrontation with a potentially disturbing existential dilemma—"Do you ever run into that guy who used to be you?"—before reaching a tentative resolution on one final note of affirmation: "Do you miss New York...? *Me too.*"

Second Order or Reflexive Nostalgia

According to Davis, second order nostalgia or *reflexive nostalgia* is accompanied by a tendency to *scrutinize* one's own nostalgic impulse. Here, via self-examination, "he or she summons to feeling and thought certain empirically oriented questions concerning the truth, accuracy, completeness, or representativeness of the nostalgic claim" (21).

Again, the songs by David Frishberg provide a telling illustration. Thus, Frishberg has revealed a tendency toward reflexive nostalgia when introducing his masterpiece, "The Dear Departed Past" (already mentioned briefly but with admiration earlier in this essay). In a performance recorded live at Vine Street in Hollywood (Frishberg, "Dear Departed Past"), he announced this tune, as follows:

Here's a song about nostalgia. It's sung by a guy who's very much like me—very hung-up on the old ways and the old days—pathologically hung-up, I guess....

But, by the time he reached his later concert recorded live in Rochester and subsequently broadcast over WBGO in Newark, Frishberg ("Live Concert") had subtly changed his mind about the normalcy of nostalgia:

Yes, I am hung-up on the old things.... It's not through any pathological, mindless nostalgia at all. I sincerely *do* believe that things used to be better. This song...is designed to be sung by someone, like me, who *really* misses everything....

Earlier, I suggested that "The Dear Departed Past" is Frishberg's masterpiece and, indeed, one of the Twentieth Century's songwriting triumphs. This piece is filled with poignant evocations of earlier days, all unified by a pervasive grounding in consumption symbolism (not unlike that found, as mentioned earlier, in "These Foolish Things"). The images strongly evoke a better world in days of yore by portraying the lifestyle associated with a reverence for the consumption experiences of a bygone era when people used to wear suspenders, drive cars with rumble seats, play the ukelele, and send away for prizes using coupons found on cereal boxes.

To cite just a few instances, named explicitly in the song, such experiences would include those with the media ("musty magazines" with "sepia-tinted scenes"), phonograph recordings of people like Ellington and Parker ("the Bluebirds and Savoys with all the surface noise"), dances ("the Lindy Hops and foxtrots"), musical instruments ("music on the uke" in which "E7 always went to A"), games ("Chinese checkers and Parcheesi"), automobiles ("the '55 Bel Air and the '37 Ford"), clothing ("tie... fly... suspenders"), champs of yesterday ("Jack Dempsey, John McGraw, Joe Louis..."), sports teams from disenfranchised towns ("the old St. Louis Browns, the Minneapolis Lakers"), and food ("a hot dog for a dime; White

Castles, seven cents"). Frishberg beautifully conveys the attitude that "things used to be better" in lines loaded with marketing imagery and consumption symbolism: I loved the '55 Bel Air / And the '37 Fords, / Complete with running boards, / And rumble seats, and fenders. In this connection, only a lyricist of Frishberg's calibre could manage to rhyme "Lindy Hops and foxtrots" with "boxtops": The Lindy Hops and foxtrots; / And here's to the Orphan Annie pin, / The secret squadron ring the mailman used to bring / For a quarter and some boxtops....

Yet, throughout this tribute to the "Dear Departed Past"—as intimated by the shift in Frishberg's spoken introductions—we sense a constant awareness that the lyricist is not necessarily the speaker in the song. Rather, reflexively, Frishberg has portrayed a worldview—one characterized by a particular consumption lifestyle—that he can scrutinize with some degree of distance and detachment even while feeling irresistibly drawn in its direction. Thus, near the beginning of the tune (to cite just one specific example), the songwriter/performer injects certain advanced harmonic progressions that happen to coincide with the question, "Can one feel a real nostalgia for a time and place one never even knew?" Comparable harmonies reappear in the song's last, touching moments— suggesting that, whatever the "narrator" insists, the "writer" himself has his artistic feet planted firmly in the current era: "But here's to the echoes of tomorrow, soon to be memories at last—memories that will someday reappear, loud and clear, in the dear departed past."

First Order or Simple Nostalgia

For Davis, as already mentioned, nostalgia of the first order or *simple nostalgia* hinges on the sense that things were healthier, happier, or otherwise nicer in the old days—the "*unquestioned* conviction that the past was better" (64). This feeling permeates many of Frishberg's songs but, not surprisingly, reaches its heights in those dealing with baseball (a sport that we have already identified as a kind of athletic metaphor for the ethos of nostalgia). Thus, as noted earlier, Frishberg's compositions called "Van Lingle Mungo" and "Dodger Blue" both consist almost entirely of recitatives that list the names of famous ballplayers from days of yore, artfully strung together to make ingenious and whimsical rhymes. Legend has it that the premiere of the latter song—at a Dodgers Oldtimers Banquet—reduced the otherwise stoic Walt Alston to tears.

However, the most remarkable of Frishberg's nostalgia-drenched baseball songs—simply called "Matty" and found on one of his most recent albums (Frishberg)—pays homage to the great right-handed pitcher, Christy Mathewson, who starred for the New York Giants from 1900 to

1916 and who shares the distinction (with Grover Alexander) of tying for third place in the all-time wins column with 373 career victories (behind only Walter Johnson's 416 and Cy Young's 511). Frishberg's obvious reverence for Mathewson appears to be widely shared by knowledgeable writers on baseball. For example, Ritter and Honig offer the following summary of the pitcher's achievement:

It was Christy Mathewson, more than anyone, who changed the public image of the game and elevated it into the mainstream of American Life. Matty symbolized the ideal All-American Boy: handsome, well educated, reserved, the embodiment of middle-class conduct and values, as well as a superb all-around athlete and the outstanding pitcher of his generation.... Few pitchers have been his equal, before or since, and surely none...has received the overwhelming adulation that was showered on Matty for his behavior off the field as well as on. (9)

Apparently, that behavior won Mathewson a reputation for unexcelled virtue. In this connection, James describes Matty's "honesty" as "so respected that umpires reportedly would sometimes ask for his help on a close play." (434)

Thus, Frishberg's "Matty" offers a tribute to Mathewson that conveys a nostalgic sense of hero worship strongly reminiscent of the aura associated with "touching greatness" (O'Guinn) and loaded with elements of the "spiritual" (Holbrook and Corfman) or the "sacred" as distinguished from the "secular" (Hirschman) or the "profane" (Belk, Wallendorf, and Sherry). Indeed, in Frishberg's song, Matty attains a sacred stature that becomes almost messianic in its magnificence.

The hero's very name, "Matty," alliterates with "mighty"—as in the line, "Matty was the mightiest of them all"—and is connected, throughout the song, to words with strong spiritual overtones such as "great," "soul," "true," "trust," "faith," "hallowed," "miracle," "swear," and even "God Himself." Some of these sacred associations are strongly reinforced by a repeated downward-falling melodic pattern that places special emphasis on the words capitalized in such phrases as "there's not a *SOUL* who would deny that you were great," "when we were *DOWN* to do or die, we'd look to you," "when a *MIRACLE* was needed, you were there," and "I'd swear that *GOD* Himself had sent His Right-Hand Man to see us through." As the lyrics proceed ineluctably toward this last revelation, the harmonic structure twice emphasizes the main message by means of key changes (always a sure-fire musical means for attracting attention and highlighting the important moments of a text). First, the song modulates briefly from F to A-natural to coincide with Frishberg's delivery of the line, "they'll tell of you, Matty; they'll remember you." Then, as the piece builds toward its final climax ("I'd swear, Matty..."), the harmonic center moves from F to A-flat (a minor third) at the critical moment ("I'd swear that *GOD* Himself had sent His Right-Hand Man to see us through; and it was you, Matty; it was you").

Thus, the harmonic progression (associated with a kind of trinity) reflects a broader transubstantiation that has metaphorically transformed Matty into God's Right-Hand Man. Here, like a trinity, the term "Right-Hand Man" carries at least three multiply charged meanings: (1) Matty was a *right-hander* (one of the best right-handed pitchers of all time); (2) Matty was a *handy* guy to have around (because he won a lot of ball games); and (3) Matty was *God's Right-Hand Man*—like Christ (who, in the words of the Nicene Creed, "ascended into Heaven and is seated at the right hand of God, the Father Almighty"). And—finally—lest we doubt this metaphoric implication of Matty's Christ-like stature, we have only to reflect on Matty's *real* name—one that is never explicitly mentioned in the song itself—specifically, *Christy* Mathewson. Thus does the spirit of "simple" nostalgia reach its apotheosis in the unconstrained hero worship of a great figure from the past.

The Present Focus: First Order Nostalgia

Interesting and profound though questions concerning the second order (reflexive) and third order (interpreted) types of nostalgia might be, my primary emphasis in the present essay concerns what Davis calls "first order" or "simple" nostalgia of the type that he characterizes as having produced a nostalgia "boom" (x), "tides of nostalgia" (57), a "nostalgia wave" (107), and "the nostalgia orgy" (104). In other words, I am primarily concerned here with what Davis calls *simple nostalgia*—that is, with basic unquestioned enthusiasms that consumers feel for objects from the past—whether people (e.g., Christy Mathewson), places (e.g., home), or things (e.g., possessions). Specifically, I shall emphasize two aspects of this "simple" nostalgia—the role of *age* in the temporal development of consumer tastes and the influence of *nostalgia proneness* as an individual characteristic.

Age and the Temporal Development of Consumer Tastes

In line with his orientation toward personal experience, Davis suggests that the kind of nostalgic impulse just described is particularly likely to fasten onto material associated with the "friendship circle" of one's late teens and early twenties (33) so that "in Western society it is adolescence, and for the privileged classes early adulthood as well, that affords nostalgia its most sumptuous banquets" (57). Accordingly, Davis argues for "the centrality of adolescent experience for nostalgia's lifelong career" (59), such that "the tides of nostalgia which nowadays almost regularly wash over middle-aged persons typically carry them back to the songs, films, styles, and fads of their late teens" (60). Further, such tides or waves of nostalgia tend to increase with advancing age: "If nostalgia most savors the adolescent years, then those most given to savoring thereof are the aging and the aged" (64). Combining these tendencies (1) for nostalgia to focus on adolescent experience and (2) for nostalgia to increase with age, we see one reason (among other possibilities) why people might retain tastes (musical and otherwise) formed in late adolescence or early adulthood throughout their later lives as consumers. Colloquially, as a manifestation of nostalgia, it appears that what you liked best when you first reached maturity may continue to please you better and better for the rest of your life.[26]

The phenomenon just described anecdotally received formal empirical treatment in research by Holbrook and Schindler ("Exploratory Findings"). In this study, consumers' musical tastes depended on the song-specific ages at which various pieces were popular. Specifically, a nonmonotonic (quadratic) relationship appeared such that preferences for musical selections peaked for those that were hits when the respondent was in the vicinity of late adolescence or early adulthood. The authors predicted and explained this finding as analogous to the phenomenon of imprinting, in which baby birds and other animals develop permanent attachments to stimuli encountered during a critical period or temporal window of susceptibility that occurs early in their lives. (For a recent comprehensive review of the literature on sensitive periods in development, see Bornstein). Drawing on the work by ethologists who discovered and reported the imprinting effect (Lorenz), they suggested that such a critical period might depend on various internal or endogenous (e.g., maturational) and external or exogenous (e.g., social) factors of the type noted by Cole and by Priasky and Rosenbaum.

An apposite study by Schuman and Scott—which came to our attention after the research just mentioned had been completed—also invoked the concepts of critical periods and imprinting to account for age-related generational differences in collective memories. Drawing on a view of generations credited to Mannheim and a notion of collective memories borrowed from Halbwachs (see also Connerton), these authors examined age-related tendencies to attribute importance to twelve events such as World War II, the Kennedy assassination, and the Vietnam War. Briefly, they hypothesized and found that maximal memorability attached to events that had occurred during an age cohort's adolescence or early adulthood:

For the majority of 12 major national or world events...that Americans recall as especially important, the memories refer back disproportionately to a time when the respondents were in their teens or early 20s. Thus the data fit well both the general hypothesis that memories of important political events and social changes are structured by age, and the more specific hypothesis that adolescence and early adulthood is the primary period for generational imprinting in the sense of political memories. (377)

Thus, the study by Schuman and Scott lends some support to the phenomenon demonstrated by Holbrook and Schindler ("Exploratory Finding"). Note, however, that Schuman and Scott focused primarily on generational differences in *cognition* (memory or recall of important events), whereas Holbrook and Schindler studied age-related differences in *affect* (positive attitude or preferences for music from one's youth). Clearly, the relevant explanatory mechanisms might differ between these two cases. Also, clearly, the phenomenon related to affect is more directly connected with nostalgia as defined earlier.

Nostalgia Proneness

The various social scientists in general (e.g., Campbell) and, in particular, the historians (e.g., Lowenthal) or sociologists (e.g., Davis) who have focused on the nostalgic "yearning for yesterday" have tended to dwell on a phenomenon that they believe has occurred at the societal level as a whole (especially during the past two decades). Thus, Davis clearly views nostalgia as a "collective" phenomenon (106) associated with a nostalgia "boom" (x), "tides of nostalgia" (57), a "nostalgia wave" (107), and "the nostalgia orgy" (104). In short, the background literature discussed thus far has tended to view nostalgia as a cultural aspect of an era or epoch.

While in no way disagreeing with Davis that nostalgic tendencies can characterize a whole group, society, or culture, I might instead mention a somewhat more neglected topic—namely, the way that nostalgia operates at the *personal* level as an *individual characteristic* that potentially *differs among people.* Thus, whereas Davis dwells on nostalgia as a cultural trend, one might also explore individual differences that result from ways in which nostalgia *varies across consumers.* In this light, work by Holbrook ("Nostalgia Proneness") has investigated the role of *nostalgia proneness* as a *psychographic variable* or a *general customer characteristic* that portrays meaningful differences among consumers.

Specifically, Holbrook ("Nostalgia Proneness") focused on developing and testing an index of nostalgia proneness intended to capture the essence of nostalgia as an individual characteristic that differs from one person to the next. In this connection, he constructed a 20-item Nostalgia Index and assessed its reliability and validity in explaining some general and specific patterns of consumer tastes. The Nostalgia Index appeared to perform reliably and validly in accounting for such aspects of consumer tastes as a preference for movie musicals as opposed to violent war stories.

Thus, it seems possible to measure the personality dimension described by Davis as typical of the sort of nostalgia-prone individual who insists that "things aren't what they used to be" or that "they hardly make them that way any more" (64). In short, one can empirically examine a way of assessing the tendency toward nostalgia proneness among those who maintain an "*unquestioned* conviction that the past was better" (64).

Conclusion

The two points just covered should help to set an agenda for future empirical research on nostalgia. In ending this essay, however, it might be somewhat inconsistent with its central theme to dwell inordinately on such a program for the future. After all, our main focus throughout has dealt not with the future but with the past, as epitomized by the nostalgic glorification of days gone by and of products long since consumed but not forgotten. Here, irresistibly, one again turns for an apposite phrase to that great self-appointed Prophet of Nostalgia—David Frishberg—who concludes his masterpiece on "The Dear Departed Past" with some words of wisdom that might well serve as the programmatic project for anyone interested in doing research on the influence of nostalgia in the lives of consumers:

> But here's to the echoes of tomorrow,
> Soon to be memories at last -
> Memories that will
> Someday reappear.

Envoi

In this essay, I have presented a series of arguments, anecdotes, and empirical observations bearing on age and nostalgia proneness as time-related influences on the development of consumption tastes. I hope that this array of what I believe are persuasive findings will have appealed to the *heads* of my readers in a manner that convinces them of the importance played by the phenomena of nostalgia in shaping consumer preferences. If so, I shall have accomplished my central purpose in writing this essay.

However, in the last analysis, there is another kind of appeal that can be made much more simply and that draws on subjective personal introspection for its power to persuade. In this latter spirit, I shall close by asking my readers to look, for a moment, deep within themselves. Engage, I ask, in a moment of subjective personal introspection.

Think back to a time, in late adolescence or early adulthood, when objects of the everyday world still seemed fresh and full of exciting possibilities. Ponder the ways in which some things seemed better then. Recall a favorite song or a film classic from that period in the old days. Remember the friends with whom it was shared—imagine their faces, their smiles, their hair, how they looked, what they wore, the surrounding sights and sounds, tastes and smells. Reminisce. And then admit that the nostalgic power possessed by this sort of consumption experience can convince not only the head but also the *heart*.

Notes

[1]The author thanks Bill Havlena, Beth Hirschman, John Howard, Ruth Smith, and Barbara Stern for their helpful comments on an earlier draft. He also gratefully acknowledges the support of the Columbia Business School's Faculty Research Fund.

[2]Nat Cole's rendition of this phrase lends it a supercharged intensity of feeling. Quite appropriately, when compiling a memorial tribute to Cole's accomplishments and depicting his lifestyle as one of the first Black entertainers to break through the color barrier and to gain a large measure of acceptance into the white society of his day, the film's producers accompanied a pictorial tour of the singer's stately mansion in Beverly Hills with a soundtrack performance of "These Foolish Things" (Cole, *Unforgettable*). In another context, the same piece recently served as a theme song for the musical soundtrack of the movie *Daddy Nostalgia*.

[3]Frishberg's international reputation did recently receive a major boost when his music was selected to open the television broadcast of the 1992 Winter Olympics, viewed by literally *billions* of people around the world.

[4]The author has seen David Frishberg live at four concerts in New York City. These performances have prompted uncharacteristically favorable reviews by the local critics.

[5]Those desperate might also try writing to Omnisound Records, Box 128, Delaware Water Gap, PA 18327; to Fantasy Records, Tenth and Parker, Berkeley, CA 94701; and to Concord records, P.O. Box 845, Concord, CA 94522.

[6]A video production of "Van Lingle Mungo," featuring Frishberg at the piano and photographs of ballplayers named in the song, appears on a recent home videotape entitled *Baseball's Greatest Hits* (Rhino Home Video, 2225 Colorado Avenue, Santa Monica, CA 90404).

[7]Later, I shall discuss another baseball-related song entitled "Matty" (dealing with the celebrated pitcher, Christy Mathewson) at considerably greater length.

[8]A more extended example, entitled "Do You Miss New York?," appears as an illustration of third-order nostalgia later in this essay.

[9]Later, we shall return to this song for more detailed commentary as an illustration of second-order nostalgia.

[10]One cannot adequately convey the musicality of Frishberg's compositions and performances in words. Suffice it to say that he undergirds his vocal delivery with a veritable pincushion of pricks, pokes, and probes from a jazzy piano style that owes much to a broad array of predecessors ranging all the way from Fats Waller and Teddy Wilson to Jimmy Rowles and Thelonious Monk. In the absence of his apposite melodies, harmonies, and accompaniments, Frishberg's lyrics might lose some of their effect.

[11]A friend who works as an investment counsellor and who publishes a periodic newsletter recently wrote about a baseball-related experience that I was privileged to share: "My first experience with this treat was in the 1950's. Actually, I remember that it was a beautiful day in April. A very close friend of mine and I were in Alabama visiting his grandmother and we were watching the Montgomery Rebels play some other farm club. At that point I was introduced to a truly fantastic hot weather repast—Grape Snow Cones with a chili dog all the way.... Just as fresh Red Snapper poached in wine sauce is raised to its highest level surrounded by the elegance of Gerard's, so a snow cone and a chili dog achieve their highest levels of attainment when you are hanging around a ball park" (Banzhaf 3).

[12]The latter revival involved an extensive search for the original little girl—now grown—who wanted to teach the world to sing and the filming of a new commercial on the same theme featuring her and her own young daughter.

[13]Though McNally's play deals primarily with classical music in general and opera in particular, the same fanatic interest in different performances appears in the desire of jazz fans to hear alternate takes of pieces played—sometimes only minutes or seconds apart—by improvisers of the stature of (say) Lester Young or Charlie Parker.

[14]This and the following several paragraphs on collecting were written in collaboration with Tiana Wimmer. The author thanks Ms. Wimmer for her excellent research inputs and insights.

[15]A more systematic definition for the present use of the term "nostalgia" appears later in this essay.

[16]See the discussion of "Do You Miss New York?," "The Dear Departed Past," and "Matty" later in this essay.

[17]Unfortunately, since the preceding description was written, this particular magazine has gone out of business and ceased publication. Nevertheless, its content serves to make the point intended.

[18]*Honeymooners* fanatics have formed their own association called The *R*oyal *A*ssociation for the *L*ongevity and *P*reservation of The *H*oneymooners or

R.A.L.P.H. Its name is, of course, an acronym for *Ralph* Kramden, as brilliantly played by Jackie Gleason.

[19]The weekly program that Nat Cole all too briefly did for television in the mid-1950s featured a segment called "Memories." Revisiting that show in its current cable reruns often makes yesterday's excursions into sentimentality seem like today's gold mines of nostalgic treasures.

[20]A big hit for Nat Cole in the 1950s, "Unforgettable" was recently revived by his daughter Natalie in a music video (and album) that featured a father-daughter duet. In 1992, forty years after the original recording, this electronic collaboration won six Grammy Awards—including those for record of the year, album of the year, song of the year, and pop vocal—duo or group. As noted by Pareles, "In an outpouring of nostalgia..., Natalie Cole's "Unforgettable," an album of songs associated with her father, Nat (King) Cole, swept every category in which it was nominated" (C15).

[21]"Try to Remember" comes from *The Fantastiks*, which has run continuously off-Broadway for over thirty years. Recently, it was "discovered" by the author's 22-year-old son, who was born a decade after the debut of the show itself. This pattern of rediscovery raises possibilities for a second-generational cycle of nostalgia.

[22]The distinction between the "simple" and "higher" orders of nostalgia appears in the next section of this essay.

[23]Indeed, the Ossianic poems were a complete fiction—nothing more than a hoax—devised by a Scottish writer named James Macpherson (1736-1796).

[24]In a sense, this progression moves from the most complex to the most simple. But it also entails progress from the most detached to the most involved. The deep personal involvement that characterizes "simple" first order nostalgia captures the essence of our present focus.

[25]I do *not* mean to imply that Frishberg *intends* to portray these or other aspects of consumer behavior. Indeed, in a letter, he has indicated that this is not the case. Rather, I simply claim that—as an acute observer of the human condition—Frishberg naturally tends to reflect these aspects of the consumption experience in his songs.

[26]However, following Lowenthal, we must also recognize that this harking back to young adulthood is only one type of nostalgia and that nostalgic longings could also fasten onto happenings that occurred before one's own arrival on the planet. Both types of nostalgia remain clear possibilities. Whether nostalgia can reach back into a bygone era from the historical past remains a question that invites empirical investigation.

Works Cited

Abrams, M. H. *Natural Supernaturalism: Tradition and Revolution in Romantic Literature*. New York: W.W. Norton, 1971.

Alexander, Ron. "One Man's Obsession of Post Created Wave of TV Nostalgia."

New York Times 2 Aug 1990: C1, C10.

Balliett, Whitney. *American Singers: Twenty-Seven Portraits in Song*. New York: Oxford UP, 1988.

Banzhaf, Harry B. "Thoughts on February." *Investment Management*. Harry B. Banzhaf & Co., 1992.

Baugh, Bruce. "Authenticity Revisited." *Journal of Aesthetics and Art Criticism* 46 (Summer 1988): 477-87.

Belk, Russell W. "The Role of Possessions in Constructing and Maintaining a Sense of Past." *Advances in Consumer Research*. Eds. M.E. Goldberg, G. Gorn, and R.W. Pollay. Vol 17. Provo: Association for Consumer Research, 1990: 669-76.

_____, ed. "Possessions and the Sense of Past." *Highways and Buyways*. Provo, UT: Association for Consumer Research, 1991.

_____, ed. *Highways and Buyways*. Provo: Association for Consumer Research, 1991.

Belk, Russell W., John Sherry, and Melanie Wallendorf. "A Naturalistic Inquiry into Buyer and Seller Behavior at a Swap Meet." *Journal of Consumer Research* 14 Mar. 1988: 449-70.

Belk, Russell W., Melanie Wallendorf, and John F. Sherry, Jr. "The Sacred and the Profane in Consumer Behavior: Theodicy on the Odyssey." *Journal of Consumer Research* 16 June 1989: 1-39.

Belk, Russell W., Melanie Wallendorf, John Sherry, and Morris B. Holbrook. "Collecting in a Consumer Culture." *Highways and Buyways*. Ed. Russell W. Belk, Provo, UT: Association for Consumer Research, 1991.

_____. John Sherry, Morris Holbrook, Scott Roberts. "Collectors and Collecting." *Advances in Consumer Research*. Vol 15. Ed. Michael J. Houston, Provo, UT: Association for Consumer Research, 1988: 548-53.

Bornstein, Marc H. "Sensitive Periods in Development: Structural Characteristics and Causal Interpretations." *Psychological Bulletin* 105.2 (1989): 179-97.

Botto, Louis. "A Night at the Opera: ...Terrence McNally's Ode to Maria Callas and the Fanatical Fans Who Idolized Her." *Playbill* 89 (Nov. 1989): 66-73.

Braudy, Leo. "In the Arts, Tomorrow Begins With Yesterday." *New York Times* Arts and Leisure Section (1 July 1990): 1-17.

Buhle, Paul. "Introduction." *Popular Culture in America*. Ed. P. Buhle. Minneapolis: U of Minnesota P, 1987: ix-xxvii.

_____, ed. *Popular Culture in America*. Minneapolis: U of Minnesota P, 1987.

Campbell, Colin. *The Romantic Ethic and the Spirit of Modern Consumerism*. New York: Basil Blackwell, 1987.

Carr, Roy, Brian Case, and Fred Dellar. *The Hip: Hipsters, Jazz and the Beat Generation*. Boston, MA: Faber and Faber, 1986.

Cherry, Christopher. "How Can We Seize the Past?" *Philosophy* 64 (1989): 67-78.

Cole, Nat "King." "These Foolish Things." *Just One of Those Things (And More)*. Capitol CDP-7-46649-2 (1987).

_____. *Unforgettable: The Complete Visual Biography of His Life and Music*.

MPI Home Entertainment, MP 1663, EMI Records (1989).

Cole, Richard R. "Top Songs in the Sixties: A Content Analysis of Popular Lyrics." *American Behavioral Scientist* 14 (Jan./Feb. 1971): 389-400.

Connerton, Paul. *How Societies Remember.* Cambridge: Cambridge UP, 1989.

Csikszentmihalyi, Mihaly and Eugene Rochberg-Halton. *The Meaning of Things: Domestic Symbols and the Self.* Cambridge: Cambridge UP, 1981.

Danet, Brenda and Tamara Katriel (1989). "No Two Alike: The Aesthetics of Collecting." *Play and Culture* 2.3 (1989): 253-277.

Dannefer, Dale. "Rationality and Passion in Private Experience: Modern Consciousness and the Social World of Old-Car Collectors." *Social Problems* 27 (Apr. 1980): 392-412.

Davis, Fred. *Yearning For Yesterday: A Sociology of Nostalgia.* New York: Free, 1979.

Fodor, Nandor. "Varieties of Nostalgia." *Psychological Review* 37 (1950): 25-38.

Frishberg, David. "Do You Miss New York?" *The Dave Frishberg Songbook.* Vol. 1, Omnisound N-1040 (1981).

_____. "The Dear Departed Past." *Live At Vine Street.* Fantasy F-9638 (1985).

_____. Live Concert in Rochester. New York, Broadcast over WBGO, Newark, NJ, (Mar. 1989).

_____. "Matty." *Let's Eat Home.* Concord Jazz CCD-4402 (1990).

Gendron, Bernard. "Theodor Adorno Meets the Cadillacs." *Studies in Entertainment: Critical Approaches to Mass Culture.* Ed. Tania Modleski. Bloomington: Indiana UP, 1986: 18-36.

Giamatti, A. Bartlett. *Take Time For Paradise: Americans and Their Games.* New York: Summit Books, 1989.

Gordon, Beverly. "The Souvenir: Messenger of the Extraordinary." *Journal of Popular Culture* 20.3 (1986): 135-146.

Gorman, James. "Nostalgia Can Choke the Ongoing Stream of Your Life." *New York Times,* Arts and Leisure Section. (1 July 1990): 16.

Halbwachs, Maurice. 1950. *The Collective Memory.* Trans. Francis J. Ditter, Jr. and Vida Yazdi Ditter. New York: Harper & Row, 1980.

Havlena, William J. and Susan L. Holak. " 'The Good Old Days': Observations On Nostalgia and Its Role In Consumer Behavior." *Advances in Consumer Research.* Vol. 18. Eds. R. H. Holman and M.R. Solomon, Provo: Association for Consumer Research, 1991: 323-29.

Hillier, Bevis. "Why Do We Collect Antiques?" *Our Past Before Us: Why Do We Save It ?* Eds. David Lowenthal and Marcus Binney. London: Temple Smith, 1981: 70-82.

Hirschman, Elizabeth C. "The Ideology of Consumption: A Structural-Syntactical Analysis of 'Dallas' and 'Dynasty'." *Journal of Consumer Research* 15 (Dec. 1988): 344-59.

Hobsbawm, Eric. "Introduction: Inventing Tradition." *The Invention of Tradition.* Eds. Eric Hobsbawm and Terence Ranger. Cambridge: Cambridge UP, 1983: 1-14.

Holbrook, Morris B. "An Audiovisual Inventory of Some Fanatic Consumer Behavior: The 25-Cent Tour of a Jazz Collector's Home." *Advances in Consumer Research*. Eds. Melanie Wallendorf and Paul F. Anderson, Provo, UT: Association for Consumer Research, 1987: 144-49.

———. "The Psychoanalytic Interpretation of Consumer Behavior: *I Am an Animal*." *Research in Consumer Behavior* 3 (1988): 149-78.

———. "Steps Toward a Psychoanalytic Interpretation of Consumption: A Meta-Meta-Meta-Analysis of Some Basic Issues Raised by the Consumer Behavior Odyssey." *Advances in Consumer Research*. Vol. 15. Ed. Michael J. Houston, Provo, UT: Association for Consumer Research, 1988: 537-42.

———. " 'These Foolish Things,' 'The Dear Departed Past,' and the Songs of David Frishberg: A Commentary and Critique." *ACR Newsletter* (June 1989): 1-8.

———. "Nostalgic Consumption: On the Reliability and Validity of a New Nostalgia Index." Working Paper. Graduate School of Business, Columbia U, 1990.

———. "From the Log of a Consumer Researcher: Reflections on the Odyssey." *Highways and Buyways*. Ed. Russell W. Belk, Provo, UT: Association for Consumer Research, 1991: 14-33.

———. "Nostalgia Proneness and Consumer Tastes." *Consumer Behavior in Marketing Strategy*. 2nd ed. John A. Howard, Englewood Cliffs, NJ: Prentice-Hall, 1992.

Holbrook, Morris B. and Kim P. Corfman. "Quality and Value in the Consumption Experience: Phaedrus Rides Again." *Perceived Quality: How Consumers View Stores and Merchandise*. Eds. Jacob Jacoby and Jerry C. Olson. Lexington, MA: D.C. Heath and Company, 1984.

Holbrook, Morris B. and Robert M. Schindler (1989). "Some Exploratory Findings on the Development of Musical Tastes." *Journal of Consumer Research* 16 (1989): 119-24.

———. "Echoes of the Dear Departed Past: Some Work in Progress on Nostalgia." *Advances in Consumer Research*. Vol. 18. Eds. Rebecca H. Holman and Michael R. Solomon, Provo, UT: Association for Consumer Research, 1991: 330-33.

Hughes, Stephen. *Pop Culture Mania: Collecting 20th-Century Americana for Fun and Profit*. New York: McGraw-Hill, 1984.

Jacobs, Dick. *Who Wrote That Song?* White Hall, VA: Bitterway Pub., 1988.

James, Bill. *The Bill James Baseball Abstract*. New York: Villard Books, 1988.

Johnson, Robert. "Classic 'Muscle Cars' Replace Model T's As Hot Collectibles: Autos From '20s and '30s Lose Value as Baby Boomers Redefine What's Vintage." *Wall Street Journal* (20 Mar. 1990): A1-A13.

Johnston, Susanna and Tim Beddow. *Collecting: The Passionate Pastime*. New York: Harper & Row, 1986.

King, Carol. "Showtime Coast to Coast." Prod. and dir. Ken Ehrlich: Ken Ehrlich Productions, 1989.

Kron, Joan. *Home-Psych: The Social Psychology of Home and Decoration*. New York: Clarkson N. Potter, Inc, 1983.

Leland, John. "The Rock 'n' Roll Generation Gap." *7 Days*. (21 Feb. 1990): 10-15.

Lorenz, Konrad Z. "The Role of Gestalt Perception in Animal and Human Behavior." *Aspects of Form*. Ed. Lancelot Law Whyte, Bloomington: Indiana UP, 1951: 157-78.

Lowenthal, David. *The Past Is a Foreign Country*. Cambridge: Cambridge UP, 1985.

Mannheim, Karl. 1928. "The Problem of Generations." *Essays on the Sociology of Knowledge*. London: Routledge and Kegan Paul, 1952: 276-322.

Marum, Andrew and Frank Parise. *Follies and Foibles: A View of 20th Century Fads*, New York: Facts On File, Inc, 1984.

McCracken, Grant. *Culture and Consumption: New Approaches to the Symbolic Character of Consumer Goods and Activities*, Bloomington: Indiana UP, 1988.

_____. " 'Homeyness': A Cultural Account of One Constellation of Consumer Goods and Meanings," in *Interpretive Consumer Research*. Ed. Elizabeth C. Hirschman, Provo, UT: Association for Consumer Research, 1989: 168-183.

McCrohan, Donna. *The Honeymooners' Companion: The Kramdens and the Nortons Revisited*, New York: Workman Pub., 1978.

Meyers, Mike. "Ads Seek Loudest Blasts from the Past." *Minneapolis Star Tribune*, (12 Aug. 1990): 1D-3D.

Miller, Cyndee. "Nostalgia Makes Boomers Buy." *Marketing News* 24 (26 Nov. 1990): 1-2.

Moriarty, Sandra Ernst, and Anthony F. McGann. "Nostalgia and Consumer Sentiment." *Journalism Quarterly* 60 (Spring 1983): 81-86.

O'Connor, John J. "Fast Forwarding Into TV's Past." *New York Times* (15 Feb. 1991): C1, C34.

O'Guinn, Thomas C. "Touching Greatness." *Highways and Buyways*. Ed. R. W. Belk, Provo: Association for Consumer Research, 1991.

Pareles, Jon. "The 70's Revisited: The Nostalgia Trail Hits Rock Bottom." *New York Times*, Arts and Leisure Section, (15 Apr. 1990): 28.

_____. "Cole's 'Unforgettable' Sweeps the Grammys." *The New York Times* (26 Feb. 1992): C15.

Priasky, Lorraine E. and Jill Leslie Rosenbaum. "'LEER-ICS' OR LYRICS: Teenage Impressions of Rock 'n' Roll." *Youth & Society* 18 (1987): 384-97.

"Remembrance of Tunes Past." *The Economist* 317 (10 Nov. 1990): 78.

Ritter, Lawrence and Donald Honig. *The Image of Their Greatness: An Illustrated History of Baseball from 1900 to the Present*. New York: Crown Publishers, 1984.

Rothenberg, Randall. "The Past Is Now the Latest Craze." *New York Times* (29 Nov. 1989): D1, D19.

_____. "NBC Planning Nostalgia Show," *New York Times* (9 May 1990): D17.

Sann, Paul. *Fads, Follies and Delusions of the American People*. New York: Bonanza Books, 1967.

Schuman, Howard and Jacqueline Scott. "Generations and Collective Memories,"

American Sociological Review 54 (1989): 359-381.

Sinatra, Frank. *Point of No Return*, Capitol CDP-7-48334-2 (1961).

_____. *September of My Years*, Reprise CD 1014-2 (1965).

Skretvedt, Randy and Jordan R. Young. *The Nostalgia Entertainment Sourcebook*. Beverly Hills: Moonstone, 1991.

Slesin, Suzanne. "Decorating With Nostalgia, Emotion and Other Intangibles." *New York Times* (21 June 1990): C1-C6.

_____. "Lasting Visions of the Home." *New York Times* (13 Sept. 1990): C1-C6.

Starobinski, Jean. "The Idea of Nostalgia." *Diogenes* 54 (Summer 1966): 81-103.

Stern, Barbara. "*OTHER-SPEAK*: Classical Allegory and Contemporary Advertising," Working Paper, Rutgers U, 1990.

Stipp, Horst. "Musical Demographics: The Strong Impact of Age on Music Preferences Affects All Kinds of Business." *American Demographics* (Aug. 1990): 48-49.

Trevor-Roper, Hugh. "The Invention of Tradition: The Highland Tradition of Scotland." *The Invention of Tradition*. Ed. Eric Hobsbawm and Terence Ranger, Cambridge: Cambridge UP, 1983: 15-42.

Wimmer, Tiana. "Investigation of Collecting Behavior." Working paper, Graduate School of Business, Columbia U, 1988.

Rumors of War:
Lyrical Continuities, 1914-1991

B. LEE COOPER

The war and song combination constitutes one of the oldest complexes in human society. They have aided and abetted each other throughout the past, and undoubtedly will continue to do so in the future.

America's twentieth century military adventures have been widely chronicled in print. However, war-time reveries are most frequently elicited through oral rather than literary resources. Popular songs, legacies of the commercial recording industry, Tin Pan Alley, ASCAP/BMI, and numerous singer/songwriters, are key items in understanding the public image of warfare in the United States. Since 1917 lyrics of war-related records have featured themes that have heartened troops, bolstered civilian morale, and defined a unique destiny for American society. The goal of national unity is unmistakable. Even so-called anti-war, pacifist, or protest songs allude to traditional ideals when challenging specific military involvement. The myth of military morality is conjured, circulated, and perpetuated in American popular music. Only by closely examining meanings of such image- driven militarism can the American public rationally decide whether war's horrors are ever genuinely justified.

Introduction

The United States is a military giant. American troops have seized naval bases in Mexico (1914), occupied Iceland and Greenland (1941), served as advisors in Greece (1947), led a United Nations police action in Korea (1950-1953), landed in the Dominican Republic (1965), halted an airfield expansion in Grenada (1983), participated in an international peace-keeping effort in Lebanon (1982-1984), bombed Libya (1986), and seized a dictator and drug czar in Panama (1989). The size, scope, and meaning of the aforementioned military activities pale in comparison to the four major U.S. crusades of the twentieth century: World War I (1917-

1918), World War II (1941-1945), the Vietnam War (1964-1973), and the Persian Gulf War (1991). Each of these four conflicts prompted a significant outpouring of popular songs. The lyrics of these war-related tunes contain key images and themes that capsule American values and beliefs about warfare. Even songs that dispute the need for immediate American involvement in overseas imbroglios—those stressing isolationist sentiments, neutrality arguments, or pacificist contentions—are crafted around the same ideals that, ironically, are championed in pro-military tunes.

What are the most prominent, persistent themes in war era songs? Ignoring contentious pre-war debates and post-war frustrations over world-wide instability and personal dislocations, there are eleven central ideas that dominate the lyrics of war-related tunes. These themes are: (1) overt hostility toward international enemies, including ridiculing leaders, stereotyping enemy nationalities, and belittling foreign soldiers as either sadists or cowards; (2) sympathy for conquered civilian populations and brave allied troops in occupied territories; (3) emphasis on long-term historical friendships between the United States, its military allies, and the invaded nations; (4) reinforcement of patriotic beliefs and emphasis on national symbols, previous military victories, and prior war heroes or national leaders; (5) support and admiration for U.S. soldiers, praise for their dedication and self-sacrifices, and grateful acknowledgment of their bravery and heroism; (6) empathy for loved ones—mothers, fathers, sweethearts, wives, and children—separated from U.S. soldiers; (7) confidence in U.S. leadership, with special praise for the wisdom of the President and for the courage of American generals; (8) support for the idealistic post-war goals of peace, prosperity, and the extension of democratic values abroad; (9) cynicism toward the articulated economic objectives and proposed post-war strategies of American politicians; (10) advocacy of resolving international disputes through non- military strategies such as economic sanctions, political isolation, and the assertion of moral superiority; and (11) anger over the appearance of anti-war arguments expressed through allegations of cowardice, unpatriotic behavior, and giving aid and comfort to the enemy. These eleven themes are invariably intertwined in lyrics and cannot be viewed as singular or discreet commentaries.

Throughout the twentieth century popular music has played a significant role in creating and reinforcing the myth of U.S. military morality. This highly subjective, ethnocentric perspective equates American involvement in international conflicts to religious crusades against infidels, to justifiable struggles against madmen, and to selfless sacrifices to advance the cause of worldwide human freedom. Nowhere do song lyrics confront pragmatic issues such as balance of power politics, policies of economic strangulation, the threat of nuclear proliferation, key resource availability, geographical spheres of influence, or imperialistic expansion of political or economic control. By an unrelenting pursuit of theologically-based patriotism the music industry and its nationalistic troubadours undermine the debates that should characterize a democratic citizenry at war. Only during the lengthy Vietnam conflict did a significant number of anti-war sentiments emerge. Not surprisingly, though, the artists' objections to Southeast Asian militarism were not grounded in rational assessments of real world politics, but in the same kind of ethical, theological stances that fuel more common pro-war lyrics.

The remainder of this study illustrates the war-time lyrical environments as generated through popular recordings between 1914 through 1991. The thematic structures outlined above are repeated time after time. The two World Wars and the Persian Gulf War are amazingly consistent in promoting the U.S. military morality myth. Only the Vietnam War, and its mixed message aftermath, presented an opportunity for Americans to experience an audio forum of contrasting images and differing ideas. Rather than being a national embarrassment, though, the music of the Vietnam era was actually the most open, democratic war-time debate of this century.

Music As Public Memory

The American public has always envisioned international warfare through the hindsight of previous military conflicts. There are four distinct periods of war-time imagery in this century. The first spans 1914-1938 and is based upon experiences gained during the First World War; the second is 1939-1963 and includes events of the Second World War and the initial portion of the Cold War period; the third is 1964-1989 and involves the Vietnam War era; and the final frame is 1990-91 and features the Persian Gulf War and its immediate aftermath.

This study examines the audio images of these four American war eras as featured on popular recordings. The lyrics reveal many of the assumptions that fuel public opinion about military policy. Commercially recorded commentaries both reflect and influence the perceptions of American society. Several persistent attitudes, topics, and themes are illustrated in war-related songs. Hindsight-driven international perspectives manifested in lyrics constitute a strange reversal of George Santayanna's warning about remembering the past. Without a forward-thinking viewpoint, a reasoned and pragmatic sense of the present, and an open perspective on the future, a democratic society is threatened by citizen grid-lock on foreign policy issues. More importantly, the President, U.S. Congress, and the State Department can also succumb to war imagery myths with even more drastic possibilities for mismanagement of America's vast military power.

Conventional wisdom asserts that while the American people may disagree about the specific reasons for becoming involved in a particular military conflict, bi-partisan popular support will unite behind any U.S. war effort. This assumption is a subset of the notion that all foreign policy is conducted on a politically nonpartisan basis. Neither proposition is historically valid. Prior to the twentieth century, Americans quarreled, complained and even killed each other during the Revolutionary War, the War of 1812, the Mexican War, the Civil War, and the Spanish-American War. Little changed after 1900. Woodrow Wilson hoped to make the world safe for democracy after 1917, but he encountered dramatic opposition from a hostile Senate when he brought his worldwide peace plan home. Franklin Roosevelt benefited from Japan's 1941 sneak attack on Pearl Harbor and Germany's maniacal leader in amassing public support for involvement in World War II. But pacificists still campaigned throughout the conflict for an immediate end to hostilities. Lyndon Johnson and Richard Nixon both encountered fierce opposition to their ever-expanding southeast Asian military adventures. Even George Bush's quick, clinical annihilation of Iraq's huge conventional military machine during the Persian Gulf War was firmly opposed by many domestic peace groups.

Reality is seldom congruent with popular opinion. Short-term memory feeds public imagery. The function of contemporary songs as image sources about specific wars in the modern era has been explored in several studies. However, the idea that songs *both* reflect and influence post-war attitudes toward military conflict is rarely investigated or discussed. The following pages present a series of illustrations depicting the lengthy shadows of war-related recordings. This study was launched with three general assumptions in mind. First, with the significant exception of the Vietnam War, popular songs have functioned to support American military policies throughout the Twentieth Century. Second, post-war feelings about the validity of previous military involvements have been reinforced through the repetition of popular war-time tunes. Finally, American public opinion is much more susceptible to popular culture imagery about wars than to critical historical analysis, scholarly reinterpretations, or rapidly changing world conditions.

Four War Song Eras

"Music is a weapon in all wars, used to
bolster morale or to heap scorn on an enemy..."
— Robin Denselow,
When The Music's Over;
The Story Of Political Pop

The experience of war is staggering. The outbreak of hostilities invariably heightens the tensions that preceded the onset of military activities. Warfare itself psychologically batters soldiers, politicians, and civilian populations alike. The eventual ceasefire leaves victors and vanquished dissatisfied, while peace negotiations and post- war power realignments are invariably less than acceptable to the warring parties. Twentieth-Century America has survived four war eras. These are World War I (1914-1938), World War II (1939-1964), the Vietnam War (1965-1989), and the Persian Gulf War (1990-present). Generations that experience war eras also experience many, many war-related songs. The perspectives on these conflicts and the results interpreted in lyrics carry forward and influence future military images.

World War I music heightened American nationalism; strengthened concern for civilians in Belgium, England, and France; increased the feeling of moral superiority toward European politicos; and created the belief that America had "saved" Europe. The music of the 1914-1938 period reinforced unity, patriotism, and faith in the U.S.. World War II era songs continued this trend. However, the post-war period became much more complicated. Expansion of atomic technology, reconstruction of western Europe and Japan, the U.N. police action in Korea, McCarthyism, the Suez Crisis, the Cuban missile crisis, and numerous international incidents attributed to the machinations of a world-wide communist conspiracy created a domestic climate of unrest and insecurity. The Vietnam War era emerged in conflict, with music reflecting the disunity, uncertainty, complexity, and limited options of even a nuclear Super Power. The music of the southeast Asian conflict was contentious and the post-war years featured a continuation of the dual perspectives of power and impotence, security and danger, and isolationistic patriotism and international humanitarianism. The Persian Gulf War, with its military brevity and patriotic zeal, found a new lyrical unity. The question that remains unanswered is whether the newest post-war period will continue the Vietnam disunity trend or mark a return to the heightened American nationalism and patriotic accord of earlier eras.

World War I Era Songs

War songs as examples of propaganda have traditionally performed one dominant function: to create a sense (maybe an illusion) of unity and shared purpose.... Reviewing the songs of the Great War, one would hardly suspect that there was anything but the most wholehearted acceptance of American involvement. And this is as it should be. The Tin Pan Alley songsmith's job was to communicate that sense of unity. The songs do not tell us that the country was divided on the issue of war....

Timothy E. Scheurer,
Born In The U.S.A.

The popular songs of the First World War were overwhelmingly patriotic, upbeat, and supportive of American soldiers. Sympathy for Great Britain and France, encouragement for President Woodrow Wilson, and commitment to defeating Germany and its allies was communicated in tunes like "Lafayette (We Hear You Calling)," "Somewhere In France Is Daddy," and "I Think We've Got Another Washington (Wilson Is His Name)." The 1915 lament "I Didn't Raise My Boy To Be A Soldier" was overwhelmed by new patriotic lyrics. These tunes included "Let's All Be Good Americans Now," "Over There" (with five different hit versions during 1917 and 1918), and "Just Like Washington Crossed The Delaware, General Pershing Will Cross The Rhine." Emotion-rousing tributes to the flag and to national honor such as "The Battle Hymn Of The Republic," "The Star-Spangled Banner," "The Stars and Stripes Forever March," and "You're A Grand Old Flag" also registered significant popular attention.

Positive perspectives of military service—duty, loyalty, and commitment—were echoed in songs aimed at soldiers, parents, and sweethearts. Service obligations were acknowledged in "America, Here's My Boy," "(Goodbye, And Luck Be With You) Laddie Boy," "Pack Up Your Troubles In Your Old Kit Bag And Smile, Smile, Smile," and "Send Me Away With A Smile." The sense of straightening out someone else's overseas problems was clearly communicated in "The Yanks Are At It Again." Homefront reactions to the dangers being faced by those loved ones who march off to Europe were contained in "Bring Back My Soldier Boy To Me," "God Be With Our Boys Tonight," and "Say A Prayer For The Boys Out There." Lyrical comments attributed to American troops were predictable: "I'm Gonna Pin My Medal On The Girl I Left Behind," "Life In A Trench In Belgium," and "Keep The Home Fires Burning." Humor wasn't overlooked, either. The G.I. viewpoint was delivered in "Oh, How I Hate To Get Up In The Morning" and "Would You Rather Be

AN ATTITUDINAL PROFILE OF FOUR WAR ERAS IN U.S. HISTORY, 1914-1991

Four 20th-Century War Eras	Pre-war Attitudes and Perspectives	War-time Attitudes and Perspectives	Post-war Attitudes and Perspectives
World War I (1914-1938)	isolationism; fear of the European alliance system; anger about economic blockades and submarine warfare; "Peace Without Victory" possible	making the world safe for democracy; fight a war to end all wars; halt trade interference by European powers	patriotic nationalism; no foreign entanglements; no League of Nations membership; return to normalcy sought
World War II (1939-1964)	neutrality; arsenal for democracy; fear of expansionism by Germany, Italy, and Japan	outrage at Japan's Pearl Harbor attack; desire to conquer the dictators in Germany Italy, and Japan	"American Century proclaimed; Marshall Plan; United Nations membership; Cold War and Iron Curtain; nuclear vulnerability; political cynicism; doubt about military superiority
Vietnam War (1965-1989)	fear of "domino effect" in Southeast Asia triggered by Hanoi's conquest of the Saigon regime	easy domination of Third World nation by naval support and air strikes; halt spread of Communism	political cynicism; doubt about military superiority
Persian Gulf War (1990-1991)	fear of Iraqi military domination of Arab states; concern about oil shortages; invasion of Kuwait; fear Iraqi nuclear capability	crush Saddam Hussein's regime and restore Kuwaiti rulers pinpoint bombing raids and blitzkreig ground victory; heightened U.N. involvement; economic sanctions were to slow	euphoria of quick victory; emerging New World Order; potential Arab/Israeli peace; praise for military leadership

A Colonel With An Eagle On Your Shoulder Or A Private With A Chicken On Your Knee."

The conclusion of the Great War provided lyrical reflection time. The European experience, particularly for young American servicemen in France, was heralded in several popular tunes: "Au Revoir But Not Goodbye, Soldier Boy," "Goodbye, France," "How Ya Gonna Keep 'Em Down On The Farm (After They've Seen Paree)," and "When Yankee Doodle Learns To Parlez Vous Francais." The humor of exchanging military ranks for civilian business roles was featured in the popular post-war tune "I've Got My Captain Working For Me Now."

The popular music of World War I was totally divorced from domestic political reality in the United States between 1914 and 1920. No references are made to the isolationist position or to fears of entangling alliances with any European powers. Neutrality was cherished. Woodrow Wilson's "He Kept Us Out Of War" presidential campaign slogan swept him back into the White House in 1916. Songs do not reflect public reactions to the sinking of the British steamship *Lusitania* (1915), to the Zimmermann telegram (1917), or to any specific military events on the Continent. After the declaration of war by the U.S. Congress on April 6, 1917, American music seemed to be motivated by patriotic tradition, British propaganda about the heartless Huns, and the rules of political commentary dictated by George Creel's Committee on Public Information. The dream of a war to end all wars was given voice in U.S. popular recordings. When the Treaty of Versailles was defeated in the Senate in 1919, American music immediately switched from military themes to the romantic, dance-oriented sounds of the Jazz Age without missing a beat. With the exceptions of The Victor Symphony Orchestra's "Patriotic March Medley" (1929) and Jimmie Rodger's "The Soldier's Sweetheart" (1927), the inter-war years were lyrically silent on the subject of warfare.

World War II Era Songs

The Second World War was a watershed period in British broadcasting, the requirements of the war effort prompting a fundamental re-evaluation of the purposes, functions, and applications of public radio service. It was a period in which the *ideological* uses of entertainment—its uses in binding people together in a common cause, its identification with and portrayal of national values, however contrived or self-regarding—were appreciated in very direct ways, and one that marked a distinct break with the principle of mixed programming and of catering for different interests and tastes within the context of one national network. As regards the broadcasting of popular music, the war years ushered in an era of greater reliance on gramophone records and considerably greater American domination of the music field as a whole.

—Stephen Barnard,
*On The Radio: Music
Radio In Britain* (1989)

The Good War. So we sum up the popular mythology centering around World War II. And so it seems it was—as wars go. There was a feeling of unity in the country. People's energies were focused again, business was humming, and the Depression was snapped. This is not to say there was not initial revulsion at the idea of another war.

—Timothy E. Scheurer
Born In The U.S.A.

As might be expected, both the singers and the songs of the Second War differed from those of The Great War. Arthur Fields, John McCormack, Nora Bayes, Billy Murray, and Harry MacDonough yielded their war-time record chart positions to Glenn Miller, The Andrews Sisters, Spike Jones, Johnny Mercer, Kate Smith, Kay Kyser, Dinah Shore, and Harry James. Although most titles and lyrics were new, popular songs still served as domestic reinforcements for the overseas war effort. Both Germany and Japan were openly ridiculed in tunes like "Der Fuehrer's Face," "Mussolini's Letter To Hitler," and "You're A Sap, Mr. Jap." Patriotism, military proficiency, and traditional American values were honored in songs such as "God Bless America, " "Remember Pearl Harbor," and "Yankee Doodle Boy." The Air Force was particularly lauded in "Comin' In On A Wing And A Prayer" and "He Wears A Pair Of Silver Wings"; the U.S. Army was depicted in more realistic terms in "(Lights Out) 'Til Reveille," "Praise The Lord And Pass The Ammunition," and "This Is The Army, Mr. Jones."

Soldiers remained the central figures in American popular songs. The inconvenience of the military draft system and the minimal pay received by U.S. troops were satirized in "Goodbye Dear, I'll Be Back In A Year" and "Twenty-One Dollars A Day— Once A Month." While fighting for the time when "(There'll Be Bluebirds Over) The White Cliffs Of Dover," a few enlisted men found romance overseas. The most popular song illustrating this situation was "Johnny Doughboy Found A Rose In Ireland." Musical salutes to "The Boogie Woogie Bugle Boy" were far out-

numbered by the sentimental feelings deploring lengthy separations
from loved ones back home. Dispatched to military theatres in
Africa, Italy, the South Pacific, and Western Europe, American
soldiers were lyrically reminded "We Did It Before (And We Can
Do It Again)" and that international peace and prosperity would be
rekindled "When The Lights Go On Again (All Over The World)."
However, the personal goals of fighting men and their sweethearts
were more accurately captured in deeply sentimental songs such as
"Cleanin' My Rifle (And Dreamin' Of You)," "I'll Get By (As
Long As I Have You)," and "It's Been A Long, Long Time."

Clearly, the Japanese attack on Pearl Harbor on December 7,
1941 was the galvanizing event for the American war effort. But
popular music ignored the political debates prior to 1941 over
isolationism, neutrality, and destroyers-for-bases deals with Great
Britain, as well as the numerous peace campaigns launched by
various groups. After the declaration of war, lyrics remained silent
on the Nisei relocation issue, on government-enforced
infringements on freedom of speech and civil rights, and even on
the atomic blasts over Hiroshima and Nagasaki. Only after Hitler
was defeated and Japan was occupied did singers begin to reckon
with the irreversible change that victory had wrought in American
life.

Between 1946 and 1964 an ever-so-slow evolution occurred in
American popular song commentaries about warfare. References to
worldwide annihilation appeared in a few country, blues, and R&B
tunes. Bill Haley's "Thirteen Women" and Ray Charles' "The
Danger Zone" illustrated this trend. But previous military
involvements were heralded in "Ballad Of The Alamo," "The
Battle Of New Orleans," "P.T. 109," and "Sink The Bismarck."
Patriotic tunes continued to be charted—"Battle Hymn Of The
Republic," "God Bless America," and "Stars And Stripes
Forever"—along with a variety of military draft melodies—"The
All-American Boy," "God Country, And My Baby," and "Greetings
(This Is Uncle Sam)." The recordings which most clearly signaled
the dawning of a new age of popular music commentary were
charted by a few popular folk artists. These tunes were: "Blowin'
In The Wind," "If I Had A Hammer," and "Where Have All The
Flowers Gone." Nuclear proliferation, the McCarthy era, Cold War
and containment policies, and the civil rights struggle of the fifties
provided the historical and social background for America's
impending southeast Asian involvement.

Vietnam War Era Songs

In early summer 1949, Americans could believe that victory in the Cold War was within their grasp. They like their wars, hot or cold, the same way they like their baseball: easily understood, brief, and with a definite score at the end so that it is clear who won.

—Walter LaFeber,
*The American Age: United States Foreign
Policy At Home And Abroad Since 1750*
(1989)

In spite of the horrors of the atomic bomb and the Holocaust, Americans emerged from World War II much as they had from World War I—confident and eager to return to normal lives full of hope in the face of future anxiety.... [Many American people]...went into Vietnam with convictions that were shaped by the mythology of World War II.

—Timothy E. Scheurer,
Born In The U.S.A.

It should perhaps be stressed that the Vietnam War was won by the Vietcong and the North Vietnamese, not pop music, but music played an important role in helping to reflect and reinforce the anti-war mood in the U.S.A.

—Robin Denselow,
*When The Music's Over:
The Story Of Political Pop*

Songs related to the Vietnam War were more numerous, more complex, more divisive, and more politically-oriented than those charted during either previous World War. This variety did not exclude tunes that championed traditional American ideals, lauded nationalism and patriotism, praised brave soldiers, and alluded joyfully to earlier military successes. These sentiments were spoken and sung in "The Americans (A Canadian's Opinion)," "Gallant Men," "Okie From Muskogee," "Pledge of Allegiance," and "Stout-Hearted Men." Yet even in the re-interpretations of traditional songs such as "Seven O'Clock News/Silent Night" and "The Star-Spangled Banner," it was clear that the times were a-changing. Confusion and argumentation thrived in popular lyrics; unrest and agitation swept the radio airwaves; unanswered questions spawned greater and greater lyrical hostility toward military activities. Songs of uncertainty included "America, Communicate With Me," "Ball Of Confusion (That's What The World Is Today)," "Eve Of Destruction," "Fortunate Son," "For

What It's Worth (Stop, Hey What's That Sound)," "2+2=?," "What's Going On," and "Who Will Answer?"

Images of soldiers also became much more complex. As always, the military draft led to unwanted separations from domestic life. However, the risk of life and limb in the jungles of Southeast Asia lacked the glamour or the sense of patriotic sacrifice for European homelands which was necessary to sustain domestic popular support. Songs frequently reflected this fact. Lyrics both fearful and satirical were presented in "Billy, Don't Be A Hero," "Dear Uncle Sam," "The Draft Dodger Rag," "I Feel-Like-I'm-Fixin'-To-Die Rag," and "Where Have All The Flowers Gone." Battlefield deaths, war's horrors, and unwarranted profiteering of munitions dealers gained lyrical attention in "Battle Hymn Of Lt. Calley" and "The Unknown Soldier." Youthful cynicism and anger echoed in "War" and "Won't Get Fooled Again." In this context, it is understandable why so many songs of peace emerged. Lyrics of pacifist tunes tended to ignore the complexities of negotiated settlements, national goals, disputed boundaries, and political objectives in favor of the immediate cessation of hostilities and the need for worldwide humanitarian healing. Songs of this genre included "Give Peace A Chance," "Imagine," "Lay Down (Candles In The Rain)," "Stop The War Now," and "We Got To Have Peace."

From the French military defeat at Dien Bien Phu in 1954 until the Gulf of Tonkin Incident ten years later, the American Government had encountered no popular music criticism related to its Southeast Asian policies. Yet the dimensions of lyrical commentary throughout the long and bloody Vietnam conflict were dramatic and detailed. From selective service practices to the My Lai massacre, no topic seemed to escape the composer's pen or the troubadour's tongue. The gentle early 1960s folk criticism of The Kingston Trio and Peter, Paul, and Mary escalated into full-throated screams for the warring to end from Barry McGuire, Bob Dylan, John Fogerty, Phil Ochs, Edwin Starr, and Neil Young.

The period from the end of the Vietnam War until the Iraqi invasion of Kuwait was unlike any other post-war period in the Twentieth Century. The war of words continued. Song lyrics perpetuated the debate about the validity of war as a means of achieving political, economic, or any idealistic ends. It wasn't that America was being torn apart by unpatriotic malcontents who happened to musicians. The public simply continued to resonate to the issues being discussed in vinyl grooves, on cassette tapes, and on compact discs. The Vietnam debate continued to rage after the Vietnam War. A few examples of songs from the inter-war period are: "Born In The U.S.A.," "Goodnight Saigon," "In America," "Still In Saigon," "Used To Be," "War," and "War Games."

Persian Gulf War Songs

No nation can survive without a myth; no nation profits from holding onto a myth
that cannot plausibly include recent historical experience. The respective result
can only be a cynical realism or a self-deluding fantasy.

—John Hellman,
*American Myth And The Legacy Of
Vietnam*

The war had greater power as a cultural event than a political one. Waiters
automatically offer tabasco sauce, which all soldiers seem to relish, at favored
military hangouts. Many Saudis are indulging their new found taste for country-
and-western music, developed after listening to Armed Forces Radio and those
illegal satellite dishes now tune in to Israeli TV—despite public warnings that the
Israeli Secret Service is trying to corrupt Saudi society over the airwaves.

—Ray Wilkinson,
"One Year Later,"

Although military and diplomatic preparations for the attacks on
Kuwait and Iraq extended over several months, the Persian Gulf War itself
was measured in days of saturation bombing and hours of successful land
force operations. Thus, the popular songs related to this conflict were
derivative rather than original. That is, images or ideas contained in earlier
hit songs were adapted to the Saudi Arabian launching site of Operation
Desert Storm. Patriotic fervor was fanned through songs like "The Star
Spangled Banner" and "God Bless The U.S.A."; support for American
soldiers was echoed in "Somewhere Out There" and "Wind Beneath My
Wings"; personal dedications from wives and sweethearts were delivered
as voice-overs on "From A Distance"; and the homefront support for
returning servicemen was articulated in the 1973 chestnut "Tie A Yellow
Ribbon 'Round The Ole Oak Tree." Disc jockeys reinforced the use of
oldies either to depict or to interpret Gulf area military activities. "Rock
The Casbah" was played as a warning to those dwelling in Baghdad about
imminent U.S. bombing raids; "Welcome To The Jungle" was dedicated
from Uncle Sam's troops to the Iraqi Army; "Another One Bites The
Dust" was played to honor the U.S. soldiers operating Patriot Anti-Missile
Batteries (so-called "Scudbusters"); and, in the war's frenzied aftermath,
"Catch Us If You Can" was the song used to describe the frantic flight of
Iraqi Republican Guard units.

For the brief pre-military period when international economic sanctions were being utilized in an attempt to force Saddam Hussein to relinquish his military control of Kuwait, a musicians' collaboration performance version of "Give Peace A Chance" was somewhat popular. However, as American policy shifted from the Desert Shield of defense to the Desert Sword of offense, such pacifist tunes virtually disappeared from the charts. The massive air strikes that defined the initial phase of Operation Desert Storm and the blitzkrieg land invasion and speedy victory produced public euphoria in the United States. General Norman Schwarzkopf was an instant hero. So were his troops. Celebrity Choir Messages were delivered in "Voices That Care." A variety of patriotic songs, very few that attained *Billboard* chart listing, praised the valor of troops, condemned the stupidity of Saddam Hussein, and promised heroic welcomes for returning U.S. soldiers. These songs included: "American Kid In Arabian Sand," "The Ballad Of Saddam Hussein," "The Beast In The Middle East," "Desert Storm," "The Flags Fly High," "Iraq Is Robbin'," "K-K-Kuwaitis," "Letter To Saddam Hussein (You Must Be Insane)," "Proud To Be An American For Freedom," "A Symbol In The Storm," "These Colors Never Run," "Welcome Home Soldier," "When Johnny Comes Marchin' Home Again," and "Who'll Put A Bomb On Saddam Saddam Saddam."

President George Bush was quick to proclaim that the shadow of the Vietnam War had finally been lifted and that a New World Order of international solidarity had commenced. Clearly, the Republican President heard little from popular music realms to contradict his preliminary conclusions. Middle East concerns voiced in earlier American song lyrics were related to oil and hostages—"The Crude Oil Blues," "Get That Gasoline Blues," "A Message To Khomeini," and "Bomb Iran." All tunes that were played concerning the Persian Gulf, though, lauded Bush's diplomacy, praised U.S. military planning and execution, and promised love, honor, and domestic tranquility to returning U.S. troops. Even such potentially embarrassing actions as playing old pop tunes like "Ahab The Arab," "The Sheik Of Araby," or "Midnight At The Oasis" over military radio stations in Saudi Arabia had apparently been avoided.

The future of post-Gulf War music remains a question mark. If President Bush's fondest wish is fulfilled, popular music will continue its uniformly patriotic stance. Lyricists and performers will forget Saigon, will ignore Baghdad, and will adopt only heroic themes when they comment on all aspects of U.S. military activity. However, another track of behavior may emerge. The failure to establish a fully acceptable peace in the Middle East might spark a new era of lyrical debate. Will Kuwait become a more democratic state? Will Saddam Hussein remain the dictator in Iraq? Will the Kurds be safe? Can Israel be successfully integrated into the body politic of the Middle East to signal a genuinely New World Order? Can the United States expect an uninterrupted flow of crude oil from its former Persian Gulf war-time partners?

Themes Featured Prominently In War-Related
Popular Songs In The United States, 1917-1991

Specific War-Related Themes	World War (1917-1918)	World War (1941-1945)	Vietnam War (1964-1973)	Persian Gulf War (1991)
1. Overt hostility toward inter-national enemies	yes	yes	yes	yes
2. Sympathy toward conquered civilian populations	yes	yes	no	yes
3. Emphasis on long-term historical associations or friendships	yes	yes	no	no
4. Reinforcement of patriotic beliefs and traditional national symbols	yes	yes	yes	yes
5. Support and admiration for U.S. troops	yes	yes	yes	yes
6. Empathy for loved ones separated from American soldiers	yes	yes	yes	yes

Specific War-Related Themes	World War (1917-1918)	World War (1941-1945)	Vietnam War (1964-1973)	Persian Gulf War (1991)
7. Confidence in U.S. political and military leadership	yes	yes	yes	yes
8. Support for the idealistic post-war goals of world peace and prosperity	yes	yes	yes	yes
9. Cynicism toward and criticism of stated political objectives and publicized military strategies	no	no	yes	no
10. Advocacy of resolving international disputes through non-military strategies	no	no	yes	yes
11. Anger over anti-war arguments	no	no	yes	yes

Preliminary Conclusions

Some would say that myth does nothing but feed fantasies and distort reality, but the crucial point about myth is that it provides a greater reality.

—Timothy E. Scheurer
Born In The U.S.A.

Some generation of mankind was eventually bound to face the task of abolishing war, because civilization was bound to endow us sooner or later with the power to destroy ourselves. We happen to be that generation, though we did not ask for the honor and do not feel ready for it. There is nobody wiser who will take the responsibility and solve this problem for us. We have to do it ourselves.

—Gwynne Dyer
War (1985)

During four major military conflicts of the Twentieth Century, popular music played a role designed to reinforce patriotism at home and among U.S. troops abroad. In three of these conflicts—World War I, World War II, and the Persian Gulf War—there was little if any lyrical debate about the validity of general military goals, about the propriety of war-time strategy, or about the honor and dignity of all Americans involved in battle field activities. The Vietnam War is an anomaly in this situation. From the inception of the conflict, anti-war lyrics burst forth with the same prominence as pro-war tunes. During the post-war periods following the two World Wars, popular music tended to downplay military themes. However, the 1946-1963 period featured a greater trend toward examining war-related phenomena than the 1919-1938 period had. Once again, the period following the Southeast Asian conflict was a hot-bed of debate and conflict about military life, American foreign policy, the results of warfare, and the domestic implications of pursuing military conquests in foreign lands. The post-war lyrical climate of the Persian Gulf conflict has yet to emerge. It would seem unlikely that a civilian population that had become accustomed to lyrical debate concerning military activity would define the coming years as free if single-minded super patriotism dominated the airwaves. The final lyrical interpretations of Operation Desert Storm have yet to be delivered by Bruce Springsteen, Midnight Oil, U2, Stevie Wonder, Don Henley, John Fogerty, Merle Haggard, Bruce Hornsby, and others who sing with the courage of their convictions.

Coda

Establishing the morality of military activity in a democratic society is contingent upon public acceptance of numerous "just cause" arguments. Lyrics of American popular songs furnish such arguments in very broad strokes. The propaganda value of oft-repeated tunes understandably exceeds the influence of singular political speeches, newspaper editorials, and magazine articles. Of course, the complexity of international relations is unrealistically simplified—if not ignored—in favor of perpetuating traditional themes that cast U.S.

military action as a moral necessity, an ethical obligation, or an historical inevitability. Honor demands human sacrifice. Freedom requires military defense. Lyrics make warfare morally palatable. The flag, historical allies, national honor, democratic values, traditions of loyal service, and images of future peace and prosperity demand continuing American involvement in the bloodiest of human enterprises.

The role of anti-war songs in America's myth-making system for justifying warfare is unique. From the end of the Second World War in 1945 to the outbreak of the precision bombing raids over Iraq and Kuwait in 1991, a few singers have "worried" aloud about nuclear annihilation ("The Danger Zone"), potential super-power confrontations, deaths of countless soldiers without positive resolution of either conflicts or tensions, international racism and imperialism ("Undercover Of The Night"), and political leaders ("Won't Get Fooled Again") or weapons dealers ("Masters Of War"). Yet the most concerned musicians—John Lennon, Ray Charles, Peter, Paul, and Mary, Barry McGuire, Bob Dylan, John Fogerty, and other— invariably communicate their lyrical messages ("Give Peace A Chance," "Blowin' In The Wind," and "Eve Of Destruction") in myth-shrouded imagery. They tout ideals of peace, brotherhood, democracy, justice, equality, freedom, and other fundamental American virtues. Not surprisingly, pro-war and anti-war songs preach the same national mythology. The fact that complicated, messy reality rarely coincides with these simple images—just as urban life in the Bronx contrasts sharply with the images proclaimed in "America The Beautiful"— tends to reinforce the theoretical morality of war. Fighting to sustain or secure universal ideals is invigorating to a democratic populace; arguing in favor of neutrality, economic sanctions, isolationism, humanitarianism, or other heavy philosophical imperatives promotes only minimal enthusiasm. Medals, parades, and the roar of canons overwhelm carefully phrased anti-war anthems. Few democratic politicians choose to openly attack those singers and songwriters who challenge the U.S. military morality myth. Instead, they wisely praise the freedom of speech principle which permits vinyl voicing of "unpopular," "illogical," or even "unwise" positions. Popular music is thus easily defused as a source of genuinely radical thought. Tradition is much more readily served by song lyrics. Military myths are especially precious to generations of veterans. The influence of popular songs on public perceptions of war is an issue worthy of further investigation.

Works Cited

Auslander, H. Ben. "If Ya Wanna End War And Stuff, You Gotta Sing Loud: A Survey Of Vietnam-Related Protest Music." *Journal Of American Culture* 4 (Summer 1981): 108-113.

Bindas, Kenneth J. and Craig Houston. "Takin' Care Of Business: Rock Music, Vietnam, And The Protest Myth." *The Historian* 52 (Nov. 1989): 1-23.

Bolger, Daniel P. *Americans At War, 1975-1986: An Era Of Violent Peace.* Novato, CA: Presidio, 1988.

Bowman, Kent. 1987. "Echoes Of Shot And Shell: Songs Of The Great War." *Studies In Popular Culture* 10 (Winter 1987): 27-41.

Boyer, Paul. *By The Bomb's Early Light: American Thought And Culture At The Dawn Of The Atomic Age.* New York: Pantheon Books, 1985.

Brown, Sheldon. "The Depression And World War II As Seen Through Country Music." *Social Education* 49 (Oct. 1985): 588-594.

Cawelti, John. *Adventure, Mystery, Romance: Formula Stories As Art And Popular Culture.* Chicago: U of Chicago P, 1976.

Chilcoat, George W. "The Images Of Vietnam: A Popular Music Approach." *Social Education* 49 (Oct. 1985): 601-603.

Chinn, Jennie A. "There's A Star-Spangled Banner Waving Somewhere: Country-Western Songs of World War II." *JEMF Quarterly* 16 (Summer 1980): 74-80.

Cooper, B. Lee. "Examining The Audio Images Of War: Lyrical Perspectives On America's Major Military Crusades, 1914-1991." *International Journal Of Instructional Media.* 1992.

_____. *Images Of American Society In Popular Music: A Guide To Reflective Teaching.* Chicago: Nelson-Hall, Inc., 1982.

_____. "Military Conflicts." *A Resource Guide To Themes In Contemporary American Song Lyrics, 1950-1985.* Westport, CT: Greenwood, 1986: 101-109.

_____. *Popular Music Perspectives: Ideas, Themes, And Patterns In Contemporary Lyrics.* Bowling Green, Ohio: Bowling Green State University Popular Press, 1991.

_____. "The Record(s) Of America At War, 1941-1991: An Audio Perspective." (Mimeographed paper presented at the annual conference of the Midwest Popular Culture Association in Cleveland, OH on Oct. 17, 1991): 1-13.

Denisoff, R. Serge. "Fighting Prophecy With Naplam: 'The Ballad Of The Green Berets'." *Journal Of American Culture* 13 (Spring 1990): 81-93.

_____. *Sing A Song Of Social Significance,* 2nd ed. Bowling Green, OH: Bowling Green State University Popular Press, 1983.

_____. *Songs Of Protest, War, And Peace: A Bibliography And Discography.* Santa Barbara, CA: American Bibliographical Center and Clio P, Inc., 1973.

Denisoff, R. Serge, and William D. Romanowski. "Gooooood Morning, Vietnam!" *Risky Business: Rock In Film.* New Brunswick, NJ: Transaction

Books, 1991: 606-51.

Denselow, Robin. *When The Music's Over: The Story Of Political Pop*. London: Faber and Faber, 1990.

Dittmar, Linda and Gene Michaud. *From Hanoi To Hollywood: The Vietnam War In American Film*. New Brunswick, NJ: Rutgers UP, 1990.

Dyer, Gwynne. *War*. New York: Crown Publishers, 1985.

Ellison, Mary. 1986. "War—It's Nothing But A Heartbreak: Attitudes To War In Black Lyrics." *Popular Music And Society*. 10 (Fall 1986): 29-42.

Elshtain, Jean B. *Women And War*. New York: Basic Books, 1987.

Geltman, Max. "The Hot Hundred: A Surprise." *National Review* 18 (6 Sept. 1966): 894-896.

Girgus, Sam. 1980. *The American Self: Myth, Popular Culture, And The American Ideology*. Albuquerque, New Mexico: U of New Mexico P.

Graff, Gary. 1991. "War Likely To Make Music, But Not Like That Of The '60s." *The Detroit Free Press* (3 Feb. 1991): IG, 4G.

Hellmann, John. *American Myth And The Legacy Of Vietnam*. New York: Columbia UP, 1986.

Hesbacher, Peter and Les Waffen. "War Recordings: Incidence And Change, 1940-1980." *Popular Music And Society* 8 (Summer/Fall 1982): 77-101.

Hibbard, Don J. and Carol Kaleialoha. "Anti-War Songs." *The Role Of Rock: A Guide To The Social And Political Consequences Of Rock Music*. Englewood Cliffs, NJ: Prentice-Hall, Inc., 1983: 55-60.

"It's Time For The Americans!" *Rhythm And News* 1 (March 1991): 3.

Jasen, David A. "The Alley Goes To War (1940-1949)." *Tin Pan Alley—The Composers, The Songs, The Performers, And Their Times: The Golden Age Of American Popular Music From 1886 To 1956*. New York: Donald I. Fine, 1988: 246-78.

Keesing, Hugo A. "Pop Goes To War: The Music Of World War II And Vietnam." (Mimeographed paper presented in April at the 9th Annual Convention of The Popular Culture Association, 1979): 1-8.

———. "Recorded Music And The Vietnam War: The First 25 Years." (Mimeographed paper presented in March at the 17th Annual Convention of The Popular Culture Association, 1987): 1-10.

Landon, Philip J. "From Cowboy To Organization Man: The Hollywood War Hero, 1940-1955." *Studies In Popular Culture* 12 (Winter 1989): 28-41.

Lees, Gene. 1968. "1918-1986: From *Over There to Kill For Peace*," *High Fidelity* 18 (Nov. 1986): 56-60.

———. "War Songs: Bathos And Acquiescence." *High Fidelity* 28 (Dec. 1978): 41-44.

———. "War Songs II: Music Goes AWOL." *High Fidelity* 29 (Jan. 1979): 20-22.

Lello, John. "Using Popular Songs Of The Two World Wars In High School History." *The History Teacher* 14 (Nov. 1980): 37-41.

Lipsitz, George. *Time Passages: Collective Memory And American Popular Culture*. Minneapolis, MN: U of Minnesota P, 1990.

Lund, Jens. "Country Music Goes To War: Songs For The Red-Blooded American." *Popular Music And Society* I (Summer 1972): 210-30.

Marsh, Dave. 1991. "Life During Wartime." *Rock And Roll Confidential.* No. 86 (Mar. 1991): 1-4.

McNeil, William K. " 'We'll Make The Spanish Grunt': Popular Songs About The Sinking Of The *Maine*." *Journal of Popular Culture* 2 (Spring 1969): 537-51.

Mohrmann, G.P. and F. Eugene Scott. 1976. "Popular Music And World War II: The Rhetoric Of Continuation." *Quarterly Journal Of Speech* 62 (Feb. 1976): 145-56.

Mondak, Jeffery J. "Protest Music As Political Persuasion." *Popular Music And Society* 12 (Fall 1988): 25-38.

Murdoch, Brian. *Fighting Songs And Warring Words: Popular Lyrics Of Two World Wars.* London: Routledge Publishing, Ltd, 1990.

Palmer, Roy. "War And Peace." *The Sound Of History: Songs And Social Comment.* New York: Oxford UP, 1988: 271-302.

Philbin, Marianne, ed. *Give Peace A Chance: Music And The Struggle For Peace.* Chicago, IL: Chicago Review P, 1983.

Pratt, Ray. *Rhythm And Resistance: Explorations In The Politic Uses Of Popular Music.* New York: Praeger Publishers, 1990.

Reynolds, Clay."Vietnam's Artistic Legacy: The Need To Understand." *Journal Of American Culture* 14 (Summer 1991): 9-11.

Rodnitzky, Jerome L. *Minstrels Of The Dawn: The Folk-Protest Singer As A Cultural Hero.* Chicago: Nelson-Hall, Inc, 1976.

Scheurer, Timothy E. *Born In The U.S.A.: The Myth Of America In Popular Music From Colonial Times To The Present.* Jackson: UP of Mississippi, 1991.

_____. "Myth To Madness: America, Vietnam, And Popular Culture." *Journal Of American Culture* 4 (Summer 1981): 149-165.

Sealey, Don. "Saudi Update." *Goldmine,* No.277 (8 Mar. 1991): 7.

Student, Menachem. *In The Shadow Of War: Memories Of A Soldier And Therapist.* Philadelphia: Temple UP, 1991.

Suid, Lawrence. *Guts And Glory: Great American War Movies.* Reading, MA: Addison-Wesley Publishing Company, 1978.

Tischler, Barbara L. "One Hundred Percent Americanism And Music In Boston During World War I." *American Music* 4 (Summer 1986): 164-176.

Turner, Donald W. "I Ain't Marchin' Anymore: The Rhetorical Potential In Anti-War Song Lyrics During The Vietnam Conflict For The Left." (Ph.D. Dissertation: Pennsylvania State U, 1982).

Van Creveld, Martin. *The Transformation Of War.* New York: Free, 1991.

Van Devanter, Lynda and Joan Furey, eds. *Visions Of War, Dreams Of Peace: Writings OF Women In The Vietnam War.* New York: Warner Book, 1991.

Waffen, Les and Peter Hesbacher. "War Songs: Hit Recordings During The Vietnam Period." *ARSC Journal 13* (Spring 1981): 4-18.

Whitburn, Joel. *Pop Memories, 1890-1954: The History Of American Popular Music.* Menomonee Falls, WI: Record Research, Inc, 1986.

_____. *Top Pop Singles, 1955-1990.* Menomonee Falls, WI: Research, Inc, 1991.

Wiener, Jon. "Give Peace A Chance: an Anthem For The Anti-War Movement." *Give Peace A Chance: Music And The Struggle For Peace.* Ed. Marianne Philbin. Chicago: Chicago Review P, 1991.

Wilkinson, Ray. " 'One Year Later." *Newsweek* 118 (29 July 1991): 28-32.

Wolfe, Charles. "Nuclear Country: The Atomic Bomb In Country Music." *Journal Of Country Music* 6 (Jan. 1978): 4-22.

Woll, Allen L. "From *Blues In The Night* to *Ac-cent-tchu-ate The Positive:* Film Music Goes To War, 1939-1945." *Popular Music And Society* 4 (Spring 1975): 77-85.

Women's Division Of Soka Gakkai, eds. *Women Against War.* New York: Kodansha International, Ltd, 1986.

Woodward, William. "America As A Culture (I): Some Emerging Lines Of Analysis." *Journal Of American Culture, II* (Spring 1988): 1-16.

_____. "America As A Culture (II): A Fourfold Heritage." *Journal Of American Culture* 11 (Spring 1988): 17-32.

Crosssing Wire Borders:
Concepts of Popular Culture in Film
& Television Studies

WILL ROCKETT

Film and television, though similar, are somewhat different voices of popular culture, and need to be studied differently.

The identification of "popular culture" as both a field of study and as what might be termed a critical posture has been one of the most significant and successful syntheses in critical discourse in the last forty years.

For a synthesis, it is: both the definition of the field and the critical perspective brought to bear upon artifacts found within that field have been codetermined by a renewed sociopolitical concern within the academy, and the coincident emergence of new critical methods in the arts (particularly, literature), together with a vigorous new view of culture from an anthropological perspective.

Now, however, the field of popular culture has matured to the point where the consideration of certain of its artifacts notably film and television has become an essentially bifurcated effort. On the one hand, film studies have proceeded along hierarchical lines, with certain films identified as "high" art, while others (especially genre films) are identified as "popular culture." Television, on the other hand, has yet to develop such a hierarchy: the medium itself is viewed as popular, and all its artifacts are treated accordingly.

This essay examines the slightly divergent directions being taken in film and television studies, within the larger context of popular culture as a field of study and as a critical posture.

The New Sociopolitical Concern
Despite their somewhat bizarre conclusions regarding cultural literacy, the failure of the university to serve the *polis*, and the illiberalization of education, E. D. Hirsch, Jr., Allan Bloom and Dinesh

143

D'Souza have got one thing right: the American professoriate has changed as significantly since the 1960s as it has done at any other point in its 300-year-old past, since Mr. Mather was made a Doctor by his Harvard colleagues.

For many members of the professoriate in the 1950s and early 1960s, the struggle that Ernest Boyer (*College*) describes as occurring between the nurturing impulse of the teacher, formed early in American higher education with its pastoral, religious roots, and the commitment to promote and protect the individual's specific discipline long had been decided in favor of the latter. As Boyer has pointed out, the influence of the German university upon the American in the 19th century encouraged faculty to begin to perceive their first obligation as not to their students, but rather to their discipline and their own research (Boyer 120-121). Together with the continued tendency of many institutions today to aspire towards the research university as a model of excellence, this has underscored the propensity in those faculty so inclined to view their task of teaching as one of transmitting to students the appropriate information specific to their own disciplines.

However, the ranks of the professoriate have been changing since the late 1960s: many a Ph.D. was forged in the 1965-1975 period within the crucible created by the anti-Vietnam, civil rights, women's liberation and gay rights movements. Now in their late 30s and early 40s, these faculty and even some administrators, especially at the chair's and dean's levels have reversed the verdict of their forebears. The vast majority see teaching as their first priority, and research as secondary, thereby stressing the need to nurture students as paramount. Moreover, significant numbers acknowledge the reality of a global community, and the need for responsible American involvement in that community; a great many would see the universities serve not the military establishment and the corporations through their research, but rather the greater commonweal, becoming engines of social change through their roles in elementary-secondary school system partnerships, and through consultantships with other governmental agencies, both here and abroad. These aspirations are not limited to a handful of our major universities: For every Harvard University John F. Kennedy Center, preparing an economic reconstruction plan for the Soviet Union, there is a SUNY Fredonia, attempting to aid Albania in a similar effort.

These new sociopolitical priorities have come into increasing force as faculty nurtured in the vibrant period of university life between the late 1960s and early 1970s move up the academic foodchain. They, in turn, are attempting to serve as mentors and role models to the next generation of

Ph.D.'s, in order to ensure that this particular cultural revolution remains in force in the universities, despite the return to a basic conservatism in the rest of America.

In sum, these faculty and administrators would concur with Bloom that the university is obliged to serve the *polis*; however, their concept of Athenian Humankind is not Bloom's austere, Platonic notion of dutiful youth, inculcated with a belief in the superiority of immutable American values he sees as defined in the Bill of Rights and the Declaration of Independence, a belief that must precede reason as a *sine qua non* to education and to the sustaining of the Republic (Bloom sees, with Plato, the latter as education's primary purpose).

Rather, these faculty believe—quite rightly, in my view—that Jeffersonian democracy, that North American recreation of the Athenian ideal, requires a citizenry capable of actively engaging in governance, at least at the level of the vote, and in the forging of Walter Lippmann's *Public Opinion*, so essential to moving our elected representatives to appropriate action. Indeed, they need to be prepared to institute, as often as once in each generation, that new sociopolitical revolution that Jefferson himself suggested might serve democracy and us all to best advantage.

Moreover, a great many of these faculty recognize that the individual is part of a greater community as well, a commonwealth of nations that has little to do with Mr. Bush's concept of a New World Order, dominated by an America dominated, in its turn, by special corporate interests. Hence, the knowledge students require to participate actively in both worlds is much broader than that advocated by a Bloom, or a Hirsch.

But in fact, it is not so much the possession of specific information that is required of these students, as it is a properly thoughtful, critical perspective on these communities.

Fortunately, such perspectives have come to the fore in recent decades, in both the social sciences and the humanities, with the establishment of new critical methods that make them possible.

The New Critical Methods

The critical methods which have been embraced over the last few decades in the study of popular culture emerged first in our departments of English language and literature, foreign languages and literatures, linguistics, psychology and philosophy. But as Dudley Andrew points out in regard to the study of film, "It is not only predictable but appropriate for film theorists to learn from the other master critiques of culture, from linguistics, psychoanalysis, ideological analysis, and critical philosophy," since film criticism came to a first resting place in North American universities within traditional humanities disciplines (Andrew 12-13). The same thing may be said of folklore studies, as well as of television studies, although the latter today often are housed in departments of communication which draw heavily upon the methods of the sociologist, creating a special tension in that field, which I shall discuss later in this essay.

Many contemporary popular culture analysts and critics have linked their methodology to a governing concept of what is usually referred to as the "ideology" embodied by an artifact; this ideology is most often understood in social and political terms, although it does admit to other interpretations. The methodology and the general approach are underpinned by the work of a kind of critical holy trinity, identified by Dudley Andrew as Saussure, Marx, and Freud; these are seen, in Andrew's words, to "form an interlocking system capable of elaborating the reasons behind all human problems and of revolutionizing personal and social behavior by reforming the human being at his deepest level, his level of signification and communication" (Andrew 240).

In effect, hermeneutics—the systematic interpretation of a work of art—has become progressively more dedicated to elucidating the sociopolitical meanings underpinning any given artifact that forms the subject of study, including matters of gender (Freud), race, and class (Marx), through engaging in an analysis that stresses the manner in which meaning is produced, or significance signified (Saussure).

For example, the horror film has been particularly susceptible to this view: Besides James B. Twitchell's interpretation of horror as dealing with the incest taboo (*Dreadful Pleasures: An Anatomy of Modern Horror*, 1985), Dana B. Polan writes of films like *Slumber Party Massacre* as opining against "What the films picture as a kind of moral decadence" (Polan 202), while Robin Wood sees slithering phallic symbols in David Cronenberg's parasites in *Shivers* (1975), signifying a heterosexually masculine- dominated culture run amuck (Wood 194). All three offer a close analysis of specific artifacts, or films, examining iconography from a perspective of signification. National and international politics as opposed to sociosexual ones can be explored as well. While historians like Daniel Leab have stressed the Cold War as a factor in producing science fiction possession/replacement films such as *Invasion of the Body Snatchers* (Don Siegel, 1956), in which the Enemy Without becomes *The Enemy Within* (J. Edgar Hoover's term for an American communist conspiracy), (Leab) others have made a very strong case for seeing many modern horror films as assaults upon the integrity of government, as identifying the dangers of the military-industrial complex (so named by Eisenhower in 1959), or as revealing the general corruption of American political life. For example, *Aliens* (James Cameron, 1986) gives us a proletarian military unit sent into space to do a dirty job cleaning up a mess which is the result of corporate greed; the workers are betrayed by the corporate liaison man who wants to salvage the monsters for possible sale to the military as killing machines, and who views the human proletarian crew as expendable in pursuing that goal. Film after film of the post-Watergate era can be and has been seen to suggest a government coverup of official responsibility for ecological disasters which spawn *Piranha* (Joe Dante, 1978) or the *C.H.U.D.* (Douglas Cheek, 1984). Human heroes, very often working alone as one Man or Woman against the "System" as well as against the more immediate source of danger that System has spawned, have to do battle with bureaucrats more concerned with obfuscating questionable government activities than with putting down the horrible threat to humanity which has arisen as a result of those activities. Finally, Robin Wood synthesizes sex and public politics, maintaining that one sees in most Hollywood films the consistent repression of social and sexual energies (the monster attacking normality) in order to preserve the existing system (normality), while one can find in only a handful of other (chiefly, horror) films a "constructive" vision of Armageddon which at least recognizes that the present order of capitalism and the nuclear family deserves to be destroyed, and indeed cannot escape destruction (Wood 164).

Together with this interest in uncovering sociopolitical meaning in the artifacts of popular culture, through an analysis that stresses the semantics of the artifact, identifying elements of iconography as significators that convey specific meanings, criticism in popular culture has turned as well to the syntax of these artifacts, which has been identified with the mythic foundations of the work. This line of inquiry has followed Claude Levi-Strauss's interest not only in myth, but also in mythic structures, rendered apparent through repetition in artifact after artifact (Levi-Strauss 226). We look for Campbell's Hero of a Thousand Faces, or Eliade's Myth of the Eternal Return, throughout the whole purlieu of popular culture, seeing in these myths the primordial roots of our own and other cultures' ideologies.

But while these new critical methods and approaches permeate studies in popular culture today, what renders them viable is the increasingly generous view of what constitutes culture itself.

The New View of Culture

To a considerable extent, the public's idea of culture—as well as that of scholars like Bloom—has remained Matthew Arnold's. Writing in the preface to *Literature And Dogma* (1873), Arnold defined it as follows: "Culture [is] the acquainting ourselves with the best that has been known and said in the world, and thus with the history of the human spirit" (Arnold 11).

Such a definition generally has limited culture to the "high" arts and those works of art widely acknowledged over a period of time to have attained to the ranks of the olympian plane. This has led to the creation of canons of works over which our faculties are now haggling, as they examine the lists of artifacts hitherto deemed appropriate for undergraduate study, and seek room for works long left off lists dominated by the products of DWEMs (Dead White European Males).[1]

While the attempt to open the canons of high culture to include the works of those deemed by many to have been excluded for reasons of gender or race is a significant development that can be attributed to the efforts of the renewed professoriate discussed above, many are still loathe to muddle or even "taint" their notion of culture (high art) with the popular arts. Yet today we are growing inexorably much more open in our understanding of what constitutes a people's culture, and what merits earnest scholarly interest, largely through the work of those who study popular culture.

Raymond Williams has reduced all definitions of culture to four general concepts:

1) "A developed state of mind as in 'a person of culture'." The "cultured" individual is one who consciously engages in the cultural activities described below in (2), in order to gain an appreciation or, better still, a real understanding of the manifestations of culture described below in (3).

(2) "The processes of this development as in 'cultural interests,' cultural activities'." This echoes Arnold's sense of culture or, better, of education as the acquiring of "culture" through contact with the great works of human imagination and intellect.

(3) "The means of these processes as in culture as 'the arts' and 'humane intellectual works'." This refers to the cultural artifacts to which one is exposed in the process of acquiring the cultured mind; they are Arnold's "great works of human imagination and intellect." Many such works constitute that portion of the material culture that is meant to portray the ideal; ironically, the others often are polemical works designed to attack what is perceived by the artist as vile in a culture. But because both kinds of works are highly self-conscious, they tell us what the members of a culture consciously value most in their ideal of themselves, rather than reveal what is valued in common practice; hence, they well may be

distorting as indicators of the actual culture of a people.[2]

(4) "The anthropological and extended sociological use [of culture] to indicate 'the whole way of life' of a distinct people or other social group." Clearly, this is the most comprehensive definition, for it embraces the other three; moreover, it welcomes popular culture into consideration, thereby avoiding the pitfalls of limiting one's study to works of high culture. (11)

This "whole way of life" encompasses every expression of a culture's values, both those acknowledged and celebrated in high art, and those observed in the actual practice of daily living. Taken together, these values constitute the culture or the ideology of the society.

One may also speak of such values as virtues, and describe, with Joseph Campbell and Mircea Eliade, the ideology or culture they form as the society's central "myth;" Edward Lowry and Joseph DeCordova follow Jung, and call it, "a sociocultural unconscious" (Lowry 346). In this way, the interest in ideology and the interest in myth and mythic structure on the part of the student of popular culture who is committed to uncovering meaning through systematic study (including both the syntactic and semantic approaches to the rendering of meaning in an artifact) in order to further the ultimate avowed goal of assisting in engineering social and human progress finds its true ground: the whole of human activity.

The Field of Popular Culture

This is the ground held today by the student of popular culture. Culture is "a whole way of life" of a given people; the artifacts to be investigated may be drawn from the vast production that constitutes that people's social practice. However, taxonomy remains a first step in a scholarly approach to popular culture, as it does in any such endeavor: Some attempt must be made to organize such an amorphous field into defined, discrete areas of study if one is to be reasonably systematic in investigation.

To begin with, limits may be established by medium. Hence, folklore (e.g., oral traditional tales and the joke) and folk arts (e.g., the "populuxe" design of automobiles and other consumer goods of the 1950s), literature, music, film, radio, and television may be focussed upon.

Secondly, as in any scholarly effort, we may choose to further narrow the field of a specific study by dividing the artifacts produced in various media into various subgroups. Genre classifications are probably the most commonly used means of doing so in film and popular literature studies; other fields develop their own approaches. For example, one of my colleagues who is interested in folk art distinguishes between the "lawn art" placed in the frontyard, and that placed in the backyard of people's homes.

Thirdly, we may choose to interpret "popular" less literally and loosely (i.e, that which is of the people), and more narrowly: that is to say, we may choose to focus upon those artifacts which have proved most successful in garnering a significant audience. This approach is particularly attractive to some students of cinema and television.

Finally, despite the reservations of some critics like Leslie Fiedler, we may choose to study those objects or artifacts we come to deem as worthy of our attention, exercising judgments based upon what are essentially aesthetic criteria which we have adjusted to meet our own purposes as students of popular culture. In effect, we narrow our field by the perspective afforded us by popular culture's critical posture.

The Popular Culture Critical Posture

This critical approach has broadened—some would say, shifted us away from—our traditional hermeneutics of aesthetic evaluation. "Ideology and system [have] replaced creativity and art as the perceived source of value in the cinema," writes Dudley Andrew (Andrew 107), in a statement equally applicable to folklore and television studies. Leslie Fiedler would have us eschew traditional approaches to aesthetics, including "all formalist, elitist...criticism," in favor of *ekstasis*, an "ecstasy of rapture or transport, a profound alteration of consciousness in which the normal limits of flesh and spirit seem to dissolve" (Fiedler 35-36). Clearly, this is a form of reader-response criticism carried to its logical end: It is the aesthetic of MTV, Madonna, and Me. I prefer to see our aesthetics as expanded in vision, rather than as supplanted by simple *ekstasis*.

To begin with, the aesthetics of popular culture accepts that a given cultural artifact must be worthy of serious study. We admit that such things have important points to make to us about our own or another culture, and that their popularity with the public argues for their intrinsic merits; we then posit a set of aesthetic principles upon which we shall base our exploration of the object.

Svetlana Alpers has identified three assumptions that underpin Western aesthetics: (1) the notion of the role or the authority of the individual maker; (2) the notion of the uniqueness of the individual work; (3) the notion of the centrality of the institution of painting (Alpers 7). To this, Lynn M. Hart has added both a clarification of the third point, namely that "The aspect of the institution of painting that Alpers stresses is its permanence, the enduring quality of the art object," and her own fourth point, namely "the primary value of abstract form... stylistic analysis and evaluation" of which "remains the dominant mode of doing art history and art criticism" in our own culture (Hart 146). To this, I would add a fifth point, namely the notion of the "artistic" worth of the work, which acknowledges the degree of difficulty obtaining in creating the work of art, and the concomitant technical mastery required of the individual artist responsible (I distinguish this from what might be termed the "genius" factor I see as lodged in the first point, the authority of the individual artist); and a sixth point, namely the usefulness of the work in helping us to understand the cultural mainsprings from which it has emerged. I believe this last point is one from which pleasure can be derived, and justify its inclusion as appropriate to a Western aesthetic since Aristotle cited it as a source of pleasure in art in his *Poetics* (Aristotle 20-21).

We can see the core principal of our own culture's values, namely the primacy of the individual, reflected in five of these six points, in both our high and popular cultural artifacts. First, we celebrate the individual artist, and identify the individual artifact with the person, be it "a Picasso painting" or "a Schwarzenegger film;" the artist, as hero, authenticates the value of the work. Second, we place a higher value upon the object which endures over a period of time as being of lasting value, such as Rembrandt's "Night Watch" or Welles's *Citizen Kane*. Third, we admire abstract form, insofar that we seek encoded subtexts in even the most "photorealistic" works of art such as Ken Danby's paintings, while more formalist abstract works like those of Klee and Mondrian receive high praise from critics, historians and theoreticians (We must add a caveat, here: The general public favors realism and Norman Rockwell or even Andy Warhol over the overt abstraction of a Henry Moore or Picasso. Artists like Van Gogh and Turner fall somewhere in the middle in popular esteem, as they become more or less accessible and recognizable). In the study of popular culture, syntax and semantics of a given film are closely examined for subtleties of significance that go beyond Rose Bud in *Kane*, while we tend to treat popular genre films collectively rather than individually, to the same purpose (This will be discussed further below). Fourth, in high culture we enshrine the uniqueness of an individual work, a value which has led to the astronomical prices paid these days for great masters' works at Sotheby's and similar venues; in popular culture, in which we enjoy thoroughly the familiarity of the genre novel or film, we still value the work which emerges from its particular genre to speak uniquely to us, and part of one's pleasure in a given work derives from recognizing the manner in which it both reflects and departs from other works in its genre. Finally, we tend to recognize some works as of greater artistic worth than others, because the skills required of a Beethoven to render a symphony are more sophisticated than those required of the anonymous troubador to compose a "Come All Ye;" the complexity of the works, together with the weight of "expert" opinion, help us reach such judgments. Hence, superb special effects in an otherwise pedestrian film like *Terminator 2* (James Cameron, 1991) may go far in redeeming our estimation of the work.

Our sixth criterion, however, does not hold such sway in high art as it does in the study of popular culture: the usefulness of the work in helping us to understand the cultural mainsprings from which it has emerged can be measured in a number of ways. This is where the popularity of a specific work may come into significant play: the more popular a work, the heartier the public embrace of it, the more relevant it may seem to a reading of the culture that produced it. This is not necessarily the case of high art artifacts, which may enjoy critical esteem in their own time, and garner only grudging acknowledgment by the public at large, based upon their endurance through time, and the authority of critics regarded as professionals who are in possession of special knowledge that renders them the fittest judges.

When we apply our aesthetic criteria to a specific area of study in popular culture, we find ourselves juggling the balances among the criteria in order to strike a cogent, comprehensive assessment of the given artifact's value. Nowhere is this more apparent than in the study of film and television.

Film & Video Studies

To begin with, the cinema and television handily meet both our fifth and sixth criteria of aesthetic evaluation. First, we recognize them as complex forms, requiring technological and technical expertise on the part of a team of artisans and artists if they are to function at all. Second, on the one hand, they are among the most popular forms of public entertainment in our culture today, with music as the only true competitor as a "democratic" art, thereby suggesting that they are truly representative of our cultural mores; on the other hand, they are mimetic art forms, and the majority of artifacts generated attempt to mirror the cultural context within which we find ourselves, if only for the purpose of providing a familiar background into which new and engaging elements may be introduced. Hence, even an historical costume epic like *The Private Lives of Elizabeth and Essex* (Michael Curtiz, 1939) may tell us much more about the people who made it and the people for whom it was made than it does about Elizabethan England, right down to their concepts of male and female beauty, for the filmmakers are offering images towards which their audience will be drawn with enthusiasm.

Hence, these two media share the same primary bases of interest to students of popular culture. However, there are significant differences. Some of these have to do with the simple matter of time.

First, film is the immediate successor to the theatre as a mimetic, dramatic medium of mass entertainment, and predecessor to television's assumption of that role in our culture. Indeed, film's history is sufficiently long enough (1895-Present) to have permitted certain works of art to be evaluated in terms of high art: critical acclaim, uniqueness of the work as proven over a period of time, endurance in our esteem and our cultural memory over that same period of time all attest to the attainment by certain works of the status of high art. In effect, popular art can become high art: Shakespeare's plays began as popular entertainments, but today are a significant part of the canon of high art. Television's briefer history (essentially, 1945-Present) is less than half that of film; and while critics write and speak of a "Golden Age" of television, they generally are referring to its formative years, to cultural significance, or to historical significance in the development of the form. I have yet to see a critical assessment of, say, Hallmark Hall of Fame or Kraft Theatre productions that would rank any of these with *Citizen Kane* or the best works of Griffith, Gance and Eisenstein.

Second, like both popular literature and high art literature, film has lent itself handily to considerations by genre and by author, thereby opening significant new avenues of critical examination.

The organization of films into various genres began early, by the public and by the popular press, in opposition to the will of the studios, which wanted people to think of a "Paramount Picture" or of an "RKO Film" in much the same way that other "products" would be identified by an appreciative public as a "Westinghouse Refrigerator," a "Ford Automobile," or a "General Electric Radio," the manufacturer's name serving as the guarantee of quality. Indeed, the studios initially fought the star system which later would lead to such great profits for them, partly to hold actors' salaries down, and partly (one suspects) out of a desire to achieve starstatus for their corporate selves. Hence, while film historians and many structural critics speak of the studios as a production system and examine how that system affected the quality and content of the popular cinema, the historians often associate studios with specific popular genre designations, such as the "Republic Western," or the "RKO Musical" (Mast 232-234).

Genre classifications such as the western, the mystery, the action film, the horror film, and science fiction are more natural divisions. The public is more apt to identify a particular genre as a favorite kind of film than the productions of a given studio. Of course, they are even more likely to combine the genre with a particular star: Edward G. Robinson and James Cagney may be identified with the gangster film of the Thirties and Forties; John Wayne, with the western and the war picture of the same period.

The identification of the individual artist with the work in film has come to extend beyond the actor-star—that is to say, the most prominently visible individual personality—to the director, through the *auteur* critical approach first promulgated by Francois Truffaut and Andre Bazin, and popularized in this country by Andrew Sarris. Curiously, *auteurism* can be seen to have emerged into popular consciousness in this country in the early 1950s, with Senator Joseph McCarthy's interpretation of certain films as the Hollywood component of a communist conspiracy designed to undermine American values, and Hollywood's sacrificing of writers and directors as those responsible for such devestatingly un-American activities.

Hitherto, most of the film-going public had seen films as creating worlds into which one escaped; the film world was deemed to be completely self-evident, and a film meant what it said on its most overt level of discourse. McCarthy, with the assistance of people like J. Edgar Hoover of the Federal Bureau of Investigation, promoted in the popular imagination the idea that mining the filmic subtext for more profound meaning was possible, and that directors and writers—the films' *auteurs*— were the parties responsible for putting those meanings there.

The advent of the *auteur* and genre approaches into serious scholarly study has been a most useful way of both organizing such study, and of justifying the study of individual films that in themselves scarcely would seem to reward or even warrant careful scrutiny. For if one examines the entire *oeuvre* of a Sam Fuller, one can see patterns emerge that are the mark of an individual artist, and a specific vision; if one examines a reasonable set of the films of a given genre, one can see sociopolitical patterns of thought and belief, repeated over and over again—evidence of their ideological or mythic significance.

Clearly, the *auteur* view is most useful to the student of film who would treat some filmmakers as artists in the traditional sense; equally clearly, genre criticism lends itself most usefully to the study of the uses of film by audiences, and the manner in which such films reflect the sociocultural ideology of that audience.

Television has not had occasion to draw upon *auteur* criticism, except in very limited fashion. Rod Serling is one of the few television writer-producers to come to mind as having generated a recognized body of work that has merited some critical attention. One can, however, anticipate Stephen J. Cannell, Diane English, Norman Lear, and a handful of other producers eventually garnering such attention in future. However, I suggest that it is doubtful that they will be entertained as "serious" or "high art" artists in the same way that, for example, Hitchcock, Hawks and Ford have been accorded such attention. Their work's worth is more likely to be valued for its sociopolitical relevance. This is due, I think, primarily to its bulk (every successful series with a five-year run generates 130 episodes), and a concomitant strong popular sense that television programming is ephemeral and "disposable": there is so much of it, and so much of it is so much like everything else. (The tendency of television networks to mine each other's schedules for patterns of new dramatic and comic productions has been recognized for quite some time.) Moreover, with certain exceptions, the various series are episodic rather than epical in structure: that is to say, the typical series of programs cannot be seen to build towards a logical dramatic conclusion. Indeed, when a long-running series like *M*A*S*H* goes into reruns, episodes separated by years during the first run of the series may appear back-to-back.

When we turn from the specific series to the television genre, we find that it opens itself as much to charges of dull, unimaginative repetitiveness as it does to an appreciation of its revelation of myth and ideology through repetition. Like the specific series, very often it is its immediacy and its relevance to very narrow temporal strips of the life of our culture that fascinate us. Hence, the portrayal of the single woman over 30 in *The Mary Tyler Moore Show* can be seen to change even as the 1970s saw our culture change, with any given season (if not episode) relevant to the given year in which the programs appeared.

Indeed, we return to time again: just as television is unlikely to open itself very soon to consideration of at least some of its artifacts as high art, as film has done, film has never had the degree of immediacy of television in dealing as pointedly with contemporary trends and values. While television news and public affairs garner at least as much critical attention as does television drama, the cinema no longer offers the newsreel, or the documentary, both of which were always at best weekly reviews as opposed to daily utterances on matters affecting the culture and the commonweal, and which derived their power with audiences through the presentation of visuals, which were welcomed even though they were offered well after an event. When television sped up the process of delivering such visuals, television's greater immediacy eventually eliminated an audience for the cinematic newsreel.

As a consequence, television has assumed a more or less rightful place in popular cultural studies as the leading indicator of shifts in sociopolitical mores and values. Rick Altman may call Hollywood genres "simply the generalized, identifiable structures through which Hollywood rhetoric flows," (Altman 29) but in point of fact this is much more true of television. And whether we read these broadcasts as setting the agenda of public discourse (i.e., what issues to think about), or even of telling us what to think about these issues as a result of an information-industrial-government complex conspiracy, the fact remains that television attempts to be responsive to what the public wants, if only because its eye is always on the bottom line of the ledger. Hence, as a barometer of the culture as it exists, television is invaluable.

It is little wonder, then, that television studies have turned so frequently to news and information programs; audience effects are the primary subject of evaluation in television drama (the effects of violence upon children being the leading query). Hence, television studies turn most often to the sociologist and the psychologist, rather than the humanities hermeneutist, for the methods used to study the medium, placing an emphasis upon our sixth criterion of a work's value in examining the sociopolitical nature of the culture above all the others. The case study, longitudinal and latitudinal surveys, even lab and field experiments are much more common in television studies than in film studies today, and are likely to remain so for the forseeable future.

In sum, film and television studies have moved into positions relative to one another within the field of popular culture that are analogous to those once held by literature and the theatre, and later by literature and theatre on the one hand, and film on the other. That is to say, film has become, like literature and the theatre before it, a medium that may generate artifacts that are apt, over time, to cross over from consideration as popular to evaluation as high art, and to call upon aesthetic criteria and critical methods appropriate to high art.

At the same time, we must remember the holistic nature of popular cultural studies. That is to say, just as an individual artifact drawn from, say, film of the 1960s may be examined within a primary context of the cinema of that period, the popular culture student acknowledges that the production of meaning in any given work is achieved in substantial part by its audience's reliance upon that broad archive of cultural knowledge, drawn from a variety of media, ever at its disposal. Hence, a knowledge of and familiarity with popular music of the period contributes significantly to the production of meaning in a film like *Easy Rider* (Dennis Hopper, 1969).

When we acknowledge in popular cultural studies that the archive constructed by the audience for understanding any given work encompasses many forms of expression,[3] and when we recognize that understanding an audience's aspirations (so often expressed and espoused in high art) is as important as understanding an audience's existent biases and values, as practiced daily in life, if we are to grasp the whole fabric of a culture, then the complementary study of film and television through their respective methodologies becomes particularly desirable.

Moreover, just as literature has informed film over the first half of our century, film today informs television to some extent, providing the latter with essential iconography and narrative structures which are altered to meet television's more immediate (and simpler) purposes. The preparation of an audience to follow enthusiastically CNN's coverage of the Gulf War owes as much to their cinematic experience of the narrative structure developed in *Potemkin* (Eisenstein, 1925), as Eisenstein's film owes to the epical structure of the *Iliad*. Each cultural form derives in part from collateral forms, distilling its own peculiarities through a synthesis of its unique medial properties and the example of associated media.

Our approach to film and to television, as to all the forms popular culture takes, must be as open as are the forms themselves to interchange. As Dudley Andrew suggests in relation to film, the various critical approaches to popular culture should enrich, rather than supplant each other, in their efforts to arrive at a better understanding of the artifacts of that culture, and the ideology-myth these artifacts represent. "Film theory today," he writes, "consists primarily in thinking through, elaborating, and critiquing the key metaphors by which we seek to understand (and control) the cinema complex...It can be done only collectively...Thus goes film theory and thus, in my mind, should it go: metaphor and critique, constantly modifying our representation of film in human history" (Andrew 11-12).

There are no tripwires that need be feared as we cross the medial borders in the field of popular culture. Indeed, I would hazard that one's critical viewpoint should admit into consideration the possible contributions to our understanding of film and television which may be made by examining both semantics and syntax and, where applicable and appropriate, the art, the artist, and the audience of popular media. Without such openness, one cannot do justice to the artifacts which one seeks to examine, and the culture one seeks to explore.

Notes

[1] The questions of multiculturalism and pluralism are enormously significant ones, worthy of considerable discussion; however, my interest here is limited to the high- popular cultures split in the academy. Please see my paper, "Anarchy & Art, Anthropology & Aesthetics: The Role of Culture & Aesthetics in Values Education" (Southern Humanities Council, March 1990) for a much more detailed discussion of this issue.

[2] For a discussion of the relationship between popular and high art in the college curriculum, see my paper, "Eddie & The Cruisers Meet Rimbaud: Salvaging Meaning From Cultural Literacy in Improving Teaching" in *Contributed Papers* (College Park, Maryland and Vancouver, British Columbia:International Conference on Improving University Teaching, June, 1989).

[3] See "Jason Dreams of Freddie: Cultural Literacy & The Production of Meaning" in *Cultural Literacy, Cultural Power*, ed. Bonnie Bradelin (Tallahassee: University of Florida Press, 1991) for a fuller discussion by me of the cultural archive, with particular reference to the film-television relationship.

Works Cited

Alpers, S. "Is Art History?" in *Daedalus*, No. 106, 114.
Altman, Rick. "A Semantic/Syntactic Approach to Film Genre." *Film Genre Reader*. Ed. B.K. Grant Austin. Texas: U of Texas P, 1986.
Andrew, J. Dudley. *The Major Film Theories: An Introduction*. New York: Oxford UP, 1976.
_____ *Concepts in Film Theory*. New York: Oxford UP, 1984.
Aristotle. *The Poetics*. Trans. Gerald F. Else Ann Arbor: U of Michigan P, 1978.
Arnold, Matthew. *Culture and Anarchy*. Ed. J. Dover Wilson. Cambridge: The UP, 1935.
_____. *Literature and Dogma: An Essay Towards a Better Apprehension of the Bible*. New York: Macmillan, 1902.
Barnard, Frederick M. "Culture and Civilization in Modern Times." *Dictionary of the History of Ideas*. Ed. Philip P. Wiener. New York: Charles Scribner's Sons, 1973.
Barthes, Roland. *Camera Lucida: Reflections on Photography*. Trans. Richard Howard. New York: Hill & Wang, 1981.
Bloom, Allan. *The Closing of the American Mind.* New York: Simon & Schuster, 1987.
Boyer, Ernest L. *College: The Undergraduate Experience in America*. New York: Harper & Row, 1987.
Clifford, J. *The Predicament of Culture: Twentieth Century Ethnography, Literature, and Art.* Cambridge, MA: Harvard UP, 1988.

Eliot, T.S. *Notes Towards the Definition of Culture.* New York: Harcourt, Brace and Company, 1949.

Fiedler, L. *What Was Literature?: Class, Culture, and Mass Society.* New York: Simon & Schuster, 1982.

Hart, Lynn M. "Aesthetic Pluralism and Multicultural Art Education." *Studies in Art Education.* 32:3 (Spring 1991), 145-159.

Inge, M.T., ed. *Handbook of Popular Culture.* Westport, Conn: Greenwood P, 1978.

Leab, Daniel. "Celluloid Cold Wars." *The Organization of American Historians Newsletter* (May 1985).

Lowry, Edward, and Richard De Cordova. "Enunciation and the Production of Horror." *White Zombie Planks of Reason: Essays in the Horror Film.* Ed. Barry Keith Grant. Metuchen, NJ: Scarecrow P, 1984).

Mast, Gerald. *A Short History of the Movies,* 2nd Ed. Indianapolis: Bobbs-Merrill, 1976.

Polan, Dana B. "Eros and Syphilization: The Contemporary Horror Film." *Planks of Reason: Essays in the Horror Film.* Ed. Barry Keith Grant. Metuchen, NJ: Scarecrow P, 1984.

Williams, Raymond. *Culture.* London: Fontana P, 1981.

Wood, Robin. "An Introduction to the American Horror Film." *Planks of Reason: Essays in the Horror Film.* Ed. Barry Keith Grant. Metuchen, NJ: Scarecrow P, 1984.

Screen Entertainment and
American Politics

DAVID PRINDLE

The argument is here made that the mass saturation in screen entertainment—motion pictures and television—experienced by American citizens during the twentieth century probably has had effects on the development of a style of politics they prefer. This idea is pursued though an historical speculation on the modern development of American politics by examining the parallels between the "classical Hollywood style" of fictional narration and post-New Deal changes in political practices.

Screen entertainment is very much with us. Beginning with motion pictures in the early twentieth century, the business of combining fiction with moving images has grown to the point that it now dominates the consciousness of Americans. By the mid-1970s, 97 percent of families owned a television set, which was turned on about seven hours a day, the average person being exposed to just under three hours. Children are especially occupied by the tube, typically watching at least four hours a day. This means that by the time the average citizen graduates from high school, he or she has spent 17,000 hours in front of the set, more than any other single life activity except sleeping. Additionally, Americans buy about a billion tickets to attend theatrical motion pictures each year and rent millions of the same movies to play on their videocassette recorders. It might be useful to speculate on the possible political implications of this mass psychic saturation (Chen; Gomery 42-57; Winn; Sterling 418).

Scholars in various disciplines have theorized about the overall impact on politics in modern societies of the barrage of entertainment its citizens absorb (Postman; Gitlin 325-333; Baudrillard). The present essay is an attempt to do so from within the tradition of political science. What is offered here is not so much a theory, as an historical speculation on the possible consequences to democracy of a citizenry which has grown up consuming the Hollywood product. The argument is that the electronic entertainment media may have indeed played a part in the development of

160

the American political system by helping to condition the way Americans think about the proper form and functioning of social institutions, and, especially, about the way the people who inhabit those institutions relate to the mass public. Thus, although most screen entertainment is surperficially apolitical, it contains an implicit set of assumptions about human action which, repeated endlessly in front of an entranced audience, have helped to mold the way we as citizens expect our leaders to behave. The argument commences with a sketch of the outlines of the American electronic theater.

Fun and Power

The screen entertainment industry was born in 1896 when Thomas Edison introduced the first motion picture projector, and it developed very rapidly thereafter as both a business and an art. The first film to tell a story, *The Great Train Robbery*, thrilled audiences in 1903, and the first permanent theater dedicated to the new form of entertainment—called a "nickelodeon" because it charged five cents admission—opened two years later. Soon there were ten thousand in the country, and by 1908 weekly attendance reportedly hit 14,000,000, or 16 per cent of the population. By the mid-1930s, over 60 percent of Americans attended a movie each week, a proportion that rose even higher in the next decade (Webb 25; Balio 3-18).

Motion picture attendance declined in the late 1940s as a result of the advent of an even more successful form of screen entertainment, television. Fewer than one percent of U. S. homes contained a receiver in 1948, but that had grown to 64.5 per cent by 1955 and nearly 100 percent by the late-1970s (Sterling 535). By that period, as already mentioned, typical citizens were exposing themselves to video information several hours a day. Since what those citizens evidently wanted to see was entertainment, the same Hollywood-based industry that had earlier occupied itself making theatrical motion pictures turned most of its energies to providing similar, if less expensive, narrative fiction for the home audience.

In summary, for the better part of a century a majority of Americans have been soaking themselves since infancy in electronic screen entertainment, produced by an industry concentrated in the Los Angeles area. It would not be too bold to hypothesize that the perceptions of physical reality, of cause and effect, and of right and wrong held by the population have been at least partly wrought in front of these glowing screens.

Outside of political science, it is a common assumption that this mass experience has conditioned the social and personal life of modern publics.

As one book on film studies has asserted in passing, "Hollywood cinema has affected nearly every sphere of Western cultural life, from building design to conceptions of physical beauty"(Bordwell 378). Anecdotal evidence of the enormous power of the screen to affect the behavior of groups and individuals has been piling up for decades (Litwak 242; Webb 191). Systematic scientific studies of the ability of the entertainment media to alter opinions, attitides, and behavior, although fraught with the usual methodological ambiguities and controversies of social research, have for half a century been providing further evidence of the influence of these media (Lowery).

For example, after analyzing data from their study of the way viewers interpret the television series "Dallas," Liebes and Katz concluded that *most* of the audience related to this melodramatic saga of a fictional rich family as though it were somehow actually taking place. With some awe, they report that their typical subject "takes for granted that JR is real, and speaks as if 'Dallas' were some sort of documentary"(Liebes 6, 9). Although reviewers of the literature on the effects of the mass media invariably caution that ordinary people are not passive vessels to be filled with media "reality", and that members of the audience "interact" with and reinterpret what they see to be consistent with their own needs, this sort of finding is thought-provoking, not to say disquieting. If people think "Dallas" is real, what must they learn from it about life, love, business, and democracy?

The hypothesis, then, is that screen entertainment has conditioned the outlooks of a large majority of the American population, and that this has had political consequences. But what, exactly, have people learned? It would seem that, while specific acts and attitudes may have been acquired, these are not the most politically important cultural habits which we owe to the screen. It is instead more the general outlook and style of our politics which has been at least partly conditioned by the movies and television. In order for this argument to be comprehensible, there must be a explanation of what that style is.

Hollywood Style

Soon after it became organized, in about 1909, the domestic motion picture industry began to evolve a specific style of fictional storytelling. This system of narrative practices had essentially been adopted as an industrial imperative by all the major Hollywood producers by 1917, and continued to virtually monopolize American movies until the 1960s. With the breakup of the studio system about that time, the monopoly ended, and American film-makers since that date have occasionally adopted one of a variety of other styles which collectively are sometimes termed those of the "art cinema." Despite the fact that it is no longer employed in every production, however, the "classical style" is still evident in the overwhelming majority of American films. It also dominates television, although not as decisively. This style has been elucidated in a pathbreaking book by David Bordwell, Janet Staiger, and Kristin Thompson (Bordwell 373-74).

The basic narrative practice of the classical style is "character centered causality." Individual human beings, motivated by psychological factors, struggle against opposing forces toward clearly-defined goals. The classical style is *individual* in the sense that identifiable people cause virtually all the action; except for bad weather or earthquake, there is almost no impersonal causation. As Bordwell, Staiger and Thompson explain it, "classical films typically present historical events as uncaused: a war simply breaks out...When history is seen as caused, that cause is traceable to a psychologically defined individual...Thus the classical film makes history unknowable apart from its effect upon individual characters." The style is *psychological* in that characters are made a consistent bundle of personality traits, which furnish motivations that drive them to action, which in turn fuels the story. The style is *goal-oriented*, in that the story begins with an announcement of something the protagonist(s) wishes to accomplish, proceeds through obstructions and clashes with characters who have conflicting goals, and ends with the protagonist (usually) succeeding or (occasionally) failing to achieve the goal. As the authors summarize, "Psychological causality, presented through defined characters acting to achieve announced goals, gives the classical film its characteristic progression"(Bordwell 12-33).

As theatrical films have declined in importance and television has become the entertainment medium of choice, the classical style has been modified, while retaining its essential characteristics. In the first place, since about a quarter of television's programming, both broadcast and cable, consists of movies, the classical style would be guaranteed a strong representation on the tube whatever the style of the other material offered (Gomery 53-54). But even given the fact that the "television style" is somewhat different from the classical cinema style, its departures are not radical enough to justify classifying it in a different category; the differences of degree do not sum to a difference in kind.

Because of its episodic, serial nature, television programming tends to close its stories with somewhat less finality than do motion-pictures, although the (nonfinal) attainment of goals is still very much in evidence. There is, additionally, a tendency in television fiction to be somewhat more cognizant of the group, as opposed to the individual character; this is pervasive in situation comedies, and still more in soap operas. Yet the basic orientation remains, for the character-groups of television are not an undifferentiated mass, but are aggregates of psychologically-defined individuals. The manner in which one television scholar characterizes the policeman-hero of one of the 1970s' most popular programs is indicative: "Kojak is a man who realizes deeply private needs and inclinations in the doing of his work. Not law-and-order simplicities, but intelligence and self-realization are what 'Kojak' celebrates." Whether or not one agrees with the aesthetic judgment, it is evident that such a character fits smoothly in with the classical Hollywood style (Thorburn 642).

Indeed, the classical style has so dominated American entertainment that it may seem natural and inevitable, and readers may have difficulty imagining screen entertainment built upon other narrative foundations. Yet foreign cultures have produced individual and group styles that violate Hollywood assumptions and discard Hollywood traditions. In the 1920s, Soviet filmmakers, of whom the best known is Sergei Eisenstein, produced movies featuring impersonal, historical causation, and lacking individuated characters. The postwar French cinema sometimes follows the same tradition. Some foreign motion pictures "create a fundamentally unreliable narration...an open and relatively improbable set of hypotheses, a dependence upon surprise rather than suspense, a pervasive ambiguity...and many gaps left yawning at the film's close"(Bordwell 13, 41). The Hollywood style, then, is not a product of nature but of human artifice, and whatever its consequences, they are not inevitable.

The American populace has therefore spent decades exposing itself to a set of ideological constructs that are not only intensely individualistic, but emphasize personal will and psychology as the basic fact of cause-and-effect in human life. It is not the intention here to argue that screen entertainment is the only medium to have exposed citizens to such a conception of social life. As long ago as the eighteenth century, the early modern novel introduced a relatively small and privileged group of readers in the English-speaking world to individualistic, character centered causality. In the years preceding the turn of the twentieth century, the growth of the cheap magazine, the dime novel, and the "yellow press" involved ever larger portions of the American population in narrative practices which could plausibly be described as forerunners of the Hollywood style. From the 1890s onward, American society was evolving in a modern direction, and the growth of electronic entertainment was clearly only part of the general movement (Watt; Mott, *A History of American Magazines;* Hart 153; Faulkner 20-21).

Nevertheless, there is reason to believe that motion pictures and television have been unusually important, indeed crucial, contributors to trends which they did not originate. This is partly because of the sheer quantitative ubiquity of the screen in the twentieth century. By the first world war, millions more people were habitual moviegoers than read books or magazines. Only the daily press reached as many citizens. By the 1960s, television had become not only the nation's chief amusement but its major purveyor of news as well, a development which led to both a decline in newspapers and an interpolation of the imperatives of entertainment into the format of news programs (Emery 443; Postman 87-88; Nimmo 25-38; Hart 183-236).

It is not only this pervasiveness that makes screen entertainment decisive, however, but its unprecedented emotional power. Theorists in a variety of disciplines have commented on, and attempted to explain, the peculiar force that movies (and, by extension, television) seem to exert on the imaginations and loyalties of citizens in every industrialized country. Most of these explanations involve variations on the idea that the filmic experience blurs the line between the unconscious and the conscious, so that individuals feel that their own fantasies are being played out before their eyes. The screen consequently exercises an influence over social ideology far more intense than do other forms of communication.(de Lauretis 67; Metz 45, 142; Mauerhofer 231-234).

There must have been a tendency to like this sort of entertainment, of course, or it would not have evolved and persisted. It is not the intention here to argue that the "ideological style" of mass entertainment is wholly an exogenous variable, thrust onto the psyche of a helpless citizenry by an alien power. It is even possible that, had the motion picture and video cameras never been invented, American popular culture would still have moved in the direction of character centered causality.

Nevertheless, whatever the tendency of Americans to take individual motivation for granted as the prime mover of social life, it must have been powerfully reinforced by their experience of the Hollywood product. And contrary perspectives and assumptions must have been at least partly suppressed through lack of nurturance in the culture of mass entertainment. Although many different and conflicting specific political agendas have been argued in the electronic theater, therefore, the overall "classical style" of reality-representation has remained hegemonic, or nearly so.

If this be accepted, the next logical question to ask is, what difference did it make? Has the American political system exhibited developmental changes which can plausibly be related to the dominance of a cultural style deriving from Hollywood? Yes.

The Old Political System

Although American culture in general and economic activity in particular have always been individualistic, and although the basic organization of national politics in the early decades of the republic was clearly of an individualist nature, by the middle decades of the nineteenth century the country had evolved institutions to counteract individualism, and create the possibility of both collective action and responsibility. Both among the informal institutions of society, chiefly the parties, and among the Constitutionally created institutions of government, accepted routines of behavior and ideas of legitimate action tended to counteract centripitality, and harness citizens and politicians to collective purposes. Moreover, these institutions and practices tended to insulate far more of the federal government from direct, personal contact with the population than is the case today.

Although de Toqueville had argued in the 1830s that Americans combatted the atomizing effects of individualism by means of free institutions and voluntary groups, (176-185) actually the chief institution knitting together our politics through most of the century was the political party. Citizens were integrated into party structure at the basic, personal level, with local organizations acting as welfare agencies, social clubs, employment bureaus, and ideological classrooms. Supporting this mass-oriented set of activities was a tight, almost military organization based on leaders' control of patronage (Rothman; Marcus; Burnham, *Critical Elections* 72-73). Leaders managed campaigns, including those for the Presidency, and usually exercised great influence, not to say control, over the behavior of candidates (Lowi 110). This also meant that leaders often dominated the actions of people who served in office, resulting in, among other things, a higher rate of party voting cohesion in Congress than has been the case lately (Sorauf 412.) Voters understood the collective nature of the sundry candidates for office, and tended to vote "straight tickets" in national elections, which usually ensured that the Presidency would be captured by the same party that controlled Congress (Burnham, "The Changing Shape 7-28). In short, parties formed nineteenth century politicians into cooperating teams, not in name only, but in fact.

The party system supplemented a set of institutional arrangements, the chief mark of which, from our contemporary point of view, was a rather subdued Presidency. Although the nineteenth century chief executive was, then as now, the nation's symbolic head of state and director of its foreign policy, his involvement in domestic policymaking was both of less intensity and of a different kind than has become the norm.

Briefly put, the President was not considered a person who should mobilize public opinion in support of a legislative program. Candidates for the nation's highest office did not even campaign on their own behalf, basically staying at home while the parties sustained drives for the votes of the few uncommitted citizens. In 1888, for instance, the eventual popular vote winner, Grover Cleveland, did no personal campaigning at all (McWilliams 179). Once in office, Presidents were relatively quiet, for many members of Congress objected if they presumed to propose legislation (Greenstein, "Change and Continuity" 390). When chief executives did dare to advocate specific policy measures, their recommendations were overwhelmingly written, and addressed to Congress, not spoken and addressed to the people (Tulis, *The Rhetorical Presidency* 46). Although Presidents might chafe under this restraint, and although they often quarrelled with members of Congress either individually or collectively, they were so integrated into the governmental team of their party that they never considered launching independent, personal quests for power.

Thus, although some strong personalities, such as Andrew Jackson, managed to impress themselves on the national consciousness, even they were very restrained by today's standards. They neither attempted to rally popular support for a legislative program, nor tried to inspire a mass following. Their relationship with ordinary citizens was oblique. If we remember them as tribunes of the people, it is largely because we have been conditioned by long habit to view our Presidents that way.

The pre-mass communications political system was thus one in which citizen contact with politicians in general and the President in particular was indirect, being mediated through the informal skein of the parties, and buffered by accepted Constitutional practices. Although national leadership could not be termed "collective" on the pattern of European parliamentary democracies, it was seldom personal and never plebiscitary. Most importantly, except in a crisis like the Civil War, the person of the President was not the focal point of the system.

As with most things that pass, the old political system did not vanish all at once. Various institutional and behavioral changes began to accumulate, beginning as far back as the 1880s, which in hindsight can be interpreted as harbingers of a new regime. With the arrival of the New Deal in the 1930s, however, the old arrangements were so wrenchingly transformed that scholars almost invariably speak of the "modern" scheme as dating from that era. Before contemplating the significance of the date, we must grasp the outlines of the new system.

The Modern System

The contemporary American political system is based upon individual, entrepreneurial politicians, of whom incomparably the most important is the President, who attempt to directly cultivate a mass constituency through the electronic media. Parties still exist, but their electoral function has been usurped by the direct primary; they no longer even pretend to exercise control over either campaigns or government activity, having evolved into service organizations for candidates. Campaigns are personalized contests between individuals, relying on idiosyncratic appeals to a constituency limited to the one relevant contest. Perceiving no teamwork among the candidates, voters exercise no consistency in their ballot choices, and straight-ticket voting and Presidential coattails are virtually extinct. Since the party label is now uninformative, voters have turned to incumbency for voting cues, resulting in re-election rates to Congress (especially the House) that flirt with totality (Fiorina; Lowi 79).

Having run as singularities, successful candidates feel no tug of association once in office, and party cohesion in Congress, while it rose slightly in the 1980s due to ideological polarization, is still well below the norms of a hundred years ago. Congressional agreement with the President is similarly unassured, especially given the fact that the President's party is usually now in the minority in Congress. Meanwhile, individual representatives seek to build personal relationships with their local constituencies by practicing "home style" and using the fragmented, dispersed Congressional power structure to bribe their districts with porkbarrel distributive legislation (Hurley 117; Fiorina).

But the single greatest difference between the modern and pre-modern political system is the status of the President. The modern public focusses on the chief executive, not only as the symbol of the nation, but as its chief policymaker. This domination of the people's political imagination is so great that one scholar has discussed the Presidency as "monopolizing the public space"(Miroff) and another has described him as a "chief priest of the American civil religion" (Burnham, "The Reagan Heritage" 6). Presidents are expected to lead public opinion, and in fact must use their ability to do so in order to overcome the Constitutional constraints on their office. It is now conventional, in fact, to observe that the President structures the agenda of our national political life (Ginsberg).

A host of structural changes has accompanied the movement of the Presidency to center stage. As Presidents since FDR have consistently taken steps to undercut party organization (Milkis), so have they attempted to concentrate as much authority of every kind as possible in the White

House. The Office of Management and Budget is now fully as important as Congress in the preparation of the budget, and is becoming increasingly politicized, moving away from neutral competence toward ideological advocacy of the chief executive's program (Burke 372). Appointment of judges is being controlled as never before by teams of White House aides (O'Brien). Bureaucratic appointments, and activities of those appointees after they enter the bureaucracy, are being scrutinized and coordinated (Sanders; Moe 245, 263). All these trends began with Franklin Roosevelt, and reached their highest development under Ronald Reagan.

In the wake of the apotheosis of the President in the public mind, and centralization of his authority, has come an obsession, not with his power and actions only, but with his person. The incumbent is now a megacelebrity whose private life and public persona are the stuff of mass fascination, so much so that one textbook speaks of "the cult of personality" surrounding the office (Dye 301-302). As the public increasingly demands to be told about the President's outlook and motivations, the management of images becomes a White House preoccupation. In the words of Theodore Lowi, "The president is the Wizard of Oz. Appearances become everything" (Lowi 151). Whereas there is reason to believe that children have for a long time embodied the "government" in the person of the President, it appears that he may also have come to be seen that way by a majority of adults (Greenstein, *Children and Politics* 32-54).

In summary, the contemporary American political system is one in which "character centered causality" is the ruling assumption. The public relates to politicians, and particularly to the President, as individuals, is fascinated with their psychological motivations, and sees them to a large extent as goal (policy) oriented. Over the course of the twentieth century, in other words, American politics seems to have elevated the classical Hollywood style into a paradigm of real-life power.

Causation?

How much of this can we lay at the doorstep of screen entertainment? Some. Historical causation, of course, is extremely complex, besides being obscure. No doubt the present political style owes much to the working-out of trends in child-rearing, family organization, economic structure, geographic mobility, religious values, and cultural assumptions that reach back at least as far as the eighteenth century. But it is perhaps not overly incautious to suggest that motion pictures and television have contributed strongly to the stream of causation by conditioning the minds of millions of people to perceive the social world in a certain manner, and by legitimating a "style" of public action. As

Jeffrey Tulis remarks in a discussion of the impact of television news on Presidential rhetoric, "the use of television for leadership purposes required prior legitimation through some set of ideas" (Tulis, *Rhetorical Presidency* 15). Certainly it did. And it is likely that the set of legitimating ideas Tulis credits for the change was acquired by watching motion pictures and television itself, not for political knowledge, but for entertainment. Over time and for most people, the style of presentation of reality they saw on the screen had come to seem "natural."

The plausibility of this argument depends partly on historical timing. If the change from the old to new style of politics had occurred before screen entertainment became a mass habit, or parallel with it, the case for causation would be weak or absent. But since most scholars place the origins of the modern system in the New Deal, which began almost two decades after the classical Hollywood style became the norm, the argument is strengthened. By 1933, watching motion pictures had practically become the national pastime, for even with theater attendance down by twenty-five percent from its pre-Depression high, the figures suggest that half the population may have attended one each week (Balio 215).

Thus, although Franklin Roosevelt built his own personal mass following with the use of radio, he was speaking to a citizenry that that been conditioned by motion pictures to expect personalistic leadership. A hundred years earlier, the impact of his genial-but-forceful persona would have been far less.

Moreover, the new style of politics, especially the celebrification of the President, became intensified with the election of John Kennedy, which occurred after television-watching had been a mass addiction for nearly a decade. Kennedy's photogenic good looks melded with his emphasis on personal vigor to exactly fulfill the public's media-induced expectations for leadership: the President as superstar.

Finally, it is probably not a coincidence that the recent culmination of the "modern" style in American politics occurred in the election and administration of a President whose own previous career had been spent in collaboration with the Hollywood style. As many observers have noted, Ronald Reagan apparently viewed the world through the prism of cinematic convention, thinking in stories and images rather than analysis. Character-centered melodrama was the basis of his world-view. Judging by his wide appeal, this mode of cognition resonated with millions of voters. Further, Reagan, who had been a celebrity most of his adult life, was an ideal subject for the hype and glorification that now accompany the job of President. His successful maintenance of popularity over eight years suggests that a life in the media prepares a person perfectly for media politics, and that he may therefore be only the first of our Hollywood Presidents.

The Future

If the foregoing speculation is accurate, it means that changes in the legitimating ideas of American politics can be at least partially predicted with reference to ongoing changes in styles of mass entertainment. And as of 1992, the most prominent recent change in screen entertainment is the advent of music videos.

Unlike traditional television programming, which, as already discussed, closely follows the classical Hollywood style, music video is a true stylistic departure. Or, more correctly, the music video presents in expanded and intensified form a style frequently found in television *commercials*, as opposed to *programs*. The "story" does not employ character centered causality, but moves like a dream through a succession of images. Individual motivation is not assumed to underly the narrative, and "events" are not presented as a chain of cause and effect. Instead, brief picture-ideas, presumably rich with emotional connotations, flash by on the screen, accompanied, of course, by the soundtrack, which is the commercial reason for the existence of the video. Thus, MTV and its epigones dissolve the classical Hollywood style into a stream of emotions that bear little traditional narrative relation to one another. It goes without saying that this new form of entertainment is enormously popular with young people (Kaplan 233-247; Kinder).

Putting aside, for the sake of speculative convenience, all other historical forces at work, then, what sort of politics can we anticipate to arise from the MTV generation? It will likely have a "postmodernist" style, relying less on individual will and more on images and emotional connotations. In other words, it will differ from the modernist style in the same way that music videos differ from Hollywood cinema, in that identifiable people will become less, and evocative symbols more important.

We may already be seeing the first stirrings of this postmodernist style in the recent development of campaign advertising. The most famous television ads of the 1988 Bush campaign, for example, the "revolving door at the prison" and the face of recidivist murderer Willie Horton, represent successful attempts to evade rational argument and simply associate Bush's opponent, Michael Dukakis, with disturbing images. This guilt-by-visual-association strategy is just what we might expect from a campaign aimed at MTV voters. The future likely holds more of the same.

If the trend continues, Presidents will not only rely on imagist appeals to win elections, but to govern. In a Presidency dominated by the MTV strategy, the person of the incumbent would recede from prominence, to be replaced by a cavalcade of images that bore no necessary relation to his character or ideology. Instead of policies, such an administration might offer "poliTV," a succession of visual symbols which were intended to convey emotional satisfaction rather than objective information or reasoned argument.

Such a vision may sound like science fiction rather than scholarly reflection. Yet many of the political events of the past decade would have seemed equally fantastic if they had been predicted in, say, 1960. As screen entertainment continues to evolve, and continues to teach millions of people about reality, almost any outcome seems possible.

Works Cited

Allen, Robert C. *Channels of Discourse: Television and Contemporary Criticism.* Chapel Hill, NC: U of North Carolina, 1987.

Balio, Tino. ed. *The American Film Industry.* Madison, WI: U of Wisconsin. 1976.

Baudrillard, Jean. *Simulations.* New York: Semiotext(e), 1983.

Bordwell, David, Janet Staiger, and Kristin Thompson. *The Classical Hollywood Cinema: Film Style and Mode of Production to 1960.* New York: Columbia U, 1985.

Burnham, Walter Dean. "The Reagan Heritage." *The Election of 1988: Reports and Interpretations.* Ed. Gerald M. Pomper. Chatham, NJ: Chatham House, 1989.

_____. *Critical Elections and the Mainsprings of American Politics.* New York: W.W. Norton, 1970.

_____. "The Changing Shape of the American Political Universe." *American Political Science Review.* 59 (March 1965) 7-28.

Burke, John P. "The Institutional Presidency." *The Presidency and the Political System.* Ed. Michael Nelson. Washington D.C.: Congressional Quarterly, 1988.

Chen, Milton. *Review of Television and America's Children* by Edward L. Palmer. *Los Angeles Times Book Review.* (20 Nov. 1988).

Cronin, Thomas E. "An Imperiled Presidency?" *The Post-Imperial Presidency.* Ed. Vincent Davis. New York: Praeger, 1980.

Dye, Thomas R. and L. Harmon Zeigler. *American Politics in the Media Age.* Monterey, CA: Brooks/Cole, 1983.

Edwards, David V. *The American Political Experience: An Introduction to Government.* 4th ed. Englewood Cliffs, NJ: Prentice-Hall, 1988.

Emery, Edwin. *The Press and America: An Interpretive History of the Mass Media.* 3rd ed. Englewood Cliffs, NJ: Prentice-Hall, 1972.

Faulkner, Harold U. *Politics, Reform and Expansion, 1890-1900.* New York: Harper and Row. 1959.

Fenno, Richard F. Jr. *Home Style: House Members in Their Districts.* Boston: Little, Brown, 1978.

Fiske, John. *Television Culture.* New York: Methuen, 1978.

Fiorina, Morris P. "The Presidency and Congress: An Electoral Connection?" *The Presidency and the Political System.* Ed. Michael Nelson. Washington, D.C.: Congressional Quarterly, 1988.

Ginsberg, Benjamin and Martin Shefter. "The Presidency and the Organization of Interests." *The Presidency and the Political System.* Ed. Michael Nelson. Washington, D.C.: Congressional Quarterly, 1988.

Gitlin, Todd. *Inside Prime Time.* New York: Pantheon, 1985.

Gomery, Douglas. "Hollywood's Business." *The Wilson Quarterly.* V. 10, #3, (Summer 1986) 42-57.

Graber, Doris A. *Mass Media and American Politics.* 3rd ed. Washington, D.C.: Congressional Quarterly, 1989.

Greenstein, Fred I. "Change and Continuity in the Modern Presidency." *Classics of the American Presidency.* Ed. Harry A. Bailey. Oak Park, IL: Moore, 1980.

_____. *Children and Politics.* New Haven: Yale U, 1969.

Hart, James D. *The Popular Book: A History of America's Literary Tastes.* Berkeley: U of California, 1961.

Hartz, Louis. *The Liberal Tradition in America.* New York: Harcourt, Brace, and World, 1955.

Heclo, Hugh. "OMB and the Presidency—the Problem of 'Neutral Competence.' " *Public Interest.* V. 38 (Winter 1975) 80-98.

Hurley, Patricia A. "Parties and Coalitions in Congress," *Congressional Politics.* Ed. Christopher J. Deering. Chicago: Dorsey, 1989.

Kaplan, E. Ann. "Feminist Criticism and Television." *Channels of Discourse: Television and Contemporary Criticism.* Ed. Robert C. Allen. Chapel Hill, NC: U of North Carolina, 1987.

Kinder, Marsha. "Music Video and the Spectator: Television, Ideology, and Dream." *Television: The Critical View.* Ed. Horace Newcomb. New York: Oxford U, 1987.

Lauretis, Teresa. de. *Alice Doesn't: Feminism, Semiotics, and the Cinema.* Bloomington: Indiana U, 1984.

Liebes, Tamar and Elihu Katz. "On The Critical Ability Of Television Viewers." Los Angeles: Annenberg School of Communications, U of Southern California, 1986.

Litwak, Mark. *Reel Power: The Struggle For Influence And Success In The New Hollywood.* New York: William Morrow, 1986.

Lowery, Shearon A. and Melvin L. DeFleur. *Milestones In Mass Communication*

174 Continuities in Popular Culture

Research. 2nd ed. New York: Longman, 1986.

Lowi, Theodore J. *The Personal President: Power Invested, Promise Unfulfilled.* Ithaca: Cornell U, 1985.

Marcus, Robert D. "National Party Structure in the Gilded Age." *Politics And Society In American History, 1865 to the Present.* Ed. James Morton Smith. Vol. 2. Englewood Cliffs, NJ: Prentice-Hall, 1974.

Mauerhofer, Hugo. "Psychology of the Film Experience." *Film: A Montage of Theories.* Ed. Richard Dyer MacCann. New York: E.P. Dutton, 1966.

McWilliams, Wilson Carey. "The Meaning of the Election." *The Election of 1988: Reports and Interpretations.* Ed. Gerald M. Pomper. Chatham, NJ: Chatham House, 1989.

Metz, Christian. *The Imaginary Signifier: Psychoanalysis and the Cinema.* Bloomington: U of Indiana, 1982.

Milkis, Sidney M. "The Presidency and Political Parties." *The Presidency and the Political System.* Ed. Michael Nelson. Washington, D.C.: Congressional Quarterly, 1988.

Miroff, Bruce. "The Presidency and the Public: Leadership as Spectacle" *The Presidency and the Political System,* 2nd ed. Ed. Michael Nelson. Washington, D.C.: Congressional Quarterly, 1988.

_____. "Monopolizing the Public Space: The President as a Problem for Democratic Politics," (ed.), Thomas E. Cronin. *Rethinking The Presidency.* Boston: Little, Brown, 1982.

Moe, Terry M. "The Politicized Presidency." *The New Direction in American Politics.* Eds. John E. Chubb and Paul E. Peterson. Washington, D.C.: Brookings, 1985.

Mott, Frank Luther. *A History of American Magazines, 1885-1905.* Cambridge: Harvard U, 1957.

_____. "The Magazine Revolution and Popular Ideas in the Nineties." Worcester, Massachusetts: American Antiquarian Society, 1954.

Mowry, George E. *The Urban Nation: 1920-1960.* New York: Hill and Wang, 1965.

Nimmo, Dan and James E. Combs. *Mediated Political Realities.* 2nd edition. New York: Longman, 1990.

O'Brien, David M. "The Reagan Judges: His Most Enduring Legacy?" *The Reagan Legacy: Promise and Performance.* Chatham. Ed. Charles O. Jones. New Jersey: Chatham House, 1988.

Orren, Gary R. and Nelson W. Polsby, eds. *Media and Momentum: The New Hampshire Primary and Nomination Politics.* Chatham. New Jersey: Chatham House, 1987.

Postman, Neil. *Amusing Ourselves To Death: Public Discourse in the Age of Show Business.* New York: Penguin, 1985.

Ranney, Austin. *Channels of Power: The Impact of Television on American Politics.* New York: Basic Books, 1983.

Rogin, Michael Paul. *"Ronald Reagan," The Movie, and Other Episodes In*

Political Demonology. Berkeley: U of California, 1987.

Rothman, David J. "The Structure of State Politics." *Political Parties In American History, 1828-1890*. Ed. Felice A. Bonadio. New York: G.P. Putnam's Sons, 1974.

Sanders, Elizabeth. "The Presidency and the Bureaucratic State." *The Presidency and the Political System*. Ed. Michael Nelson. Washington, D.C.: Congressional Quarterly, 1988.

Sorauf, Frank J. and Paul Allen Beck. *Party Politics in America*. 6th ed. Glenview, IL: Scott, Foresman, 1988.

Sterling, Christopher H. and John M. Kitross. *Stay Tuned: A Concise History of American Broadcasting*. Belmont, CA: Wadsworth, 1978.

Thorburn, David. "Television Melodrama." *Television: The Critical View* Ed. Horace M. Newcomb, 4th ed. New York: Oxford U, 1987.

Tocqueville, Alexis. de. *Democracy In America*. New York: Washington Square P, 1964.

Tulis, Jeffrey K. "The Two Constitutional Presidencies." *The Presidency and the Political System*. Ed. Michael Nelson. 2nd ed. Washington, D.C.: Congressional Quarterly, 1988.

_____. *The Rhetorical Presidency*. Princeton, NJ: Princeton U, 1987.

Watt, Ian. *The Rise of the Novel: Studies in Defoe, Richardson and Fielding*. Berkeley: U of California, 1957.

Wayne, Stephen J. "Great Expectations: What People Want from Presidents." *Rethinking The Presidency*. Ed. Thomas E. Cronin. Boston: Little, Brown, 1982.

Webb, Michael, ed. *Hollywood: Legend and Reality*. Boston: Little, Brown, 1986.

Winn, Marie. *The Plug-In Drug: Television, Children, and the Family*. New York: Viking Penguin, 1985.

Young, James Sterling. *The Washington Community, 1800-1828*. New York: Columbia U, 1966.

Images of the Western
in Selected Vietnam Films

W. J. HUG

Nothing sours the American people quite so much as a great dream turned into a nightmare. As Hug points out in the following paper, such was the Vietnam debacle. It was the American frontier transplanted to another culture, and one that did not fit.

Film makers have often portrayed twentieth-century America at war in images reminiscent of the nation's frontier past. Gary Cooper's Sergeant York, the peaceable, soft-spoken primitive whose skills in the wilderness make him a hero in the trenches, is a son of the Leatherstocking transported to the Western Front. Slim Pickens as the fanatical cowboy bomber pilot of Stanley Kubrick's *Dr. Strangelove* begins the nuclear holocaust with an apocalyptic last ride astride a warhead. In more recent films about America at war—those depicting the war in Vietnam—the nation's conquest of the frontier and its involvement in Southeast Asia have been linked with particular consistency. From John Wayne's *Green Berets*, with it Special Forces camp called "Dodge City," to Kubrick's *Full Metal Jacket*, wherein marines in Vietnam joke about themselves as players in a western movie, references to the American West and the western recur time and time again.

One likely explanation for this recurrence lies in the fabric of broad correspondences between the circumstances of the Vietnam War and those of the conquest of the American frontier. As John Hellmann has shown in *American Myth and the Legacy of Vietnam*, these correspondences made Southeast Asia a latter-day correlative or extension of the American West, and the American soldier a correlative of the western hero. Both the frontier experience and the Vietnam experience involved American military efforts to extend and maintain socio-political "spheres of influence." In both cases, the targets were primitive, non-Anglo-Saxon cultures inhabiting primeval landscapes. Both cultures were stereotypically assumed to be ethnically inferior—"redskins" in one instance, "gooks" in the other—and therefore in special need of Americanization, particularly the South Vietnamese, who after the French withdrawal from Indochina lay in danger of communist subversion. In the American West and in Southeast Asia, the nation's military effort was relatively large-scale, bureaucratically managed, and fought with technologically advanced weapons, from repeating rifles and gatling guns to napalm; in contrast, native responses generally consisted of sporadic guerilla campaigns frequently conducted with more primitive weapons, like bows and arrows or booby traps. While western fiction and films often highlight later stages of the Americanizing process—the arrival of settlers, the establishment of law and order in small, frontier communities—the initial stages—subduing the wilderness and the natives, confining them to reservations—are always assumed facts and thus part of every western's context. In Vietnam films, these initial stages are consistently in the forefront, as the narratives highlight American soldiers' combat experiences against the Viet Cong or North Vietnamese regulars, or their relations with the Vietnamese natives in the rural villages.

Perceived in these terms, stories about Americans on the frontier and stories about Americans in Vietnam involve similar tensions. Most broadly, these can be subsumed within the tension between civilization and wilderness; in more specific terms, they may include the tension between white and non-white, between the technological and the primitive, between complex and distant bureaucracies and simpler, localized administrative structures. The play of these tensions emerges most vividly in the stories' protagonists. Like the archetypal American hero of the West, the American hero in Vietnam is almost inevitably a man in the middle: he must choose whether to employ his considerable skills in violence to promote the spread of the American Way with its promise of safety, stability, and equality on the one hand and its imperialist and capitalist ambiguities on the other, or to retreat in favor of the wilderness, where good and bad emerge in far more elemental forms. In the majority of westerns and in at least one Vietnam film—Wayne's *Green Berets*—the issue is simple, even simplistic, a choice so obvious as to leave no choice. The American Way, as embodied in the stoical sheriff or the tough Special Forces commander, is so virile and morally upright as to be irresistible, while the denizens of the wilderness—whether they be red or yellow—are so savage as to be utterly repulsive. However, in some Vietnam films as in some of the more ambitious westerns, the choice is not this clear-cut. In these works, the American endeavor to civilize the wilderness is distinctly flawed, perhaps by administrative corruption or clumsiness, or a powerful individual's obsession. In western narrative, the scheming banker, the swindling Indian agent, and the rapacious cattle baron have appeared so often as to be cliches. In stories about Vietnam, the noncom or the commander with a we-must-destroy-the-village-in order- to-save-it mentality has become more and more familiar. On the other hand, the wilderness in such works often has a pastoral allure embodied in the nomadic or agrarian simplicity and close-knit communities of the Indian or Vietnamese villagers.

Confronted with situations as complicated as these, the hero's choice becomes a far more difficult proposition. The moral awareness which is essential to his heroism enables him to distinguish the flaws in the pioneer endeavor and the appeal of the wilderness. His growing alienation from endeavor makes his participation in it more and more of a dilemma—he cannot accept the very system he feels duty-bound to defend. In the best Vietnam narratives as in the best westerns, the dilemma is irresolvable. The hero may die fighting for a cause he sees as tainted, or, having defended it successfully, he may withdraw, into the wilderness and/or perhaps into himself. In these situations he becomes a figure of potentially tragic stature.

Of course this summary of correspondences between western and Vietnam narratives identifies only in the broadest terms the characteristic tensions of civilization and wilderness and the hero's involvement with them. These issues may be handled in very different ways from one story to another. Narrative structure, point of view, portrayal of character, socio-political perspective may all vary widely, as may the mode of presentation—i.e., tragic, epic, elegiac, comic, parodic, etc. To take three instances from western narrative as examples, Cooper's romantic saga of the Leatherstocking is certainly tragic and elegiac; Owen Wister's pseudo-realistic novel *The Virginian* is, in terms of its happy resolution in the hero's marriage, classically comic; Mel Brooks' postmodern send-up of the western, *Blazing Saddles*, vacillates between the parodic and the satiric. Yet all three adhere generally to the suggested paradigm. Less diversity has emerged in Vietnam films produced thus far. Since the war became such a painful element in the national consciousness, the notion of portraying American soldiers' experiences in Vietnam in an upbeat fashion has seemed grotesque. Nevertheless, some diversity has emerged. In two of the more ambitious films yet made about the Vietnam War, the correspondences between Americans on the western frontier and Americans in Southeast Asia are given distinctly different modes of presentation. In Michael Cimino's *The Deer Hunter*, the dilemma of the young Green Beret Michael Vronsky (Robert DeNiro) is portrayed in tragic and elegiac terms reminiscent of Cooper. In Francis Coppola's *Apocalypse Now*, Colonel Kilgore (Robert Duvall), the swaggering leader of an air Cavalry unit, is depicted in terms of the western mock-heroic.

Since *The Deer Hunter's* release in 1978, many reviewers and critics have noted the deer hunter/Deerslayer parallel (Auster and Quart 7; Pease 255; Wood 277): like Natty Bumppo as well as his literary and cinematic progeny, Michael Vronsky is a solitary hero uncomfortable in his society and allied with the wilderness, from which he derives his skills in violence and his strict code of behavior. These are embodied in Michael's notion of "one shot," his catch phrase for the grace, skill, and integrity necessary to stalk and kill a deer with a single bullet. Circumstances dictate that he, like the Leatherstocking, must defend his society against the primitive inhabitants of the wilderness; Michael emerges from the conflict a melancholy and perhaps even tragic figure whose fate raises troubling questions about the society he has fought for. Some critics have taken *The Deer Hunter's* relations to the western still further, linking the film not only with Cooper's novels but with the classic Hollywood westerns of John Ford and Howard Hawks, works with far less ambivalent social and political implications (Wood 277-281; Britton 15-18). In these discussions, *The Deer Hunter* emerges as something of a swan song for the Hollywood western, a eulogy for the simplicity and vigor of the frontier endeavor as depicted in such films. Though the parallels drawn between Cimino's film and those of Ford and Hawks are sometimes far-fetched (*The Deer Hunter* and *Rio Bravo*?), they have been valuable not only in defining *The Deer Hunter* within its cinematic tradition, but in suggesting the possibility of broad correspondences, of the sort outlined above between western and Vietnam narratives. And perhaps this comparative approach may be taken further still: by extending it here, I hope to illuminate two facets of Cimino's film that it seems to me bear more examination than they've received up to now—Michael's on-again/off-again relationship with Linda (Meryl Streep), the former fiancee of his best friend, Nick; and the notorious Russian Roulette sequences. If the film is indeed as strongly influenced by the western as this discussion and others suggest, then these situations should come clear when considered according to the established formulae of western narrative.

Michael's relations with Linda constitute an innovative and poignant variant on a classic predicament in western stories: the hero's dilemma over the wilderness code and a woman. From the inception of the western in Cooper's novels, the hero's devotion to the wilderness has been challenged by the allure of love and an easy domesticity. When in *The Deerslayer*, Natty refused the passionate Judith Hutter, he established for those western heroes to follow their obligation to fulfill their code despite the attractions of a woman. Owen Wister's Virginian, Jack Shaefer's Shane, Larry McMurtry's Augustus McCrae, and countless forgotten others have held true to form, and so does Cimino's deer hunter. Michael's affection for Linda thrusts him into the same sort of quandary as the more traditional western heroes, but with several crucial distinctions. These emerge vividly when Michael's dilemma is set against Shane's, for his circumstances and Michael's are particularly similar.

Both heroes must choose whether or not to follow the wilderness code and thereby save the men to whom the women they love are bound. If Shane abandons the code, if he allows the farmer Joe Starrett to fight for himself against the land-hungry cattleman Fletcher and his hired guns, Starrett will be killed; then Shane can slip easily into a relationship with Marian, Starrett's pretty young wife, whose strong attraction to him has become apparent, even to Starrett himself. Similarly, if Michael abandons the code and does not return to Vietnam to save his friend Nick, who has gone AWOL and vanished, he ensures a relationship with Linda, Nick's fiancee. Of course both men make the noble choice, sacrificing love for the sake of the code and friendship. But here the similarity ends: Shane's decision is simple, instantaneous, and successful; Michael's is complicated, lengthy, and ends in crushing failure. These differences constitute an ingenious and perverse twist upon a characteristic situation in the western, a twist that projects Michael's western heroism into a realm which only the Deerslayer and a few other western heroes achieve: the realm of tragedy.

When Michael returns from Vietnam to his home in the Pennsylvania steel town of Clairton, his faith in the wilderness code of "one shot" has been profoundly shaken. During his tour of duty, he, Nick, and another hometown buddy, Steve, had been captured by Viet Cong, who forced their prisoners to play Russian Roulette against one another. Through his courage and skill in violence, Michael managed to free himself and his friends by persuading their captors to allow him and Nick to play one another. But his scheme took a brutal toll on both his companions. After the three escaped the POW camp on a piece of driftwood floating in a nearby river, Steve's legs were shattered when he fell from an American helicopter attempting to rescue them. Nick was traumatized by the Russian Roulette game he and Michael had played, and upon his release from a military hospital goes AWOL because he is psychotically compelled to play it over and over. Just before leaving Vietnam, Michael sees him watching Russian Roulette in a Saigon gambling den; Nick's irrational actions—grabbing the pistol from one of the players, putting it to his own head and firing an empty chamber, then disappearing into the crowd—have shown Michael the disastrous effects of their escape on Nick. After he comes back to Clairton, his hesitancy in facing the friends whom he,

Steve, and Nick had shared suggests that these consequences of his acts linger in his mind.

By all indications, Michael's guilt over the fates of his buddies, in contrast to his own relative well-being, prompts him to abandon the code. Instead of hunting deer, the activity which for him had been emblematic of it, he now pursues Linda, though before Vietnam he'd always avoided women. He does go hunting once after his return; however, the idea is not his but an old friend's, and he can no longer approach the hunt with his former conviction. He had always taken pride in his ability to perform the ritual acts of the hunt with skill and grace—stalking his prey silently, killing it cleanly, with a single shot. Now he is unable to complete the ritual. Having stalked his deer and set up an easy kill, he cannot bring himself to fire the decisive shot. Instead, after staring into the eyes of his prey, he fires into the air and cries in admission of his failure to fulfill the code successfully—both in Vietnam and now in Clairton—an ironic "OK." At this point, Michael has utterly given it up; he has, so to speak, hung up his gun. And, in fact, when Michael returns from the abortive hunt to the cabin where he and two friends are staying, he is without his rifle.

But for Cimino's hero as for his more traditional western predecessors, discarding the gun and the code is tantamount to discarding one's character and integrity. Ironically enough, Michael determines to take up the code once more at the moment when his temptation to dismiss it forever is greatest. His change of heart occurs in a short, inconspicuous, but pivotal scene set in his house trailer. He and Linda have just become sexually intimate, and, as she lies sleeping beside him, he gazes not at her but at a deer's head mounted on the wall. The two images, his sleeping lover and his hunting trophy, effectively embody the alternative ways of life before him, the same alternatives that so many western heroes have confronted previously, and Michael remains true to tradition. To accept domestic happiness with Linda would be to turn his back on Steve and Nick and their sad plights, for which he feels largely responsible. Thus, Michael leaves his sleeping lover, walks out to a pay phone and calls Steve, who because of his paraplegia has holed up in a V.A. hospital refusing to see family or friends. The gesture confirms Michael's sense of guilt for all this, and his determination to attempt once more the heroic control basic to the code.

In this decision, he affirms his role not only as the western hero who opts for the code instead of love, but also as tragic hero, the strong and noble man whose assertion of his own will brings not triumph but destruction. Though Michael draws Steve out of his isolation and returns him to his family, his efforts to save Nick fail far more terribly than before.

He returns to Saigon during the fall of South Vietnam to find Nick addicted to heroine as well as Russian Roulette, and apparently incapable of remembering Michael or their home. In a last-ditch effort to jar Nick's memory and convince him to come back to Clairton, Michael buys his way into a Russian Roulette game with Nick, so that the two friends will face one another just they had done during their escape from the Viet Cong. As each raises the pistol to his head and fires an empty chamber, Michael vows his love for Nick, and begs him to stop the game. He describes to his friend the beauty of the Pennsylvania mountains where they had hunted deer, and recognition sparks in Nick's eyes. But the rush of memory is unendurable: Nick quickly raises the pistol, utters "one shot"—the symbolic phrase for the wilderness code—and, as Michael watches helplessly, fires the loaded chamber into his head. The "one shot" that had been the emblem of the western hero's grace, skill, and integrity in violence is transformed horribly into the emblem of his tragic failure (Britton 20).

Thus, Michael's classic western heroism and his tragedy are in large part the results of his pivotal decision to leave Linda. The western hero's rejection of love for the sake of the wilderness code—a choice which conventionally leads to heroic triumph—culminates here in utter defeat. Such a fate is perhaps more compelling even that that of Michael's ancestor, the Deerslayer: for Natty Bumppo, as for many western heroes to follow him, adherence to the wilderness code is effective in saving others, and usually himself, in violent situations; for Michael, it proves disastrously unreliable.

If *The Deer Hunter's* striking mixture of western heroism and tragedy becomes clearer in the light of western literary and filmic tradition, so too does the conclusive moment when these qualities of Michael's character collide. In most westerns, the hero's distinctive features display themselves most vividly in the moment of the shootout, the ritual of confrontation in which the hero coolly and aesthetically dispatches the villain. This conventional climax, like the hero's dilemma over love and the wilderness code, was established in Cooper's *The Deerslayer* (Cawelti 203). During the novel's famous seventh chapter, Natty is attacked by an Iriquois brave and undergoes his initiation into manhood through single combat so stylized as to be ceremonial. R.W.B. Lewis' summary of the conflict highlights its formal symmetry:

The adversaries, peering around from behind trees, bow courteously to one another; they exchange words and proposals; each gesture and act of preparation has an air of solemn formality. They fire simultaneously—it is like a kiss. (104)

The quality of ritual in the Deerslayer's initiation emphasizes its serious and complex implications. Natty is of course relieved that he has emerged the victor, but his newly demonstrated capacity for killing people places upon him profound moral responsibilities he had not borne before. Thus, as the dying brave christens the youth-hunter Deerslayer as the man-warrior Hawkeye, he is thrust into a far more complicated moral realm.

Though the site of the shootout would change from the woods to some small town's saloon or dusty street, the formal manner of the participants, first articulated in Natty's initiation, would reappear in countless westerns to follow; time and again the hero's cool demeanor and the artistry of his violence emerge conclusively through ceremonial combat with the villain. However, the moral complexities originally associated with the event would largely disappear: in the majority of subsequent westerns, the shootout becomes merely the highpoint of a story's physical violence, foreshadowed by a series of preliminary skirmishes. But in a handful of the finest westerns, works like *Shane*, *The Searchers*, *The Man Who Shot Liberty Valance*, and *Hombre*, the ambiguity of the shootout reappears. In such stories, writers and/or directors still create innovative and powerful variants on the gunfight, variants which renew its classic significance as the solemn moment when opposing desires or alliances within the hero collide. Oftentimes, the hero's personal feelings—about either his adversary or the people whom he defends—are at odds with his moral imperative to fight. Like Pat Garrett (James Coburn) in Sam Peckinpah's *Billy the Kid*, the hero may have to subordinate friendship with his opponent to his obligation to the law. Or, like Paul Newman's "Hombre," he may be alienated from those whom he saves.

Perceived in light of the original gunfight in *The Deerslayer* and its variations in these and other subsequent westerns, the conclusion of *The Deer Hunter* becomes resonant, for the film's final Russian Roulette scene emerges as an ingenious and gripping reworking of many of the conventions surrounding the shootout. As in many westerns since Cooper's, the final confrontation has been foreshadowed by preliminary conflicts: Michael and Nick had played Russian Roulette once before, during their escape from the Viet Cong; later they'd both attended Russian Roulette games in Saigon. The setting recalls those of earlier gunfights as well (Hellmann 175). Shootouts often take place in a saloon, with its familiar drinking and gambling; two of the three Russian Roulette scenes occur in a Saigon gambling den amidst a drunken crowd betting on the outcomes. The demeanor of the opponents is reminiscent of the formal air adopted by Natty and the Iriquois brave; as Michael and Nick face one another quietly across a small table, a single pistol laying between them, their solemn manner contrasts starkly with the chaos that initially surrounds them. Most importantly, this shootout, like those in the finest westerns, is laced with ambiguities. We have seen already how Michael's adherence to the code culminates not in success, as it does for so many western heroes, but in tragic failure; other complications, which ironically recall traditional westerns, appear as well. Michael's predicament in facing Nick across the Russian Roulette table constitutes a cleverly convoluted play upon the familiar conflict between the hero's personal feelings for his adversary and his moral imperative to fight.

Though his devotion to the code and his desire to save Nick ultimately coincide, Michael must engage in an act that apparently denies his affection for Nick; in order to have any chance of saving him, Michael must make Nick an opponent, and even become a potential accessory to Nick's death. This conflict between Michael's wish to save Nick and his obligation to adhere to the code and face him in Russian Roulette becomes more wrenching still when we consider the nature of the relationship between the two men. They had been closest friends, living together, working together, sharing a mutual reverence for deer hunting, loving the same woman; they are, in effect, two halves of a single self—they are doubles. Thus, as Michael faces Nick across the Russian Roulette table, he risks not only literal suicide if he fires the loaded chamber, but psychic suicide through loss of a portion of himself if Nick does. These complex personal implications make Michael's dilemma a deviously contorted version of the western hero's predicament in facing an old friend in a gunfight, though few previous treatments of this situation involve such vicious circumstances or psychological intricacies.

These various correspondences culminate in a debased and absurdist rendering of the traditional shootout, a revision which, given its setting and the experiences of the two "adversaries," generates strong and ironic political implications. By the end of the film, Russian Roulette and American involvement in Vietnam have become so closely linked as to be identical, a fact reviewers and critics have often noted. Michael and Nick played Russian Roulette as means of getting weapons to kill their Viet Cong captors; during their recoveries they each attended Russian Roulette games in Saigon; now they play Russian Roulette once more, as Saigon burns. This consistent and direct association suggests that in Vietnam, the shootout, an archetypal gesture of American heroism, became nothing more than Russian Roulette, an illogical and potentially disastrous gamble. Moreover, Michael's tragic separation from Nick, whose life was so thoroughly interwoven with his own that the two were halves of a single self, reflects the profound rift in the national consciousness caused by the war. The nation's self was ruptured by Vietnam just as was the shared self of the two Vietnam veterans.

The subsequent sense of personal and, through metaphoric extension, national loss is conveyed powerfully in the film's ending, depicting the events surrounding Nick's funeral in Clairton. Here an elegiac quality akin to that which permeates Cooper's novels emerges as, after the funeral ceremony, Michael and his friends gather at the tavern that before the war had been their favorite watering hole. The tragedy of the western hero's failure through adherence to the code is poignantly addressed in the film's final scene, wherein the group, in a communal effort to come to terms with Nick's death, join in a muted, uncertain rendering of "God Bless America." Far from being an affirmation of confident patriotism of the "my-country-right-or-wrong" sort, it is instead a cathartic expression of loss and a plea for help. As Robert Hellmann has noted:

In contrast to the proud assertions of "The Star-Spangled Banner" and "My Country, 'Tis of Thee," "God Bless America" is a humble acknowledgement that the divine favor seemingly manifest in the American landscape can be achieved only if spiritual consciousness will guide America on its uncertain nighttime journey. Michael and the other characters make a half-conscious call for grace...(187)

Ultimately the song functions as a multi-faceted lament, literally for Nick, metaphorically for the western hero's tragic failure and for the absurd gamble of the cause he fought for.

If Cimino's *Deer Hunter* portrays the western hero tragically and elegiacally to mourn America's endeavor in Vietnam, Francis Ford Coppola's *Apocalypse Now* portrays him satirically to ridicule it. Though neither of Coppola's main characters—the military assassin Captain Willard (Martin Sheen) or his victim Colonel Kurtz (Marlon Brando)— is depicted overtly in western terms, both are caught up in versions of the western hero's classic predicament. In his own way, each is at odds with the pioneer cause he fights for, the American effort to civilize and democratize the wilderness. Willard has witnessed and understood the absurdity of the war effort, yet for him no other sort of life is any longer possible. As he admits in the film's voice-over, he'd gone stateside after his first tour in Vietnam only to find himself incapable of returning to the domestic roles of husband and father, so he and his wife divorced. Furthermore, the nation as he thought he'd known it no longer existed, so he'd asked for another tour in Vietnam. Like the western hero unsuited to civilized life and suspicious of civilization, Willard returns to the wilderness. Kurtz, the special Forces colonel whom Willard is assigned to kill, represents an analogous case. Frustrated at the bureaucratic clumsiness of the American war effort and at the bureaucrats' pretensions to a lofty morality in conducting it, he surrenders to the primitive ferocity of the wilderness. Kurtz becomes a renegade, crossing into Cambodia so that he may carry on the war with the utter savagery he believes essential to victory.

To draw forth these western implications latent in his major characters and to comment on the Vietnam conflict itself, Coppola creates a minor character who is explicitly, even bombastically western—Colonel Kilgore (Robert Duvall), head of the air cavalry unit that carries Willard and his boat on one leg of his quest to kill Kurtz. Unlike these men who have found themselves at odds with America's pioneer endeavor in Vietnam, Kilgore revels in it, to the point of arrogance. As Gilbert Adair has noted, Kilgore plays to the hilt the historical and cinematic role of swashbuckling cavalry officer leading the fight against the savages on the frontier (148). His uniform, his style of leadership, his relations with his men, and even his enthusiasm for surfing suggest an extravagant and ultimately satiric rendering of the George-Custer-cum-Roy-Rogers western hero of the Saturday matinees—a simplified, homogenized descendant of the classical western hero, utterly pleased with his part in the ambivalent conflict of civilization and wilderness. Kilgore's dandyism in dress and manner recalls the flashiness of the historical Custer and of the Hollywood cavalry officers who were his progeny. The broad-brimmed Stetson, the yellow dickey reminiscent of the cavalryman's bandanna, the pistol and holster on the hip, the swaggering oblivion to personal danger—all ironically conjure the heroic image of the gallant soldier conquering the western plains. He strives to impart the western mystique to his command as well, maintaining a company bugler also replete with Stetson, and even orchestrating nights around the campfire. In a scene recalling countless western films, Kilgore strums a guitar as he and his men lounge around a fire amidst the Asian wilderness, drinking and swapping stories of their exploits. In battle he is every bit as fearless as his idealized and vacuous predecessors; after his unit attacks a Vietnamese coastal village and lands to mop up, he stands upright, oblivious to enemy artillery and small-arms fire, while his men duck for cover. All of this, in a film about another time and another war, could be straight heroism; in Coppola's depiction of Vietnam, however, it becomes mock-heroic. The conventional elements in Kilgore's character are so overstated—particularly from the more skeptical perspective that grew out of Vietnam and Watergate—as to be bombastic pretense. Kilgore becomes the satiric embodiment of the corrupted pioneer endeavor he defends.

This larger significance emerges most vividly in his primary motive for attacking the coastal village. Though he initially considers the tactic because the village presents a logical site to drop Willard and his boat, the Colonel decides upon it only when he recalls the heavy surf off the village beach. He is, as it happens, an avid surfer, and Lance, one of Willard's men, had been nationally recognized in the sport back in the States. From Kilgore's perspective, an attack on the village represents above all else the chance for the two of them to catch some waves. The Colonel's fanatical enthusiasm for a fashionable sport associated with the glitzy western playgrounds of Southern California and Hawaii represents the film's strongest assertion that Vietnam was a debased pioneer endeavor. As embodied in Kilgore, the bombastic cowboy-beach boy, the quest to conquer the wilderness has lost all relation to the ideals of bringing civilization and democracy to a virgin land; it has become instead the utterly illogical expression of an arrogant consumer society's will to power. The beliefs associated with the settlement of the Old West have given way to the consumer appetites associated with the New West, and Kilgore, its mock-heroic embodiment, fights to promote the latter values, not the former.

As an addendum to the Kilgore episode, Coppola inserts a later reference to the western which magnifies this depiction of the decadence implicit in America's pioneer efforts in Southeast Asia. After Willard and his companions aboard the patrol boat leave Kilgore, they refuel at a supply depot where that same night troops are to be entertained by *Playboy* playmates. Once the crowd has gathered, a helicopter emblazoned not with military insignia but with a bunny descends upon the stage, a large platform surrounded by brightly-lit phalluses. The girls emerge clad in scanty cowboy and indian outfits, to bump and grind to a driving rendition of the old rock'n'roll standard "Suzie Q," then slip coyly into the waiting 'copter when the troops, roused to a mating frenzy, storm the stage. Here again, the opposing concepts of old and new America are imagistically suggested. While the playmates' costumes inevitably recall the conflict of civilization and wilderness in the Old West, the idea is quite literally "burlesqued" by the performance of those who wear them. The playmates, as they parody one American pioneer effort, taunt the libidos of soldiers fighting in another. Far from offering the troops solace and renewed resolve, they arouse tension, frustration, and ultimately chaos. Through the playmates as through Kilgore, Coppola's film suggests that in Vietnam the ideals which provided intellectual and moral bases for one frontier endeavor have been undercut by the self-centered desire for gratification in this other.

Though *Apocalypse Now* and *The Deer Hunter* approach the Vietnam conflict through different modes of western presentation—the satiric as opposed to the tragic and elegiac—their mutual reliance on images and themes from the western produces visions of the war that dovetail. Both films employ the western to comment on perceived absurdities of the American involvement: Coppola's lampoons them, while Cimino's laments them. In their depictions of the nation's effort in Vietnam as failed extension of America's effort on the frontier, the two films not only resonate with ironic echoes of Wayne's *Green Berets*; they define a *leitmotif* for later Vietnam films like Oliver Stone's *Platoon* and Stanley Kubrick's *Full Metal Jacket*. Through the character of Barnes (Tom Berenger), a sergeant fanatically committed to the war, Stone associates visual and aural imagery reminiscent of the frontier with a militant right-wing stance. The film's more urban and politically liberal white characters have no recognizable accents and spend their free time smoking marijuana as they listen to rock music; Barnes, however, speaks in a thick western accent, plays poker and drinks whiskey saloon-style, while he listens to country-and-western music, most notably Merle Haggard's "Okie from Muskogee." The corruption of this latter-day cowboy's jingoist notion of Vietnam as a new frontier emerges vividly after he allows an atrocity in a Vietnamese village: when Elias (Willem DaFoe), a kindly and liberal sergeant outraged at the crime, threatens him with court-martial, Barnes kills his accuser and blames the Viet Cong for the death. As another embodiment of America's pioneer endeavor gone wrong, Barnes is not far removed from Kilgore.

Kubrick's *Full Metal Jacket* handles western references in similar and sometimes more overt ways. In fact, two particular scenes late in the work explicitly define the historical, psychological, and cinematic relations between the Old West and Southeast Asia which all these films address. Preliminary allusions to the West and the western establish the motif: the opening credits roll to a country-and-western song "Goodbye Sweetheart, Hello Vietnam" proclaiming "America has heard the bugle call" just as it had on the frontier—both Kilgore and Barnes would love it. The film's central character, an anonymous marine draftee (Matthew Modine) does swaggering imitations of John Wayne's cowboy *persona*, for which he earns the name "Joker" from his drill instructor; another draftee whom we learn comes from Texas is christened "Cowboy." Later, after Joker has arrived in Vietnam, a fellow marine has his camera snatched as he and Joker haggle with a prostitute outside a Saigon cafe called the "Las

Vegas": moral decadence in Vietnam is linked to the most famous resort town of America's New West and the decadence often associated with it.

These seemingly random allusions—and in fact the western references in every film we've considered—are thrust into context by two scenes near the end of the film. Joker, now a reporter for *Stars and Stripes*, is sent with a camera crew to cover a marine counterattack in the city of Hue during the Tet offensive. As he and a cameraman film a unit of troops huddled behind a pile of fallen brickwork, they come upon a marine whom Joker had known in bootcamp. With a wry gallows humor, the soldier peers into the camera and asks Joker in a tone of mock-reverence, "Is that you, John Wayne?" His buddies immediately pick up on the joke and extend it:

> "I'll be General Custer."
> "I'll be a horse"—this from a black marine.
> "Who'll be the indians?"
> "We'll let the gooks be the indians."

This little scene, lasting less than a minute, comically condenses the complex of interrelations between the frontier and Vietnam which Kubrick's film and these others to varying extents address; Kubrick's verdict on the American involvement emerges in an episode that soon follows. After shooting the combat footage, Joker and his crew tape interviews with several marines concerning their feelings about the War; among them is another of Joker's friends from bootcamp, Cowboy, the soldier from Texas. In light of the previous western allusions in the film, his comments, which posit an implicit contrast between his home state and Vietnam, take on particular significance. "I hate Vietnam," he says, peering into the camera in quiet, puzzled disappointment; "there's not one horse in this whole country." In Cowboy's frustration at a petty disparity between Southeast Asia and his home in what was once the Old West, Kubrick creates an ingenious miniature of the disillusionment that permeates all of these films. In one way or another, the War in Vietnam becomes in each of them America's failed effort to resurrect the frontier. The western will probably remain a viable motif in representations of the nation's future conflicts.

Works Cited

Adair, Gilbert. *Vietnam on Film from the Green Berets to Apocalypse Now*. New York: Proteus, 1981.

Auster Al and Leonard Quart. "Hollywood and Vietnam: The Triumph of the Will." *Cineaste* 9 (1979): 4-9.

Britton, Andrew. "Sideshows: Hollywood in Vietnam." *Movie* 27/28 (1980/81): 2-23.

Cawelti, John G. *Adventure, Mystery, and Romance: Formula Stories as Art and Popular Culture*. Chicago: U of Chicago P, 1976.

Hellmann, John. *American Myth and the Legacy of Vietnam*. New York: Columbia UP, 1986.

Lewis, R.W.B. *The American Adam: Innocence, Tragedy, and Tradition in the Nineteenth Century*. Chicago: U of Chicago P, 1955.

Pease, Nick. "*The Deer Hunter* and the Demythification of the American Hero." *Literature Film Quarterly* 7 (1979): 254-259.

Wood, Robin. *Hollywood from Reagan to Vietnam*. New York: Columbia UP, 1986.

"They Shall Take Up Serpents": Images of American Snake Handlers in Visual Media

STEPHEN J. PULLUM

America is a Janus-land reaching out for visions of the future while at the same time clinging tenaciously to practices of the past. To some of us many of these elements of the past are irrational and seem hard to justify. Yet if we are to understand American culture we need to take these rituals into account and try to understand them.

And these signs shall follow them that believe; In my name shall they cast out devils; they shall speak with new tongues; They shall take up serpents; and if they drink any deadly thing, it shall not hurt them; they shall lay hands on the sick, and they shall recover.

The above quote, taken from Mark 16:17-18 of the King James Version of the Bible, is the foundation for the sometimes-forgotten religious practice in America of handling poisonous snakes. Believing that this passage is an injunction from Jesus, snake handlers, as they are popularly called, are a sect of Pentecostal and Holiness churches who live predominantly in Southern Appalachia. Some can be found even in Indiana and Ohio and as far north as Michigan (Kane, "Ritual Possession" 293; Hunter 778).

As a religious practice, snake handling in this country finds it roots in an individual named George Went Hensley, an illiterate preacher from East Tennessee. Having begun the custom around 1909 in the isolated mountain community of Sale Creek, Tennessee, just north of Chattanooga, Hensley introduced snake handling to the Church of God in Cleveland, Tennessee, around 1912 with the approval of its overseer Ambrose J. Tomlinson. By 1917, Tomlinson, in his annual address to the church, suggested that "under the proper conditions," snake handling was an acceptable religious practice but that it was in no way to be "a test of salvation" (Hunter 778; Kane "Ritual Possession 293; Kane, "Snake Handlers" 699). In 1919, after

George Defriese, one of Hensley's disciples, was bitten by a rattlesnake at Sale Creek, the ensuing controversy forced Hensley to leave, even though Defriese did not die. Upon moving to East Pineville, Kentucky, about 17 miles west of Harlan, Hensley eventually became pastor of the Pine Mountain Church of God where he introduced snake handling (LaBarre 12; Maguire 174). After a lifetime of controversial practice in several states, Hensley eventually died of a snakebite received in a service on July 24, 1955, near Altha, Florida. He was 75 years old (Gerrard 22; Kane, "Holy Ghost People" 260; Maguire 174; Kimsey 90). By 1953, as a result of the influence of Hensley and his disciples, snake handling had become so pronounced in the South that several states passed laws against it, including Kentucky (the first to do so), Georgia, Virginia, Tennessee, North Carolina, and Alabama. Municipal ordinances in Bartow, Florida, and Greenville, South Carolina also banned the practice (Kane, "Snake Handlers" 698; Kane, "Holy Ghost People" 258). Today, West Virginia is the only state in which snake handling is legal.

Hunter suggests that by the 1940s, snake handlers were receiving national attention (Hunter 777). Kane, on the other hand, argues that snake handlers were receiving media attention as early as the 1930s (Kane, "Ritual Possession" 293). Similarly, Maguire argues that snake handlers have been studied by journalists and academicians for over 60 years (Maguire 166). In his *Bibliography of Religion in the South*, Lippy points out that studies on snake handlers have ranged anywhere from Pelton and Carden's conclusion that snake handling is an inauthentic practice of Christianity to Kane's argument that, among other things, snake handlers are not psychotic or neurotic. Lippy also reveals that, in a controlled study, Gerrard concluded that snake handlers practice this custom as a release from the mundane affairs and frustrations of daily living. According to Lippy, others have contended that snake handling is a ritual in which individuals engage to verify the scriptural promises of Mark 16:18 and, thereby, validate their salvation (Lippy 304-5).

Whether snake handling has received public attention since the 1930s or the 1940s is not relevant here. What is significant is that, to date, no one has examined how snake handlers have been portrayed in various visual media through the decades. Given this fact, an interesting question for the communication scholar is this: "What images of Snake Handlers have emerged in various visual media within the last fifty to sixty years?" My purpose, therefore, in the following pages is to address this question.

Recognizing that nowadays "we are bombarded by messages from radio, television, film, newspapers, magazines, and a host of other media which bring with them a 'rhetoric' all their own," Medhurst and Benson argue, "It is important that we learn more about these new 'languages'...if we are to be able fully to understand and appreciate the messages they bring" (Medhurst vii-viii). Since, as Barthes contends, "The press photograph is a message," (Heath 15) and since as Eco argues, "A movie is a text," (Eco 231) both photographs and films (whether documentary or fictional) are legitimate purviews of analysis for the rhetorical critic since both have the potential to influence audiences to view the world in a particular way. In an attempt to address the question, "What images of snake handlers have emerged in visual media within the last fifty to sixty years," I analyzed various photographs from the following print media: *Time* ("Any Deadly Thing" 25), *Life* ("Holiness Faith Healers" 59-62), *Saturday Evening Post* (Kobler 26-7, 153-4, 156), *Foxfire 7* (Wigginton 370-428), *Southern Voices* (Campbell 41-48), *Dictionary of Pentecostal and Charismatic Movements* (Hunter 778), *Trans-Action* (Gerrard), *Theology Today* (Daugherty 232-43), *Quarterly Journal of the Library of Congress* (Maguire 166-79), *Appalachian Heritage* ("Snake Handling" 29-32), and *The Knoxville Journal [Newspaper]* (Bean 1A, 7A). In addition to photographs from the above periodicals, I analyzed images in the documentary film *Holy Ghost People*, a report aired in 1987 by "World News Tonight," and a 1991 report by *A Current Affair*.[1] The above visual artifacts were chosen because of their availability and because of their potential impact on mass audiences.

Barthes suggests that "analogical reproductions of reality" such as photographs and cinema often contain, in addition to what he refers to as a first-order message, a "supplementary message." In other words, such 'imitative arts' comprise a denoted and a connoted message. The denoted message is the "analogon itself," the first-order message that "completely fills its substance and leaves no place for the development of a second-order message." It is the "perfection and plenitude of its analogy" and needs no description. Simply put, it is "objectivity."

The connoted message, on the other hand, is one of three types of second-order messages that results from the way the image "has been worked on, chosen, composed, constructed, [or] treated according to professional, aesthetic or ideological norms...." It is a "modification of reality itself, of...the denoted message" and is not peculiar to just the photograph. "The photographic paradox can then be seen as the co-existence of two messages," explains Barthes, "the one without a code (the photographic analogue), the other with a code (the 'art,' or the treatment, or the 'writing', or the rhetoric, of the photograph)...." Since the connotation of a visual message "is realized at the different levels of ...production" and is that "plane of expression and...content" that needs "decipherment," Barthes suggests that when analyzing visual artifacts, one should take into account one or more of the following elements: trick effects, pose of the subjects, objects, photogenia (i.e. lighting, exposure, printing), aestheticism, syntax (e.g. ordering of photographs), and text that occasionally accompanies the visual artifact (Heath 16-25). The following discussion, therefore, will focus on these components of photographs and film in an attempt to suggest both denotative and connotative messages that possibly emerge.

Snake Handlers as Working-Class Whites

From an analysis of various photographs, films, and news reports, one of the most salient images about snake handlers is that they are working-class whites who, although they may not be living "from hand to mouth" possess relatively little of this world's riches. This can be seen in their homes and houses of worship, dress, and hairstyles. Every visual image of snake handlers is that of a caucasion—and usually, though not always, male. Blacks are never depicted.

One of the earliest photographs of a snake handler, dated September 12, 1946, in *The Quarterly Journal of the Library of Congress*, shows Franklin Sergent of Harlan, Kentucky, headed to work with his mule and sled. Sergent is wearing a white shirt with overalls. On the hillside behind him stand six, small, frame houses of unpainted weathered boards. Each house contains a brick chimney but no electricity. At least five of them sit on stilts, judged to be four or five feet high, to keep them level against the hillside. None of the houses is underpinned. Near one of the houses, a single clothesline stretches across the dirt yard strewn with an old barrel and other debris. What looks to be an outhouse can be seen outside a wire fence marking the parameter of the yard. Farther out are fields of weeds through which Sergent and his white mule are walking. The caption reads, "Franklin Sergent starts out with mule and sled to haul coal for the PV & K Coal Company, Clover Gap Mine, Harlan County, Kentucky, September 12, 1946" (Maguire 179). The entire scene, with all of its objects, conjures up the notion of ruralism and poverty.

In another picture dated September 15, 1946, from the same periodical, approximately twenty people, most of whom are children, are waiting to walk through the door of a church building that looks to be no larger than one room. The building is standing on blocks and is constructed of badly weathered boards nailed vertically. The dirt yard outside has been worn down by pedestrian traffic. Many of the boys are wearing overalls. As a whole, this scene likewise suggests that snake handlers are at best rural and at worst poor (Maguire 178).

Such images in visual media have changed little with the passing of time. One picture published in *Foxfire 7* in 1982, for example, shows a small white concrete-block meeting house with the sign "The Church of God" painted across it in large bold letters. What is particularly revealing about this picture is that in the foreground, just below the weed-infested embankment on which the building rests, is a 1963 or 64 junked Chevrolet Impala automobile. The car, resting partly on an old board, has no tires, no window in the front passenger's side, no hood, and no headlights. Litter is lying all around it on the dirt ground. Certainly a picture of the building could have been taken without the junked car, but the photograher (and by extension the editor), in capturing the car, is implicitly suggesting the poorness and ruralness of snake handlers (Wigginton 372).

Even as late as 1987 and 1991, when viewing the buildings where snake handlers worship, one is impressed by their rural, simplistic flavor. When reporting on snake handlers in 1987, ABC news showed the interiors of three meeting houses of snake handlers. One building in north Georgia had unpainted plywood ceilings, pressboard floors, and bare windows. Plaques and signs with slogans hung on the walls. The inside of another building in Haywood County, North Carolina, was small and was finished in white dry wall. Although the inside of the meeting house in Jolo, West Virginia, was the most modern with its paneled walls, tiled ceilings, and ceiling fans, it, too, was approximately the same size as the other buildings in the report and contained plagues and slogans on the walls. Although here one does not detect a conscious attempt on the part of ABC News to emphasize these buildings, one still receives the impression that snake handlers are simple, common folks with little financial wherewithal. When *A Current Affair*, on the other hand, reported in 1991 on the snake handlers of Jolo, West Virginia, it was careful to pan the countryside, consciously showing the simple homes and cars owned by the people in the community, before zooming in on the outside front of the Jolo church. It pictured a small building, approximately the same size as the buildings in photographs and news reports of other snake handlers. What was particularly revealing was the dirty white outside siding. An unprofessionally painted indistinguishable sign hung over the front door. Just outside the double front doors was a dirt and gravel parking lot. When reporters took their camera inside, they were careful to pan the interior, showing five or six rows of wooden pews and another two or three in the back which were blue. These pews were divided by a single narrow isle in the middle. A coat hung on a side wall. At one point, the camera paused momentarily on a pew occupied by five people, allowing the viewer to ingest the image of the people themselves. More will be said about these people's dress in a moment, but the point to be understood here is that, doubtless, the producer was trying to show viewers the simplicity and ruralness of snakehandling as seen in the objects surrounding them (*A Current Affair*; *Holy Ghost People*; Campbell 48; Daugherty 239; "Snake Handling" 29-32; Hunter 778; Gerrard 25-7).[2]

One of the most revealing pictures suggesting the poorness of snakehandlers is a color photograph in *The Knoxville Journal* of a Hamblin County, Tennessee church. Here is depicted a one story, tin-roof building made partly from stucco and block and partly from badly weathered boards. One is particularly taken by the chipped and curling paint on the eave of the front porch and the dirt ground in front of the steps. Barthes contends that the text accompanying photographs (e.g. headline, title, caption, etc.) "most often simply [amplifies] a set of connotations already given in the photograph" (Barthes 27). The text surrounding the above picture amplifies the image. The writer refers to it as "a hardscrabble place lined with rusted-out trailers in tramped-out, litter-strewn yards" near an "auto graveyard and car-shredding operation that has spit up a mountain of mangled vehicles" (Bean 1A). Hence, both picture and text suggest that those who attend church here are poor.

One can observe the standard of living of snake handlers not only in their meeting houses but also in their personal appearances. One of the earliest images that suggests snake handlers are people of meager means is found in *Life* magazine in 1944. Four pictures on the opening page of the story show closeups of four different people: three males and one female. All three males have weathered faces and unkept hair. All are wearing plain, white shirts. Two photographs show the men with open collars. The lone female has shoulder-length hair, no makeup, and no jewelry and is wearing a plain dress. The text surrounding these photographs refers to these people as "Virginia Mountaineers," "illiterate mountaineers," "Coal miners," and "self-appointed, unordained parson," thus emphasizing the image of common people. In fact, most photographs in periodicals analyzed in this study since 1944 show men with weathered, rudy complexions and open-collar shirts. Not a few have uncombed hair. Women are almost always depicted as having long hair (sometimes pinned up), no makeup or jewelry and wearing simple dresses. In the 1991 report by *A Current Affair*, when the camera was taken into the assembly at Jolo, West Virginia, as it panned the interior, pausing momentarily on the five congregants sitting on a pew, viewers saw three women wearing long hair, simple dresses, and no make up. One man wore an open collar shirt while another sported a bright blue wind-breaker jacket and rolled up shirt sleeves. *A Current Affair* also showed a closeup of a male snake handler judged to be approximately sixty to sixty-five years old whose face was wrinkled and weathered. Two of his lower front teeth were missing. He wore a brown flannel shirt. In fact several men in this report wore flannel shirts, which is typical of the dress of male snake handlers in other photographs. Uncombed hair fell across his forehead just above the left eye. Again, the image was that of a working- class, rural individual.

Snake Handlers as Uneducated

Perphaps the most salient image about snake handlers is that they are uneducated. At the beginning of the film *Holy Ghost People*, for example, after the narrator has introduced snake handlers and viewers are taken on a vicarious tour through the community to see their depressed living conditions, the film cuts to four monologues (each approximately two minutes long) of adherents of this religion. This is the producer's way of introducing the viewer to the personality of snake handlers. One quickly notices the low educational level of these people. All four have heavy rural accents and simplistic speech. The following testimony of one of the interviewees is typical of the way these individuals talk:

I got the Holy Ghost when I wuz about thirteen. And, uh, God was really good to me and, and, and, I had very much troubles. I'z a very mean feller and, its like, and, uh, but God wuz good to me, and he, he let me outta jail and I promised'eem if I got out at I would serve'eem. When I did get out it wuz probably month maybe two months before I ever repented, but when I did repent I could feel the quickenin' power that comes with the Holy Ghost. But I didn't have the evidence of speakin' in tongues like I had before. And, uh, I prayed to God fer might'en neared a year and seeked the Lord. And I thought that he wuz uh foolin' with me and I hadn't never got the pow'r back.... I wondered about the tongues see because without the evidence of speakin' in tongues why we we ain't got it see and that's, I, what, I wuz concerned with. And so, uh, I prayed and seeked God, and I couldn't get no piece of mind about it, and but course I would dance under the pow'r and the quickenin' pow'r would get on me but, thank God, one night it wuz in a meetin and it wuz a young girl 'air and she wuz a playin the pianer [pronounced pie-an-er] and, uh, she, uh, come off the platform and a cryin' and went to the alter and started repentin' and the Holy Ghost moved up on me and I went over and laid hands on her and the Holy Ghost come up on'er and she started speakin' in tongues, and I come outta there speakin' in tongues myself. I got, I got what I been lookin' fer. Thank the Lord. And ever since'en I been satisfied that God ain't been foolin' with me no more. I'm satisfied that he's really, uh, delivered me from all my...sins. Thank God. Thank God. (*Holy Ghost People*)

The image of snake handlers as uneducated can also be found in periodicals. In the *Saturday Evening Post*, for example, the caption over one picture of a man holding a fistful of snakes reads, "Holding a handful of writhing rattlesnakes aloft, a 'saint' proclaims his unique faith. 'We shore don' aim to get bit,' one cultist said. 'If it happens, hit just means we ain't been payin' attention to the Lord' " (Kobler 26). In 1947, *Time* showed a lone picture of an open-collar preacher holding two large rattlesnakes over his head. In an attempt to illustrate that the preacher was uneducated, the text below the picture reported the man as saying, "I ain't had this power but about a month now. But I got the power now—I got the 'nointing!" ("Any Deadly Thing" 25)

In an attempt to present the reader with some flavor of how contemporary snake handlers speak, thereby illustrating their degree of literacy, the caption beside the picture of a man holding open his Bible in *Foxfire 7* reads, "'Believin' is part of th'faith.... I can't understand why th'people can't see it. Right there it is in th' Bible. You boys ought'a read that and study that so's you can teach that and say, 'now people, that's the Lord's sayin'. Ain't it?' " Numerous quotes like this one can be found in the story accompanying the photographs in this work (Wigginton 373). In short, many of the texts surrounding the photographs suggest that snake handlers are uneducated and common people who inhabit rural areas of Appalachia. This becomes even more pronounced when one views the interviews conducted by television reporters. In attempting to justify the practice of snake handling, for example, Billy Summerford, a church member in West Virginia suggested in his heavy rural accent in an interview on *World News Tonight*, "If Jesus said, 'Thou shalt rassle grissle bears, I would rassle a grizzly' " (*World News Tonight*). Thus, the speech of these individuals, often captured on film, suggests not that they are not intelligent but that many of them are not highly educated.

Snake Handlers as Religious Aberrations

In addition to being portrayed as poor, uneducated individuals, snake handlers have also been depicted in visual media as extreme religious aberrations. In 1957, for instance, *Saturday Evening Post* showed six pictures of snake handlers, each containing no less than two snakes. One man was depicted as having five or six snakes draped around his neck. Others were shown with uplifted hands. In the lower right-hand corner of the lead photograph is a smaller photographic insert of a bottle of strychnine and a can with a wick in it. What appears to be a trick effect implies to the viewer that not only do these people handle snakes, but they also engage in other non-traditional practices of drinking poison and handling fire. The title under the picture reads, "America's Strangest

Religion." In this article, snake handlers are referred to as a "weird cult" who "test their faith against the serpent's sting." "Some die in agony," suggests the text, "but the rest come back for more." Words such as "unorthodox," "supercharged," "frenzy," "hysteria," and "excesses" permeate the text to describe these people (Kobler 26-7, 153-4).

In describing what takes place at a typical snake handling service, *Saturday Evening Post* recounts how one member "grasped the copperhead between his tattooed fingers." As the saints "surged around the open [snake] cages," they talked in tongues "jerking from head to feet." One member reportedly "thrust a rattler into his shirt front" while another "heaped a pair of rattlers on his head" and tied another one "into knots." He then dropped it to the ground before crouching over it and bringing "his smoldering eyes to within an inch of its darting tongue" (Kobler 153). Doubtless, the writer is attempting to amplify the images in the photographs through the accompanying text.

Similar images can be found in *Life* magazine. Eight out of ten photographs show people either handling snakes or fire. Several show individuals dancing around as they hold snakes aloft. The dominant picture on the first page of the story shows a large rattlesnake resting between the pages of an open bible held high in the air. The text which accompanies these pictures reinforce the images of religious aberrations. Expressions such as "glassy-eyed members of a religious cult" and "hysterical saints" describe these believers. The text also suggests that these people "scream in...a frenetic gibberish to which the cultists resort when their religous fervor moves them beyond intelligible speech." "Hysterical," "hypnotized," and "primitive emotional appeal" are other terms that help to reinforce the visual imagery. One caption under a man with a snake coiled around his neck reads, "Chanting and swaying as snake encircles neck, cultist seems hypnotized. Another man tore off shoes and trod on snake." The caption under another picture of a woman with her face to a fire protruding from a jar of kerosene reads, "In fanatic frenzy, girl passes her face through the flame." Clearly, the image portrayed in the photographs and in the texts is one of fanatacism and fringe religion (*Life* 59-62). The reader is left to wonder who in his or her right mind would perform such bizarre acts.

In film, the image of snake handlers as extreme religious aberrations is no different. One segment of *A Current Affair*, for instance, depicts a man in a red flannel shirt earnestly rubbing two snakes across his eyes and over his face while the reporter, Steve Dunleavy, satirically suggests, "Believers warn that if you are not certain that your destination is heaven, then please refrain from rolling snake eyes." In another segment, when focusing on how often those who are bitten actually die, *A Current Affair* showed the testimony of the mother of a 19-year-old girl who died after being bitten. What is revealing about this testimony—which is typical of other media testimonies—is the practice of not seeking medical help after a snakebite. "Well I knew she was in God's hands," said the woman. "I really didn't think, though, that she'd die.... We don't believe in a doctor but that's everybody's priviledge. Now we ast her if she wanted a doctor and she said no" (*A Current Affair*). Such testimonies give the viewer the impression that snake handlers are not typical, even among Pentecostals, because they will not see a doctor even when bitten by a poisonous snake and faced with the possibility of dying. Again, viewers are left to ponder just what type of person would refuse medical attention in a life-threatening situation.

Snake Handlers as Devout

Closely related to the above notion is the image that snake handlers are deeply religious. Perphaps this is best seen in some of the photographs in the magazine *Southern Voices*. Here snake handlers are often shown in soft focus, almost silhouette, with the sun or some point of bright light over their heads. One woman, for example, is depicted in soft focus with eyes closed and mouth open as if she were crying. Shining brightly on her forehead is a light from above her. The source of the light is not known, but the viewer is left with the impression that God, represented by the bright light, is pleased with her devotion since he is shining on her. Further, Fiske argues that soft focus is a "motivated sign for sentiment." In other words, soft focus equals soft-hearted (Fiske 85). Thus snake handlers are here depicted as being sincerely devout. Another picture shows a man standing with hands raised in praise against a white backdrop. Perhaps the photographer is trying to convey the notion of sincerity and love of God. The text that accompanies these photographs elaborates on the piousness depicted therein. In fact, the whole story surrounding these photographs is one contrasting the sincerity and piousness of snake handlers with that of supposedly stale, cold, mainline churches. The author notes, for example, that, "even in their errors and misinterpretations, they are closer to the truth of the Gospel than mainline Christianity and should be left alone" (Campbell 48).

Often snake handlers are depicted as being so devout that they are willing to disobey the laws of the land to practice their religion. The caption under a *Saturday Evening Post* photograph of several people holding large snakes reads, "Gathered on the Kentucky-Virginia state line—a point from which they easily elude police—believers manipulate timber rattlers and copperheads, chanting" (Kobler 27). In the text surrounding the photographs in *Southern Voices*, the writer relates how two snake handlers stood before a judge who warned the men not to handle snakes until after an appeal. The men reportedly responded, "But judge, we can't promise you that. We don't have the authority to promise you that" (Campbell 46).

Snake handlers' devotion can also be found in the pictures of their snake cages. These usually advertise a particular verse from the Bible or religious slogan. For example, one picture in *Trans-Action* shows a man from Scrabble Creek, West Virginia, opening a box that reads, among other things, "Galatians 6-2 to 9." Another picture shows a box that reads, "Are You Ready" (Gerrard 25, 17). Other photographs usually contain Bibles, showing their source of inspiration and suggesting their devotion to God's literal word (Maguire 168; Kobler 26-7; "Holiness Faith Healers" 59, 61; "Snake Handling" 29). Barthes argues that when analyzing the connotative messages of photographs, one should look at the pose of the subjects (Heath 22). Often snake handlers are shown in worship with their eyes closed, mouths open as if singing or praying, and hands held over their heads, thus signifying spirituality, purity, or devotion to God ("Snake Handling" 29-32; Gerrard 26). In film one also receives the impression that snake handlers are devout. For example, in 1987, in a report by ABC's *World News Tonight*, Bob Elkins, pastor of a snake handling church in Jolo, West Virginia, said, "We trust the Lord when we take'em up, and we trust the Lord to heal our bodies if they bite us." (*World News Tonight*) Clearly, the image that is often portrayed in visual media is that snake handlers are highly devoted to their religion.

Conclusion

While the primary intent of this essay has been to discuss images of snake handlers, a few points about the media that depict them should also be observed. First, snake handlers have received much coverage in visual media throughout the twentieth century. Second, more visual imagery about snake handlers is found in print media (i.e. magazines, journals, and newspapers) than in television and documentary film. Moreover, little if any portrayal of snake handlers is found in fictional films. Finally, while there is an occasional trick effect, an occasional photograph with manipulated lighting, exposure, and focus, and an occasional ordering of the photographs to relay a particular idea, by and large, most images emerge largely as a result of the poses of individuals, objects within photographs, and their accompanying texts. In fact more shaping of reality may come from contiguous texts than from the pictures themselves. The few film and television reports analyzed also relied heavily upon objects to introduce snake handlers to viewers. Moreover, there appears to be a conscious effort on the part of media to introduce snake handlers by showing viewers their physical surroundings, dress, and the like rather than through photogenia, trick effects, and syntax.

According to Barthes, these visual artifacts have symbolic significance. Fiske points out that in Barthes scheme, an object "becomes a symbol when it acquires through convention and use a meaning that enables it to stand for something else." A Rolls-Royce, for example, is a symbol of wealth. Hence, if a man were forced to sell his Rolls-Royce, this would be symbolic of the man's financial failure (Fiske 91).

Many of the objects found in photographs and films about snake handlers indicate poorness, simplicity, aberration, or commitment to one's faith. For example, the small, unattractive block buildings and modest homes that borderline on shacks which constantly appear signify simplicity and lack of wealth. Likewise, overalls, flannel shirts, and open collars worn by male snake handlers symbolize a type of agrarian simplicity. Just as a Rolls-Royce is a sign of wealth, junked cars and other debris seen in many of the photographs and films, symbolize poverty. Mayonnaise jars and fruit jars of strychnine and kerosene that occasionally emerge represent ordinariness. For women, long, straight hair symbolizes modesty and a fervent commitment on their part to I Corinthians 11:15, which teaches that long hair is a woman's "glory." Lack of makeup indicates lack of sophistication and perhaps a conscious effort not to become entangled in the fleeting vanities of this life. The absence of jewelry on both men and women might very well represent lack of sophistication but also suggests a lack of wealth. Like long hair, long, simple dresses symbolize modesty. Doubtless, poisonous snakes often seen in media represent the devil, and it is through taking up these serpents in an act of faith that snake handlers symbolically triumph over Satan, thus not only showing religious aberration but devotion. Bibles frequently found in visual media symbolize God's infallible word and the final authority for snake handlers' practice. Thus, snake handlers are shown to be biblical literalists. This is especially true whenever they are pictured holding snakes in open bibles held aloft as if to be showing God that they have faith in everything they read in His word, especially Mark 16: 17-18.

A final way that signs operate in the second order for Barthes is through myth. For him, a myth is—to use Fiske's words—"a story by which a culture explains or understands some aspect of reality or nature." It is "a culture's way of thinking about something, a way of conceptualizing or understanding it…a chain of related concepts." Visual imagery merely "activates the chains of concepts that constitute the myth" (Fiske 87-8). If this be the case, then the myth of snake handlers as told by photographs and films for the last 60 years is not a flattering one. Society probably views them as poor, uneducated whites who live in rural areas and who are strangely devout.

In 1981, Maguire wrote that "over the next few years" scholars will be given the chance to test Gerrard's hypothesis that snake handlers engage in such activities because it is "one of the few meaningful goals in a future dominated by the apparent inevitability of lifelong poverty and idleness." Maguire believed that, for the first time, snake handlers are "enjoying middle-class prosperity" due to "high-paying jobs" resulting from the revitalization of coal-mining. She also pointed out that their children are receiving more education than they once did (Maguire 178). If this be the case and if snake handlers continue their practice, it will be interesting to see how, if any, their images in visual media change in the coming decades.

Notes

[1]The film *Next of Kin* was also analyzed but not used in this study because, although there were scenes of an individual handling snakes, it was not done in a religious setting. Therefore, I choose to exclude this film.

[2]For similar images of the churches of snake handlers, see "Holy Ghost People, " Campbell 48, Daugherty 239, "Snake Handling" 29-32, Hunter 778, and Gerrard 25-27.

Works Cited

A Current Affair. ABC, WWAY. Wilmington, N.C., 17 July 1991.
"Any Deadly Thing." *Time* 8 Sept. 1947: 25.
Bean, Betty. "Church Mum on Snakebite Death." *The Knoxville Journal* 16 July 1991: 1A, 7A.
Campbell, Will D. "Come: A Study of Appalachian Folk Religion." *Southern Voices*. Mar./April 1974: 41-48.
Daugherty, Mary Lee. "Serpent-Handling as Sacrament." *Theology Today*. 33.3 (1976): 232-43.
Eco, Umberto. "On the Contribution of Film to Semiotics." *Film Theory and Criticism*. Eds. Gerald Mast and Marshall Cohen. New York: Oxford UP, 1979: 231.
Fiske, John ed. *Introduction to Communication Studies*. 2nd ed. New York:

Routledge, 1990: 85.

Gerrard, Nathan L. "The Serpent-Handling Religions of West Virginia." *Trans-Action*. 5.6 (May, 1968): 22.

Heath, Stephen, trans. *Image, Music, Text*. By Roland Barthes. New York: Hill and Wang, 1977: 15.

"Holiness Faith Healers: Virginia Mountaineers Handle Snakes to Prove Their Piety." *Life*. 3 July 1944: 59-62.

Holy Ghost People, (video) dir. Peter Adair, producer Blair Boyd, 1983.

Hunter, Harold D. "Serpent Handling." *Dictionary of Pentecostal and Charismatic Movements*. Eds. Stanley M. Burgess and Gary B. McGee. Grand Rapids, MI: Regency Reference Library, 1988: 778.

Kane, Steven M. "Holy Ghost People: The Snake-Handlers of Southern Appalachia." *Appalachian Journal* (Spring, 1974): 260.

_____. "Ritual Possession in a Southern Apalachian Religious Sect." *Journal of American Folklore* 87 (1974): 293.

_____. "Snake Handlers," *Encyclopedia of Religion in the South*. Ed. Samuel Hill Macon, GA: Mercer UP, 1984: 699.

Kimsey, Don. "The Jaws of Death: Snake Handler's Tragic End" *The Atlanta Journal* 8 Jan. 1973: 9D.

Kobler, John. "America's Strangest Religion." *Saturday Evening Post* 28 Sept. 1957: 26-27, 153-54, 156.

LaBarre, Weston. *They Shall Take Up Serpents: Psychology of the Southern Snake-Handling Cult*. New York: Schocken Books, 1969: 12.

Lippy, Charles H. *Bibliography of Religion in the South*. Macon, GA: Mercer UP, 1985: 304-05.

Maguire, Marsha. "Confriming the Word: Snake-Handling Sects in Southern Appalachia." *Quarterly Journal of the Library of Congress* 38 (1981): 174.

Medhurst, Martin J. and Thomas W. Benson, eds. *Rhetorical Dimensions in Media: A Critical Casebook*. Dubuque, IA: Kendall/Hunt Publishing Company, 1984: vii-viii.

"Snake Handling." *Appalachian Heritage* (Spring 1978): 29-32.

Wigginton, Elliot. "The People Who Take Up Serpents." *Foxfire 7*. Ed. Paul Gillespie. New York: Anchor P, 1982: 370-428.

World News Tonight. reported by Al Dale, ABC, WRTV. Indianapolis, Feb. 1987.

Words as Power:
Noah Webster and the Politics of Language

GARY L. JONES

If "In the beginning was the Word," as the Bible teaches us, language, as countless politicians and ministers have recently demonstrated, may be the universal music. A picture may be worth a thousand words, as the proverb attests, but there are far more people working in words than in pictures. Words are the power of politics. With them rides success, without them failure.

While most people in the United States today are accustomed to using the name *Webster* as a synonym for the word *dictionary*, few know of the man to whose dictionary they refer. That his first name was Noah, not Daniel and that he may rightly be regarded one of America's Founding Fathers are facts not a part of American popular culture. Despite the success of the great *An American Dictionary of the English Language*, which even today stands as a monument to the man, Americans have, by and large, paid only the scantest attention to Webster's contributions to the emerging American republic, a contribution that went far beyond the compilation of his great dictionary.

But it is not just the "common folk" who have been inattentive to Webster; scholars too have failed to note his contribution. It is not only that his contribution to the development of the American polity and to a distinctly American culture has been "forgotten" as has been argued is the case with his contributions to the study of language (Southard 12). Rather, his contribution to political life and thought has been, it would seem, summarily dismissed and ignored by historians of the subject. An examination of the standard histories of American political thought reveals only passing reference to—never any extended treatment of—Webster.

The neglect of this incredibly versatile and prolific writer is doubly unfortunate, for not only does Webster's thought have a particular relevance for an understanding of the development of contemporary American political culture, it contains some remarkable insights, even if only dimly perceived, into the nature and function of politics and the role of the political theorist himself.

To be sure, Webster did, in large part, bring this neglect on himself. First of all is the personality of the man himself. Throughout his life he was self righteous, dogmatic, and given to self-promotion in all that he wrote (*Noah Webster's American Spelling Book* 15). In old age, he became bitter, cantankerous, and unpleasant, all of which stem from his realization that he had drifted outside the mainstream of American life and thought and, perhaps more importantly, that he was not receiving the welcome into the nation's ruling circles that he so ardently sought. Secondly, during the course of his life he was attracted by, reflected upon, and wrote about an extraordinary number of subjects: history, politics, language, science, journalism, and education. In some, such as his theories on the spread of pestilential diseases, his observations were rather far-fetched; in others, such as his theory of government, rather pedestrian and unoriginal. The net effect was the creation of the image of a dilettante rather than of someone to be taken seriously.[1] Finally, there is, what may be called, the apparent failure of political programs that he himself thought was manifested in the election of Thomas Jefferson in 1800 and the rise of political parties.

But perhaps the most important reason for failing to note Webster's importance has to do with the success of his dictionary itself. It was to become so firmly established as *the* American dictionary that all of Webster's other accomplishments are obscured in its shadow—even his *The American Spelling Book*, which, during its time, was an immensely popular book selling over one hundred million copies in more than 150 editions. Were it not for our failure to grasp the "political" character of that astonishing accomplishment, Webster would surely be known to us today as an important contributor to the American founding.

Long before he ever began work on his famous dictionary (he was 70 when it was published), Webster had established himself as a leading (some would say notorious) representative of nationalistic and, later, Federalist thought. For nearly 20 years, from 1782 to 1800, he toiled with enthusiasm and dedication to instill in the hearts and minds of his fellow Americans the political ideals and principles acquired in his youth— particularly those acquired in the revolutionary and nationalistic atmosphere of Yale College in the 1770s. As a fervent Federalist writer, and later editor, Webster was deeply involved in the political affairs of the emerging new nation, "joining Alexander Hamilton, John Jay, Rufus King, Oliver Wolcott, Jr., and others in their attempts to control, direct, and contain the flow of events" (Rollins 1).

During this period Webster wrote several essays which were explicitly political in content. In "Observations on the Revolution in America" (1783) and "Sketches of American Policy" (1785) he sought to defend the American Revolution and to set a new course for the United States. "An Examination into the Leading Principles of the Federal Constitution" (1787) was an eloquent and impassioned defense of the new Constitution which, as Robert Peters has noted, "does not suffer by comparison with certain numbers of the *Federalist Papers*" (*A Collection of Essays and Fugitiv Writings*). But as time wore on Webster became increasingly less hopeful about the future course of the political system. "The best evidence of this increased anxiety," Richard Moss writes:

was his 1794 essay *The Revolution in France*.... On the surface, the essay (published as a pamphlet) seems a calm consideration of the impact and future consequences of revolution in France, but a deeper reading reveals Webster's growing concern about the changes taking place in American life. (*Noah Webster* 62)

By 1800, with the success of the Jeffersonian forces, Webster's disillusionment with the course of American politics was complete and he embarked upon a new strategy; that which would eventually result in the publication of his dictionary in 1828.

But it is precisely at his point that historians and Webster's biographers go astray. Typical of the misunderstanding of this new strategy are the following assessments by the editors of collections of his essays:

Disillusioned by what he considered the demoralization of American politics, Webster turned, with the century, from political action to moral criticism, his shining vision of the new America tarnished. With increasing piety and diminishing humanness, Webster moved away from the affairs of men to the pursuits of the mind and the spirit. (*On Being American* 4)

And:

His withdrawal to New Haven in 1798, an act of great significance in Webster's life, was a symbolic retirement to the sidelines of national affairs and marked the beginning of the career that made him famous. His political comments, thereafter, though frequent and militant, served only to emphasize his failure to follow in the flood of democratic sentiment that was sweeping America. (*On Being American* 10)

And, finally:

Hamilton's ascendancy within the Federalist party after 1797 and Jefferson's election in 1800 soured Webster on politics and drove him to the privacy of his study, where his great dictionary of 1828 was to take shape. (*A Collection of Essays and Fugitiv Writings* 1)

What these observers fail to grasp is that Webster was not, in 1800 and thereafter, dropping out of the political affairs of the new nation, he was simply moving to a new *political* sphere, that of the mind and, more basically, language. The failure to grasp the political impulse (an impulse of which Webster was, if only intuitively, aware) which drove him after 1800 is the result of too narrow a conception of what politics is and of the relation of theory to practice.

The point being made here can perhaps be best understood by referring to the political thought of Antonio Gramsci, who was much more explicit on these matters than was Webster. What is probably the most important aspect of his political theory for our purposes is his broadening of the conception of the state and politics.

For Gramsci, politics and the state are not and cannot be reduced to force. He recognized, as few political theorists since the Greeks seem to, that in politics more is involved than power. It is true, he wrote, that "the first element [of politics] is that there really do exist rulers and ruled, leaders and led. The entire science and art of politics are based on this primordial, and (given certain conditions [those of class society]) irreducible fact" (*Selections from the Prison Notebooks* 352). But, the exercise of coercive force is not the only, nor is it even the most important, form of political activity. In fact, to focus on the pursuit and exercise of power, or the coercive apparatus of society, i.e., government, laws, and "policies," obscures more than it explains.

Thus, the theory of politics developed by Gramsci conceives political activity as being more complex than the simple exercise of brute force and has as its core ingredient a theory of hegemony—a theory which seeks an explanation of the foundations of social and political life not in the coercive apparatus of the state alone, but in cultural phenomena as well.

The basic premise of the theory of hegemony as developed by Gramsci in his prison notes, and, as we shall see, anticipated by Webster, is deceptively simple and is one with which few people would disagree: "That man is not ruled by force alone, but also by ideas" (Bates 351). Gramsci understood, as perhaps only Thorstein Veblen before him had, "that the rule of one class over another does not depend on economic or physical power alone but rather on persuading the ruled to accept the system of beliefs of the ruling class and to share its social, cultural, and moral values" (Joll 16). There are, then, in Gramsci's analysis, at least two basic forms of exercising political rule: direct domination and hegemony (*Selections from the Prison Notebooks* 57-58).

As a form of expressing the supremacy of the dominant class, hegemony is an intellectual and moral leadership based on the consent of the led, a consent which is obtained through the diffusion and popularization of the world view of the dominant class (Bates 352). It refers to the "spontaneous" loyalty that any dominant class obtains from the masses by virtue of its social and intellectual prestige and its supposedly superior function in the world of production—perceptions carefully manufactured by the dominant class itself. The world view of the dominant class exerts a directive influence on the subaltern classes, as Gramsci called them, precisely because they have embraced it as their own. In fact, the aspirations, beliefs, needs, in sum the entire life of the subaltern classes is impregnated with the ideology of the dominant class. Thus, the cultural leadership—i.e., the intellectual and moral direction—of the dominant social grouping is an important mechanism for performing the vital function of preserving a sense of ideological unity or, perhaps more precisely, harmony in the community and results in less reliance on coercive power, i.e., force, as a form of political and social control.

Recognition of the importance of cultural leadership and influence led Gramsci to reassess the nature of the state which could no longer be reduced to the instruments of force. This reassessment resulted in the identification of two great levels or compartments of the state. In this respect he wrote:

What we can do, for the moment, is to fix two major superstructural 'levels': the one can be called 'civil society,' that is the ensemble of organisms commonly called 'private,' and that of 'political society' or 'the state.' These two levels correspond on the one hand to the function of 'hegemony' which the dominant group exercises throughout society and on the other hand to that of 'direct domination' or command exercised through the State and 'juridical government.' (*Selections From the Prison Notebooks* 12)

And:

...the State is the entire complex of practical and theoretical activities with which the ruling class not only justifies and maintains its dominance, but manages to win the active consent of those over whom it rules. (*Selections From the Prison Notebooks* 244)

"Political society" is composed of all those public institutions—the government, courts, police, and army—which are involved and employed in direct domination, i.e., the formulation and enforcement of "public policies." "Civil society," on the other hand, is composed of all those "private organisms"—schools, churches, social clubs, newspapers and magazines, and, now, television—that contribute to the formation of social and political consciousness, to the definition of reality in a given society. As Thomas Bates has suggested, "civil society is the marketplace of ideas, where intellectuals enter as 'salesmen' of contending cultures. The intellectuals succeed in creating hegemony to the extent that they extend the world view of the rulers to the ruled, and thereby secure the 'free' consent of the masses to the law and order of the land" (353). That is, hegemonic rule is rule by consent, but that consent is not really free—it is manufactured or created. In this regard Gramsci writes:

> Ideals and opinions are not spontaneously 'born' in each individual brain: they have a centre of formation, of irradiation, of dissemination, of persuasion,—a group of men, or a single individual even, which has developed them and presented them in the political form of current reality. (*Selections From the Prison Notebooks* 192, cf 259)

Hegemony is present, and society is, in consequence, stable, when the underlying population has embraced the world view of the dominant class as their own (i.e., when it has become the "common sense" of the society); and it is this acceptance of the received ideas that makes the subaltern classes willing participants in their own subjugation.

Consequently, any class aspiring to supremacy "will always attempt to secure a hegemonic position, i.e., to gain political legitimacy by weaving its own cultural outlook deeply into the social fabric"; (Adamson 149) and once the world view of the group has trickled down and solidified into "common sense" its position of supremacy is secure. However, its position of superiority, once attained, can only be maintained through the most careful attention to its hegemonic position. It must, if it wishes to sustain the existing class relationships, take pains to assure that the hegemonic world view that sustains those relationships is coherently produced and disseminated throughout the whole of society.

Obviously, then, the most important "political" activity of the dominant social group is an educative and formative one. Politics must become more than the simple exercise of coercive power, it must become, as well, an act of persuasion; it must become an essentially educational activity. As V.G. Kiernan has pointed out:

> In practical terms, Gramsci attached very great importance to education. He might be called an educationalist to his fingertips, for whom schoolroom-learning and politics, culture and the conduct of life, were all parts of one endeavor. ("The Socialism of Antonio Gramsci")

By "educating" the masses the dominant social group interposes an intervening variable, a "filter" so to speak, between the masses and the objective situation made up of all sorts of wants, expectations, and dreams which screens out certain parts of the objective situation and emphasizes others. By so doing, it gains a common acceptance of a particular conception of reality, one which justifies, even demands, its continued supremacy. What needs to be emphasized in this regard is that this educative activity is fundamentally political and constitutes an important activity of the "state." As Gramsci explains it:

The enormous development of activity and organization of education in the broad sense in the societies that emerged from the medieval world is an index of the importance assumed in the modern world by intellectual functions and categories. (*Selections From the Prison Notebooks* 10)

And:

...the state is not agnostic but has its own conception of life and has the duty of spreading it by educating the national masses. But this formative activity of the state, which is expressed particularly in the education system, as well as in political activity generally, does not work upon and fill up a blank slate. In reality, the state competes with and contradicts other explicit and implicit conceptions, and folklore is not among the least significant and tenacious of these; and hence it must be "overcome." (Gramsci 191)

The all important task of "educating" the subaltern groups falls on the shoulders of the intellectuals who act as salesmen in the marketplace of ideas. Thus it is the intellectuals who are the central actors in the political arena for it is they who, in the final analysis, secure the predominance of one class or group over others by establishing that group's claim to be the *de facto* ruling class by virtue of its superior qualities in the realm of culture, politics, and ethics. Through their efforts, the perceptions and interests of the privileged group—the rulers—become the basis for moral judgment and action of the lower social orders.

Now, one of the most important, or rather most fundamental, ways in which this is accomplished is through establishing and maintaining a "national" language. Since, as Robert Pattison has suggested, "in practice our notions of order in the world and in ourselves are inseparable from the language in which we frame them," (*On Literacy* 22) language presents us with an important and potent instrument of political power, for by imposing their norms of language use and their notion of "literacy" upon society, the dominant social group is able to impose their values and beliefs on society at large. Language is, in other words, a central ingredient in the hegemonic apparatus of society, serving as the bedrock of its unity. Any group, then, wishing to gain a position of dominance in a society must seek, in all ways possible, to establish its linguistic usage as the only one worthy of becoming the "common" language of the nation, proclaiming its universality and emphasizing the parochialism of all others. Clearly, then, while insistence on "correct" linguistic usage may appear on the surface to be nothing more than academic pedantry and/or a form of snobbery, it proves to be, from this perspective, a profoundly political act.

Admittedly, this discussion of Gramsci's theory of hegemony, as incomplete as it has been, has proven to be a rather long digression. It, has, however, been necessary in order to establish the proper perspective for discerning and assessing the nature and importance of Webster's contribution to American political thought and culture and its relevance is, hopefully, evident. That is, it is only through the notion of hegemony that we are able to see that Webster's whole life was dedicated to the achievement of a particular social and political vision.

If we persist in the traditional habit of breaking Webster's career into two discrete periods—an early "political" period and a second, after 1800, in which he was engaged in purely "literary pursuits" we are doomed to misunderstand his political thought and to seriously underestimate his genius and the nature and importance of his contribution to the American polity. It is true that Webster was disappointed in his failure to get his political program written into the laws and policies of the land and that this led him to become less optimistic about the capacities of the American people to govern themselves. But his dismay over what he called the demoralization of American politics did not cause him to lose faith in his vision. His "withdrawal" to the "privacy of his study," while a result of disillusionment, did not constitute a retreat from politics; it was but a change in tactics, a shift in emphasis from what Gramsci terms the arena of "political society" to that of "civil society."

While it is true that Webster did not explicitly spell out a theory of hegemony as Gramsci was later to do, it is evident from his voluminous writings that he did indeed grasp, even if only intuitively, the essentials of such a theory and that, more importantly, he acted upon them throughout the whole of his writing career. Once this is recognized it is possible to discover the unity in the multifarious writings he produced over his lifetime and to more adequately assess his contribution to American political thought and culture.

His explicitly political writings, while important for understanding his response to the events of the times, are but one aspect of his political thought (Moss 116).[2] His writings on history, geography, science, education, and language are equally important aspects of his political thought. as Richard Moss has written:

Almost everything Webster wrote had a political element in it. His schoolbooks, for example, were intended to educate children, but they were also political tracts designed to create a certain political attitude. As a journalist, politics was never very far from his mind. Even his dictionaries were political. They were motivated by feelings of nationalism and a desire to use language to create a stable republic. (Moss 49)

Once the political character of these other writings is grasped it is possible to note Webster's awareness that men are not ruled by the force of law alone, but also by ideas. Nowhere is Webster's grasp of the idea of hegemonic rule more evident than in his thoughts on language. Clearly, as early as 1783 Webster was aware of the importance of language as an instrument of hegemonic political rule. With his *A Grammatical Institute of the English Language: Part I* (that is the *American Spelling Book*) Webster sought "to promote the honor and prosperity of the confederated republics of America" by providing a national standard of American English. In this regard he wrote in the preface:

In the progress of society and improvement, some gradual changes must be expected in a living language, and corresponding alterations in elementary books of instruction become indispensible: but it is desirable that these alterations should be as few as possible, for they occasion uncertainty and inconvenience. And although perfect uniformity in speaking is not probably attainable in any living language, yet it is to be wished that the youth of our country may be, as little as possible, perplexed with various differing systems and standards. Whatever may be the difference of opinion among individuals respecting a few particular words, or the particular arrangement of a few classes of words, the general interest of education requires that a disposition to multiply books and systems for teaching the language of the country should not be indulged to an unlimited extent. (*Noah Webster's American Spelling Book* 18)

The ideas implicit in that work are made explicit in two later collections of essays, *Dissertations on the English Language* (1789) and *A Collection of Essays and Fugitiv Writings* (1790). In the latter he wrote principally of the importance of education:

The education of youth is, in all governments an object of the first consequence. The impressions received early in life, usually form the characters of individuals; a union of which forms the general character of a nation.

The mode of education and the arts taught to youth, have, in every nation, been adapted to its particular stage of society or local circumstances. (*A Collection of Essays and Fugitiv Writings* 1)

America is, in this regard at a particularly critical juncture because it is but on the brink of nationhood:

While these States were a part of the British Empire our interest, our feelings, were those of Englishmen; our dependence led us to respect and imitate their manners, and to look up to them for our opinions. We little thought of any national interest in America; and while our commerce and governments were in the hands of our parent country, and we had no common interest, we little thought of improving our acquaintance with each other, or of removing prejudices, and reconciling the discordant feelings of the inhabitants of different Provinces. (*A Collection of Essays and Fugitiv* 35)

Further:

Our constitutions of civil government are not yet firmly established; our national character is not yet formed; and it is an object of vast magnitude that systems of education should be adopted and pursued, which may not only diffuse a knowledge of the sciences, but may implant, in the minds of the American youth, the principles of virtue and of liberty; and inspire them with just and liberal ideals of government, and with an inviolable attachment to their own country. (*A Collection of Essays and Fugitiv* 3)

The American republics may have achieved independence from Great Britain through political and military means, but their future political and commercial prosperity, and, we might add, the fate of the newly established national government among them, hinges on their establishing a sense of nationhood, that is, a national identity; and the principle vehicle by which this is to be accomplished is education.

Webster's immediate concern here is, of course, with the future of America and with the implementation of a particular social and political vision, but it is important to note that the principle upon which he proceeds is, in his mind, universal: "there is," he maintains, "no state in which [education] has not an inseparable connection with morals, and a consequential influence upon the peace and happiness of society (*A Collection of Essays and Fugitiv* 3).

Education will bring about the peace and happiness of society by transmitting to its members a particular, or more appropriately, a common world view. Now, if the members of a society "are to acquire *ideas*, it is certainly easier to obtain them in a language they understand, than in a foreign tongue (Webster, *A Collection of Essays and Fugitiv* 7; cf *On Being American* 170). This being the case, the question of language, or more precisely, language use and language instruction, becomes the quintessential political question, and this is precisely the conclusion to which Webster is drawn. In an essay entitled "A Dissertation Concerning the Influence of Language on Opinions and of Opinions on Language," written in 1788, he argues:

> But if it can be proved that the *mere use of words* has led nations into error, and still continues the delusion, we cannot hesitate a moment to conclude, that grammatical enquires are worthy of the labor of men. (*A Collection of Essays and Fugitiv* 222)

There is more, however, to the study of language than its contribution, as important as that may be, to a liberal education, it must lead also to "an adequate idea of the influence which a uniformity of speech may have on national attachment," (*Dissertations on the English Language* 33) for the political harmony of any community is "concerned in a uniformity of language" (*Dissertations on the English Language* 20). Uniformity in language is, in the end, the glue which holds society together and he who would determine the course of social life would bend every effort to "discovering" and disseminating "the *rules of language itself*, and [elaborating] *the general practice of the nation* [which] constitute propriety in speaking" (*Dissertations on the English Language* 27). By controlling language one is enabled to control and direct the opinions of men and thereby their behavior as well.

Notes

[1]Indeed, this is the conclusion to which Richard J. Moss in an otherwise sympathetic treatment is seemingly drawn.

[2]If Webster's status as a political theorist were to be based solely on the theoretical powers of his explicitly political writings, we could but conclude that he was not a particularly powerful political thinker. His "Observations on the Revolution in America," "Sketches of American Policy," "An Examination into the Leading Principles of the Federal Constitution," and "The Revolution in France" while illuminating and often eloquent simply are not great political theory—paling to insignificance when compared to the contributions of Hamilton, Madison and Jefferson.

Works Cited

Adamson, Walter L. *Hegemony and Revolution: Antonio Gramsci's Political and Cultural Theory*. Berkeley: U of California P, 1980.

Bates, Thomas R. "Gramsci and the Theory of Hegemony." *Journal of the History of Ideas*. 36 (April-June, 1975): 351-366.

Gramsci. Antonio. *Selections from Cultural Writings*. Ed. David Forgacs and Geofrrey Nowell-Smith and trans. William Buelhower. Cambridge: Harvard UP, 1985.

_____. *Selections From the Prison Notebooks*. Ed and trans. Quintin Howell and Geoffrey Nowell Smith. New York: International Publishers, 1971.

Joll, James. *Antonio Gramsci*. New York: Penguin Books, 1978.

Moss, Richard J. *Noah Webster*. Boston: Twayne Publishers, 1984.

Pattison, Robert. *On Literacy: The Politics of the Word from Homer to the Age of Rock*. New York: Oxford UP, 1982.

Rollins, Richard M. *The Long Journey of Noah Webster*. Philadelphia: U of Pennsylvania P, 1980.

Southard, Bruce. "Noah Webster: America's Forgotten Linguist." *American Speech*. 54 (Spring 1979): 12-22.

Kiernan, V.G. "The Socialism of Antonio Gramsci." *Essays on Socialist Humanism*. Ed. Ken Coats. Nottingham: Spokesman Books: 63-89.

Webster, Noah. *A Collection of Essays and Fugitiv Writings 1790*. Intro. by Robert K. Peters. Delmar, NY: Scholar's Facsimiles and Reprints, 1977.

_____. *Dissertations on the English Language*. Intro by Harry R. Warfel. Gainesville, FL: Scholar's Facsimiles & Reprints, 1951.

_____. *Noah Webster's American Spelling Book*. New York: Bureau of Publications, Teachers College, Columbia U, 1962.

_____. *On Being American: Selected Writings, 1783-1828*. Introduction. By Homer D. Babbidge Jr. New York: Frederick A. Praeger Publishers, 1967.

Crime and Detection Writing:
Expanding Mirror of Society

RAY B. BROWNE

Whether crime is the result or cause of the criminal, there is no doubt that society is getting heavy with the cause and the effect. Where there is a phenomenon there undoubtedly will be an author writing on the subject. There can be no doubt that crime is very much with us daily and nightly. What authors have to say on the subject reveals their state of mind and the culture in which they live. They may also be revealing a very grim future.

Crime fiction under the name of the detective genre dates from the short stories of Edgar Allan Poe in the nineteenth century ("The Murders in the Rue Morgue," 1841; "The Mystery of Marie Roget," 1842-43; "The Purloined Letter," 1844). But stories of the commission of crimes and the apprehension and punishment of the criminals are as old as even the earliest societies.

Western—that is Christian—society has been dominated from the start by the violence associated with the beginning of mankind as reported in the Bible. Apparently mankind has always rebelled against restrictions. The first record of man's breaking the law and the resulting interrogation and punishment comes in Genesis, when God questions Adam about being ashamed of being naked: "Who told thee that thou wast naked? Has thou eaten of the tree, whereof I commanded thee that thou shouldst not eat?" God pressed the issue. Then he interrogated Eve about how she discovered that she and Adam were naked. Had she broken the law and eaten of the tree of knowledge? Punishment of having broken the law was swift and severe—expulsion from the Garden of Eden, the longest life-sentence on record!

In this same tradition the first family was the setting for the first murder, when Cain killed his brother Abel, and was the scene of the first murder investigation, when God questioned Cain about his fratricide. "What has thou done? The voice of thy brother's blood crieth unto me from the ground," He said. Then God rendered the first recorded judgment

217

and sentence, in the Christian tradition, for murder without trial by jury. Fratricides are common in primitive cultures (especially in Greek, Buddhist, Irish, Icelandic and Maroi) (Thompson) and generally have been dealt with summarily, as Cain's was. God's first judgment set a precedent for later recorders of murders, especially in American hard-boiled detection fiction. God's icy judgment drove such a writer as Mickey Spillane to unrelenting execution. He borrowed the title of one of his books from the Bible—*Vengeance is Mine!* (1950; "Vengeance is mine; I will repay, saith the Lord." Romans XII, 19)—and replicated God's behavior in his first novel, *I, The Jury* (1947).

In this earliest of his crime novels, Spillane has Mike Hammer, his detective, gut-shoot his lover, Charlotte Manning, as she temptingly undresses before him, like Eve, after he determined that she had murdered his best friend, a man who had lost an arm defending him in the South Pacific during World War II. Hammer's comments as he executes Charlotte sound like the judgment of God: "No, Charlotte, I'm the jury now, and the judge, and I have a promise to keep. Beautiful as you are, as much as I almost loved you, I sentence you to death." Hammer's determination to act as detective-judge-executioner permeated all of Spillane's detective fiction and has remained, though with much less intensity, in much hard-boiled crime fiction down to today. This tradition of making the criminal pay for his/her crime is one of the major characteristics distinguishing American crime fiction from that of other countries. In the British puzzle-type crime fiction, for example, finding the culprit satisfies the author and reader in solving the puzzle. In the American style, however, perhaps driven by a puritanical social involvement society dictates that the guilty must pay for their crimes. Generally the detective turns the criminal over to the society for prosecution, instead of being judge as well as jury. American society needs to be cleansed of the corruption, the authors seem to be saying, and this demands prosecution. But the fire for prosecution is tempered by an empathy and humanity which insists that the victim and society understand motivations. "That crime, but for the grace of God, I might have committed," seems a precautionary proverb in the minds of most Americans, especially as society becomes increasingly competitive and driven by the hopes of accomplishment by all individuals.

In societies other than the Judeo-Christian the mystery has long traditions also. For centuries the Sphinx, for example, crouched on the Egyptian sands, asked passersby a simple question ("What walks on four feet in the morning, two at noon and three in the evening?") and executed those so unaware of symbols and metaphors that they did not know the answer. The Sphinx' riddle was a common motif in other cultures, especially the Greek, Persian and Hindu (Thompson). Execution for ignorance, like execution of a messenger for delivering bad news, though it seems harsh, has persisted through time since the beginning of frustration and unhappiness at the outcome of events, and it continues to drive the violence of many societies today.

From the beginning in all societies, it seems, violence and homicide—Darwin's law of survival of the fittest—have been endemic, a given of *homo sapiens* life, as in all forms of life. Through crime fiction we might understand the drives and rationales of violence, American authors increasingly are insisting, for if we do not understand the violence of the past we will be condemned to suffer from and perpetuate it.

Stories about crime and its aftermath have generally reflected the social attitudes of society. At first such stories were wrapped in large contexts, part of a larger story, though at times even a prime mover which was concerned with society in a larger setting. Melville's *Moby-Dick*, Dostoevsky's *Crime and Punishment* and Charles Dickens' various stories are excellent cases in point. Edgar Allan Poe, working for different ends, demonstrated that a great deal of intensity could be generated by reducing those elements which did not contribute directly to the development of the crime plot. For a hundred years afterwards English crime fiction—called closed-door, Golden-Age or "cozy" crime fiction— continued this tradition. Growing out of the remarkably successful stories of A. Conan Doyle and encouraged by the unparalleled success of Agatha Christie this type of detective fiction has gained great popularity.

But American crime fiction, after 50 years of following rather closely the English type in the works of such writers as S.S. Van Dine (Willard Huntington Wright) and John Dickson Carr changed course. In the middle of the nineteenth century, American popular writing in general developed a style strongly influenced by the vernacular prose of everyday life, and the hundreds of dime novels, taken over during the first half of the twentieth century by the pulp magazines, set the course for subject matter and treatment of crime fiction. Some of America's strongest popular writers of crime fiction developed in the pages of those cheap, thrilling magazines.

The change was given great impetus in the novels of such splendid writers as Dashiell Hammett (1894-1961) and, later, John D. MacDonald, who developed the American recognition of the artificiality of the British tradition and turned crime stories into a tradition that concerned the people who were a part of the crime scene. Raymond Chandler (1888-1959) voiced the American attitude when he wrote in his well-known manifesto, "The Simple Art of Murder," that murder is a dirty business, usually committed not in an English country house but on the mean streets of a city, and it should be written about and with that understanding and point of view. "It is not a fragrant world," he wrote, "but it is the world you live in, and certain writers with tough minds and a spirit of detachment can make very interesting...patterns of it." Chandler's story and detective are peculiarly American and, through that Americanness universal, as an extended quote from his statement demonstrates:

...Down these mean streets a man must go who is not himself mean, who is neither tarnished or afraid. The detective in this kind of story must be such a man. He is the hero, he is everything. He must be a complete man and a common man and yet an unusual man. He must be, to use a rather weathered phrase, a man of honor—by instinct, by inevitability, without thought of it, and certainly without saying it. He must be the best man in his world and a good enough man for any world. I do not care much about his private life; he is neither a eunuch nor a satyr; I think he might seduce a duchess and I am quite sure he would not spoil a virgin; if he is a man of honor in one thing he is that in all things.

...He is a relatively poor man, or he would not be a detective at all. He is a common man or he could not go among common people.... He talks as the man of his age talks—that is, with rude wit, a lively sense of the grotesque, a disgust for sham, and a contempt for pettiness.

The story is this man's adventure in search of a hidden truth, and it would be no adventure if it did not happen to a man fit for adventure. He has a range of awareness that startles you, but it belongs to him by right, because it belongs to the world he lives in. If there were enough like him, the world would be a very safe place to live in, without becoming too dull to be worth living in. (*The Simple Art of Murder*, 1950)

Though there is in this well-known statement much that will not stand up under present-day scrutiny—such as the "honor" and sexual restraint of the crime fighter—there is more than a mere liberalizing of the subject to be written about in crime fiction and a new language in which to write it. There is a realization that fiction—crime or any other—should not be a hot-house flower concerned only with an artificial existence and expressed in artificial language, but should instead be a chronicle of society. Crime fiction, at least in Chandler's eyes, is perhaps more nearly the fiction of the world than any other. "It belongs to the world [the detective writer] lives in," he said.

Chandler's statement had a liberalizing, genre-breaking influence on the kinds of crime fiction that has developed. British writers like P.D. James and Ruth Rendell, not to mention scores of others, have seen beyond the borders of their formula. But essentially the new subject of crime fiction and the way it is to be treated has been an American creation. Hundreds of American writers, those in pulp fiction, in paperback and hardback editions felt the new freedom and followed enthusiastically.

To American author Ross Macdonald (1915-1983) the main difference between the so-called elite novel and the popular one may be substantially in size of reading audience. He felt that the new-crafted novels of Hammett and Chandler equal those of any other writer in addressing the human situation. "I still believe that the subject of most modern novels including mystery novels is psychological truth in the widest sense, expressed more or less symbolically, and that social truth is best revealed by the novelist through individual characters and their conflicts," he wrote.

Because of such insights, Macdonald is perhaps the pivotal figure in opening crime fiction into general fiction. Through his plots, his symbols and metaphors, Macdonald demonstrated his compassion for all Americans, and through them for all people. His tool was popular crime stories.

I have a very strong feeling that it's the duty of a writer, or at least of this particular writer, to write popular fiction. Ideally, a community tends to communicate with itself through its fiction, and this communication tends to break down if there are Mandarin novels written for Mandarins and lowbrow novels written for lowbrows, and so on. My aim from the beginning has been to write novels that can be read by all kinds of people. (qtd. in Wolfe, Carroll 149)

Crime novelists, Macdonald said, have an awesome responsibility to society and are willing to shoulder it.

We are willing to accept responsibility [for society] and its attendant pains, responsibility for what happens to us and for what happens to other people. We are no longer spiritual colonials or provincials dependent on other men's experience for our knowledge of the world and of ourselves.... As we become custodians of the human conscience, it is scarcely surprising that self-examination and self-inculcation are the theme of so much modern American writing.... On the lower level, the mystery novel which deals honestly with private and public evil carries this theme to a mass audience.

Elsewhere he wrote that his purpose in writing was "to throw insight into lives," with a background that is "psychological and social rather than theological." His reach perhaps exceeded his grasp but not his desires. His books "explore guilt, justice, mercy, exile, new beginnings, the closed circuit of time, the family romance,...the tension between causality and revolt...and, crucially, the spider web of consequences spun from the abdomen of Oedipus" (qtd. in Wolfe, Leonard 2).

Most immediate of all, however, was Macdonald's realization that the American Frontier was disappearing, as it had been officially closed in 1890, and with it came a geographical tightening of the American Dream. Macdonald chose to situate his novels in Southern California because that is where the American Dreamer is faced with the hard realization that he/she can go westward no farther and is there congested like lemmings and must learn to live under these "un-American" conditions. In choosing this hot-house of crowded human conditions, Macdonald was prescient in anticipating a globe of 5-10 billion people where no one can move without jostling another, with the resulting irritation and vulnerability and bias toward violence.

With such precedents, crime fiction and the ever-growing audience that it continues to attract has in the last twenty years pushed toward a liberalizing, genre-breaking influence on the kinds of fiction that are developing. If authors of such a tightly structured genre of fiction as that about crime and punishment realize that they can break the rules by which it is written, they come to assume eventually that there are in fact no unbreakable rules of composition. As long as the subject matter remains recognizably the commission of crime (usually violent and generally murder, since murder is mankind's greatest concern) and a (usually) successful apprehension of the perpetrator, then the readers of crime fiction will have their wishes fulfilled.

The switch-off has not always been easy. Traditions in fiction die slowly, especially when tradition is as formulaic as that in crime fiction and has been immensely successful since Doyle's Sherlock Holmes and Christie's Hercule Poirot. With such success there seemed little need to change a successful formula, to tinker with a machine that was not broken.

But it is difficult to keep in line a large number of writers whose interests span the whole of existence. Their mere numbers threaten the boundaries of the genre. Though crime fiction tends to be written on contemporary affairs, especially by Americans, in fact there are at least 800 writers of all nationalities writing on historical events and historical characters. Ellis Peters, (Edith Pargeter) for example, writes on figures and episodes of the 12th century. The most famous case of such a book was Umberto Eco's *The Name of the Rose*, which centered on a 14th century figure and events in the Italy of that time. Numerous authors use historical figures, like Lillian De La Torre who has Dr. Samuel Johnson—of the 18th century British Dictionary fame—as her protagonist, and Robert Lee Hall has Benjamin Franklin snooping around amongst murderers.

Most authors, however, tend to write most of the time on contemporary events and figures because by and large readers are most interested in the present or the immediate past. There are additionally at least 100 writers who tie in their crime fiction to the future. Foremost perhaps among such writers is Isaac Asimov, whose books demonstrate the author's projection of today's society into a more advanced technological age, and his detectives are therefore concerned with using advanced technology in their efforts to solve crimes.

But it is not the science fiction writers of crime fiction who are advancing the genre to its fullest. Horizons in the genre are being pushed back most successfully by authors interested in the humanities[1]—in mankind's plight and relationship with one another, with genders, with race and nationalities.

There are, as mentioned earlier, numerous writers in the British tradition who are doing it successfully. But advances in the genre of crime fiction are most dramatically being made in American crime fiction, more than in any other language. This is not difficult to understand since there are more Americans writing—by a three to one margin—than those of any other country. American writers are responding to several new-found freedoms.

In the first place, many new voices and an increased volume from areas long under-represented are being heard. There are at least 100 female authors working today and the number is growing more rapidly than that for men. There are Canadian, Japanese, Russian, German authors producing today. Australian aboriginals have at least two major voices in Arthur Upfield, of whose 36 books 29 concern the super mental power of the half-black-half-white detective Bony, and Jon Cleary, who has written on every aspect of life including the adventures of an out-back Aborigine police officer. Afro-Americans through the years have had several spokespersons, including whites Ed Lacy (1911-1968) and Judson Philips (b. 1903), and popular African-American writer Rita Mae Brown, currently writing. The most powerful Afro-American voice of crime fiction was Chester Himes (1909-1984), but John Ball (1911-1988), a white, created an unforgettable literary and television Black detective, Virgil Tibbs, in his novel and the TV series *In The Heat of the Night* (1965).

American Japanese and Nisei have had several spokespersons, especially E.V. Cunningham (Howard Fast, b. 1919), who sets his half-dozen novels among the Japanese in Pasadena and downtown Los Angeles, and the problems faced by a Nisei detective, both in his police department and the white city at large. John Ball again, who was nothing if not a writer whose interests encompassed the world, wrote at least two crime novels—*Five Pieces of Jade* (1972) and *The Eyes of Buddha* (1976)—centering on Japanese and Nepalese (and Blacks and their problems in a white society). Ball's wife, Nan Hamilton, feeling that Japanese and Niseis in the U.S. have never received quite a square deal, wrote at least two crime novels—*Killer's Rights* (1984) and *The Shape of Fear* (1986)—featuring the Japanese-American L.A. detective Sam Ohara and his sergeant Ted Washington, a Black.

Native Americans have had a least half a dozen authors covering their brushes with the law. Among them, Tony Hillerman, the dean of American crime writers, in a series of some dozen books is methodically probing the life and culture of the American Indian in deep psychological and cultural studies. Hillerman is totally dedicated to realism and authenticity in his novels. A source of pride for him is that his books are used by the Navajos and Zunis in their schools, and Hillerman has been sharply questioned by the Indian elders about who gave away their secrets to him. He knows whereof he writes and reports the real meaning of life among these Indians.

Among the general authors most are trying not only new characters and new locales but new subjects and new approaches. Ralph McInerny, a professor of philosophy at Notre Dame University, has written three series of crime fiction and is now branching out into a more general and "philosophical" series. John D. MacDonald, before his death, extended his vision beyond mere story telling, on which he prided himself, and wrote about social and environmental subjects. Ross Macdonald, one of the half-dozen leading crime writers of America, searched into the mythology of father-son, son-father relationships and the very heart of human intercourse. Andrew Greeley, a priest deeply concerned with the plight of human existence and the salvation of the human soul, has evidence from his thousands of readers that his works—including his crime fiction—draw readers back to the Church and God.

In many ways one of the more daring of the crime fiction authors in breaking into new territories is George C. Chesbro, an upstate New York ex school teacher who is investigating the twilight zone between life and death, especially in those people who are brain-dead but physically alive.

Crime fiction continues to branch out in other ways. Robert R. McCamoen's fascinating *Boy's Life* (1991), for example, is ostensibly an autobiography of growing up in a small Alabama town. But the story is held together by the murder of an ex-Nazi whose identity is about to be discovered, and the impression this murder makes on a 12-year-old boy and his development into manhood. The story is a Tom Sawyer kind of adventure tied together by a murder and its eventual solution.

Another example of how far crime fiction is ranging is *The Buzzards Must Also Be Fed* (1991), by Anne Wingate, the author also of much more conventional crime stories. In this one, police Chief Mark Shigata solves a murder mystery, but the story is far more than such a type narrowly defined. Instead it is a romance-fantasy which is a projection of what people should be rather than what they are. The conventional crime story is left far behind.

So crime fiction is driven to radiate out in all directions. The genre is now exfoliating from crime fiction to general fiction about crime and as such is moving toward becoming again mainstream fiction as it was in the nineteenth century before Poe and his followers separated it into a single entity.

The number of authors and their approaches reveal the trend. Of the sum of books being published in the U.S. in 1991 20 percent were crime fiction. Of the number of authors in the U.S. in the total, at least one-third were writing crime fiction of one kind or another. The attitude of these authors is significant. Most are "serious" and are trying to do their best. Those in America, especially, are concerned with the trends in society and are trying through their writing to influence society. They do not look upon crime fiction as an inferior, merely formulaic, type of fiction that only hacks utilize, but look upon themselves as craftspersons and their work as being worthy of the most serious consideration.

Early in his career, Ross Macdonald, as we have seen, concluded that in a democratic society an author should write democratic literature, and he chose crime fiction as his statement. The English crime-fiction author P.D. James had a similar experience. "I...saw the writing of detective fiction with its challenging disciplines, its inner tensions between plot, character and atmosphere, and its necessary reliance on structure and form, as the best possible apprenticeship for a serious novelist," she wrote. Experience forced her to grow into a new realization. Each of her books became, in her words, "a landmark in my gradual realization that, despite the constraints of this fascinating genre, a mystery writer can hope to call herself a serious novelist." Mark Twain, with five crime stories, had learned the lesson long before: *A Double-Barreled Detective Story* (1902); *A Murder, a Mystery and a Marriage* (1902); *Simon Wheeler, Detective* (1963); *The Stolen White Elephant* (1882); *Tom Sawyer, Detective and Other Stories* (1896). Henry James, though he condescended to popular literature, wrote three unsurpassed crime stories: *The Other House* (1896); *The Turn of the Screw* (1898); *Two Magics* (1898). The versatility of the motif was demonstrated by William Faulkner in at least five of his books: *Sanctuary* (1931); *Light in August* (1933); *Absolom, Absolom!* (1937); *Intruder in the Dust* (1949); and *Knight's Gambit* (1949).

What an ever-growing number of authors continue to learn, the reading public increasingly recognizes. Fiction is without bounds and all types grow from the same seed. All types to one degree or another are representations of the society in which they are written. Hierarchical and totalitarian societies develop fiction that perpetuates the hierarchy or totalitarian government. Democratic societies on the contrary demand democratic literature. The history of American fiction demonstrates the thrust of this development.

There is nothing new in these observations, though they are not always accepted. Well over a hundred years ago someone writing in *Blackwood's Edinburgh Magazine* recognized what is becoming more and more obvious:

> Popular literature is a reflection of the period in which it flourishes—its active as well as its meditative life—its politics and its romance, and we rest assured that there is not a movement in it, not a force, not an atom of life which has not its counterpart in contemporary history.... Literature, in fact, now implies far more than it did before. It is now a complete representation of society.... It is to the historian what the dial-plate is to the time piece; it is a perfect index of the innumerable processes at work throughout the whole frame of society.

Half a century later the eminent British man of letters Andrew Lang, known to all for his books of fairy tales, commented in a similar vein:

> The popular novelists of England or America are serious men [and women]; they occupy at least in their own opinion a position which, since the days of the Great Hebrew Prophets, has been held by few sons of earth. Now and again they descend, as it were, from the mountain and wearily tell the world the story of their aims, their methods, and their early struggles, before they were discovered by interprising publishers, before their books provided the text of many a sermon....

About Arthur Conan Doyle, one of his favorite authors, Lang commented: "It may be said with gratitude that he aims at entertaining rather than at instructing his generation. We venture to think that the contemplative and speculative elements in his nature are subordinate to the old-fashioned notion that a novelist should tell a plain tale" (*Quarterly Review* 158-9; qtd. in Orel 219-220).

Crime fiction is the most democratic of all popular fiction since it concerns one of the two certitudes of life: all people must die, and increasingly violence with its many motivations and methods of expression seems to be the vehicle of death touching more and more of us. Crime at one time was essentially an effort to get something from another or to voice some kind of emotion. Now it is likewise a political statement. It is also all-pervasive, ranging from the highest levels of humanity to the meanest. Crime-violence seems to be one ingredient of capitalist-democratic society that is insatiable. The more one has the more one wants.

George Gerbner, who has spent a lifetime clocking acts of violence on TV and in movies has some sobering statistics:

> The moderate viewer of prime time in the U.S. sees every week an average of 21 criminals (domestic and foreign) arrayed against an army of 41 public and private law enforcers.... An average of 150 acts of violence and about 15 murders entertain us and our children every week, and that does not count cartoons and the news.... Most likely there will be bodies of women, violated often just as curtain-raisers to the real "he-man action." (Raboy 102)

Gerbner reminds us that entertainment need bear no resemblance to reality. But numerous cities in the U.S.—Washington, D.C., New York City, Detroit and Chicago, to name only four—easily have more than one murder per day. Generally the media picture what the public want to see. A program that does not please the public is quickly scuttled. Disturbing questions are thus raised.

Since crime fiction mirrors the many sides of society there can be no doubt that in the future more and more authors will turn to that type of story as their method of expression, and that the current trend in the expansion of that genre to encompass all forms of fiction will continue. The Twenty-First Century seems an open invitation for such fiction to expand and in so doing turn full circle and become again the general fiction in which it began.

Notes

[1] For a full discussion of this aspect of crime fiction see Ray B. Browne, *Heroes and Humanities: Detective Fiction and Culture* Bowling Green, OH: Bowling Green State University Popular Press.

Orel, Harold. *Critical Essays on Sir Arthur Conan Doyle.* New York: G.K. Hall, 1992.

Raboy, Marc and Bernard Dagenais. *Media, Crisis and Democracy: Mass Communication and the Disruption of Social Order.* Newbury Park, CA: Sage. 1992.

Works Cited

Carroll, Jon. "Ross Macdonald in Raw California." *Esquire* June 1972: 149.

Chandler, Raymond. *The Simple Art of Murder.* Boston: Houghton Mifflin, 1950.

Leonard, John, "Ross Macdonald, his Lew Archer and other Secret Selves." *New York Times Book Review* 1 June 1969: 2.

Orel, Harold. *Critical Essays on Sir Arthur Conan Doyle.* New York: G.K. Hall, 1992.

Lang, Andrew. *Quarterly Review* July 1904.

Raboy, Marc and Bernard Dagenais., eds. *Media, Crisis and Democracy: Mass Communication and the Disruption of Social Order.* Newbury Park, CA: Sage. 1992.

Thompson, Stith. *Motif-Index of Folk-Literature: A Classification of Narrative Elements in Folktales, Ballads, Myths, Fables, Medieval Romances, Exemplar, Fabliaux, Jest-Books and Local Legends.* Rev. and Enlarged. Bloomington: Indiana UP, 1966.

Girl Scouts, Camp Fire Girls, and Woodcraft Girls: The Ideology of Girls' Scouting Novels, 1910-1935

SHERRIE A. INNESS

That the literature by and about the female gender, more than half the population of the U.S., has been kept out of the canon is one of the ironies of our culture. American poet William Cullen Bryant, writing in another context, commented on this phenomenon:

> Truth, crushed to earth, shall rise again;
> The eternal years of God are hers;
> But Error, wounded, writhes in pain,
> And dies among his worshippers.
>
> (The Battle-Field, Stanza 3)

Even American men cannot forever overlook the obvious.

In his article "The Boy Scout Handbook," Paul Fussell argues that scholars are not paying adequate attention to many literary works that do not qualify as masterpieces. "It's amazing how many interesting books humanistic criticism manages not to notice," Fussell comments. "Staring fixedly at its handful of teachable masterpieces, it seems content not to recognize that a vigorous literary-moral life constantly takes place just below (sometimes above) its vision.... The culture of the Boy Scouts deserves this sort of look-in" (3). At this point, I agree completely with Fussell. Certainly, humanist criticism (or Marxist or Lacanian or feminist criticism) has managed to overlook or disregard a vast number of texts that do not achieve "masterpiece" status. Feminist critics (as well as others) have challenged the established canon of Anglo-American literature, but, for the most part, old great books have been replaced with new great ones. Thus, in an American literature survey course, Melville, Faulkner, Hemingway,

Emerson, and Hawthorne are commonly taught along with Sarah Orne Jewett, Mary Wilkins Freeman, Jean Toomey, Agnes Smedley, Charles Chesnutt, and a host of other writers being touted as desirable additions to the canon. Literary critics, however, have had a more difficult time getting past what I call the "masterpiece mentality": a mindset in which the critic must proclaim a text's "greatness" in order to justify its right to be read, criticized, and inserted into Norton anthologies. This strategy has been and continues to be a highly successful way to alter the traditional canon, but it fails to challenge the notion of canonicity itself and of the literary masterpiece. Thus, a vast variety of texts still fail to find a home or a voice in literature departments, creating a lopsided, elitist view of literary history.

I am not, however, in complete accordance with Fussell's argument, particularly when he seems to suggest that scholars neither have to pay close attention to the historicity or the ideology of a particular text. Fussell analyzes the rhetoric of *The Official Boy Scout Handbook* (1979), and has nothing but praise for its high moral standards. Furthermore, he lauds the "pliability and adaptability of the scout movement" that have helped it to exist for so long. Although he admits that the term "free world" appears too frequently in the Handbook, Fussell quickly bypasses this phrase to discuss the "slightly archaic liberal" politics of the Handbook (6), praising the book's ethics as the best gauge "for measuring the gross official misbehavior of the seventies" (7). "The generously low price of $3.50 [for the Handbook]," Fussell remarks, "is enticing, and so is the place on the back cover where you're invited to inscribe your name" (8). But are we *all* "invited" to inscribe our names? Certainly, women and girls are not invited (perhaps they are supposed to inscribe their names on the Girl Scout's Handbook), while boys who refuse to pledge allegiance to the flag need not sign, because they will be quickly hustled out of scouting. Before we sign on the dotted line, perhaps we should learn more about Scout ideology and its origins. Fussell establishes an overly-simplistic dichotomy between the upright morals espoused by the Handbook and the general decay of American government and civilization. We have to go beyond this bipolarism and examine the ideology behind the scouting movement, and how scouting was perceived by the mass public at various times, because textual criticism of popular texts gains in depth and breadth if grounded in historical research.

To this end, I will examine in this essay the beginnings of the Girl Scout/Camp Fire Girl movements in the United States, particularly their representation in popular, U.S. girls' series fiction from 1910 to 1935.[1] The hundreds of Girl Scout, Camp Fire Girl, Junior Guide, and Woodcraft Girl novels as well as the hundreds of Boy Scout and Camp Fire Boy novels that were published during this period are an important source of information about changing gender roles and United States imperialism. Also, we will find that the commodities of a capitalist system (in this case, serial novels) can function to promote and sell the system of which they are a part.

From analyzing these novels and the early development of scouting for girls, we will be better able to understand that the scouting movement functions as a disciplinary agent of the state that controls and regulates the movements of youths; as Foucault informs us, "discipline fixes; it arrests or regulates movements; it clears up confusion; it dissipates compact groupings of individuals wandering about the country in unpredictable ways" (219). Compact groupings of individuals, however, that act in predictable and socially-sanctioned ways are one of the essential sources of power for the state. Whether scouts, members of the military, or college students, organized groups help to ensure obedience to state regulations and controls. Although scouting in fiction and in reality might offer girls a fleeting feeling of agency, ultimately scouting is only one of many state-sanctioned institutions that produces more malleable subjects for the nation. Thus, a reader should hesitate before inscribing her name on the official Boy/Girl Scout Handbook and question whether its ideology is, as Fussell implies, "enticing."

History of the Scouting Movement² and Popular Scout Fiction
The scouting movement originated in England when Lord Baden-Powell established scouting for boys in 1908. After his military campaigns in South Africa, Baden-Powell sought to create a pseudo-military society for boys that would provide the discipline of a military unit during a non-war period. Boy scouting was a clever combination of paramilitary style (uniforms, badges, and military organization) and imperialist ideology (emphasizing the "natural" dominance of the Anglo-Saxon races over all other peoples) combined with a large dose of camping and woodmanship that proved to be remarkably attractive to large numbers of boys, and girls, too. Thousands of girls wrote to Baden-Powell, pleading to be included in scouting activities. Although Baden-Powell, a strong believer in male supremacy, had no intention of allowing girls into the Boy Scouts, a separate group—the Girl Guides—was founded in England in 1910, and imported to the United States as the Girl Scout movement in 1912. From slightly different roots, the Camp Fire Girls began in 1910 in the United States. Both the Girl Scouts and the Camp Fire Girls spread rapidly across the globe. Girl Aides developed in Australia while Peace Scouting was organized in New Zealand. By 1912, there were an estimated 60,000 Camp

Fire Girls, and Camp Fire circles were established in Japan, Canada, Siam, Panama, Scotland, the West Indies, and several other countries (Buckler 83-84).

The interest in scouting was reflected in the massive production of commodities with a scouting theme. Scouting quickly became a capitalist enterprise. For example, *The Vacation Book of the Camp Fire Girls* (1914) assures its reader that the Camp Fire Outfitting Company stocks everything from short skirts and bathing suits to outing hats, middies, and bloomers for the well-dressed Camp Fire Girl (32). The scouting craze reached such grand proportions that numerous Girl Scout and Boy Scout moving pictures were filmed, while hundreds (if not thousands) of scouting serial novels were published by such firms as Lothrop, Lee & Shepard, A.L. Burt, D. Appleton, Cupples & Leon, and Penn Publishing. Only a few of these novels received official sanction from the organization that they represented; I.T. Thurston's novel, *The Torch Bearer*, was one of the few officially endorsed Camp Fire stories (Buckler 88), while Lillian Roy's novel *Norma: A Flower Scout* was published with the approval of the National Girl Scouts. The lack of official endorsement, however, did not hinder scouting fiction from becoming tremendously popular. It is extremely difficult (if not impossible) to get exact reader statistics for these early twentieth-century series novels, but we can judge their popularity from other sources. Certainly, the companies producing the five to fifteen novels in a typical series would not have been so eager to publish these works if they did not sell. Moreover, authors would not have maintained and copied the standardized format for a scouting novel unless it was a format that was marketable.

A scouting novel (when I refer to "scouting" I also include Camp Fire novels) was a rationalized, standardized product. A typical book was approximately 225 pages long, hardbound, stamped on the cover with a colored picture of a group of girls engaged in some scouting activity, and it cost a nominal fifty to seventy-five cents. The words "Camp Fire" or "Girl Scout" were inevitably prominent in the title. Furthermore, the reader was obviously expected to read, and even urged to read, all the novels in a particular series. Commonly, the texts would self-consciously refer to the other novels in a series and urge the reader to purchase them. For example, in Lilian Garis' *The Girl Scouts at Rocky Ledge*, a group of Girl Scouts (Betta, Doro, Pell, Alma, and Treble) are discussing the merits of the last books in the series that centers on their scouting exploits:

They were referring to the first volume, 'The Girl Scout Pioneers,' but others of the group spoke up for their particular choice of the series, naming, 'The Girl

Scouts at Bellaire' and 'The Girl Scouts at Sea Crest.'
'You may have those,' offered Doro, 'but I perfectly love this.' She held up the
last book published. It was entitled 'The Girl Scouts at Camp Comalong.'

This brought about a general discussion of the entire series, and although the
method being used is not usually employed to remind readers of the other books
in a series, perhaps, since the girls were speaking for themselves, it will be
accepted. (74)

The fictional scouts sold themselves. Also, the novels sold their readers on
the importance of scouting activities. In Amy Blanchard's *In Camp with
the Muskoday Camp Fire Girls* (1917), the author writes in the foreword,
"To those girls who know nothing about the joys of camp life such
experiences as those of the Muskoday Camp Fire Girls must come as a
revelation.... The doings of the Muskoday Camp Fire Girls I hope may
inspire others" (np). Similarly, the narrator in Lillian Garis' *The Girl Scout
Pioneers* questions the reader, "Have you ever been called upon to lead
others? Do you know the joys of using your own personal power in a well-
organized and carefully directed plan?" (143). The reader is not expected
to read passively, but to view her reading experience as a direct reflection
of the potential enjoyment that she could receive from joining a Camp Fire
or Girl Scout troop.

It is unlikely, however, that any real scouting troop could meet with a
tenth as much adventure as does a fictional scouting troop. Always
undaunted, always high-spirited, fictional scouts go through dangers that
would be insurmountable to non-scouts, their only worry being that their
new uniforms might get wrinkled. In *The Camp Fire Girls Go Motoring*
(Frey), the plucky girls are involved in several car accidents, have an
automobile stolen, drive a thousand miles with no chaperon, and escape
from a burning building, yet are still chipper enough to sing camp songs
on a dismally wet, cold night, while in Julianne DeVries' novel, *The
Campfire Girls as Federal Investigators*, the girls charter a private yacht,
fly in an airplane, and discover who is smuggling foreign goods into the
United States. Not all scouting novels paint such an unrealistic picture of
scouting; in *Lucile, the Torch Bearer* (Duffield), the title character enjoys
"fishing on the banks of the stream...swimming—tramping—canoeing"
(115), while Olive in *Camp Fire Girls in War and Peace* (Hornibrook)
benefits from "hiking, climbing, sleeping out on mountain-tops, or by the
seashore" (24). Girls are lured into scouting because serial fiction depicts
scouting as offering girls escape from stereotypical gender roles, and a
great amount of physical freedom. As I will explain in the next section of

this essay, the degree of liberty allowed to girls does not hinder the scouting movement from working to construct suitably socialized bourgeois women.

Domestic Training:Building a Better Mother

James F. Page, in his book about juvenile organizations entitled *Socializing for the New Order (1919)*, points out that "if girls are to possess the highest type of feminine traits which will enable them to serve adequately the needs of society, they must pass through the race history of women, as the boy to attain to maximum proficiency must recapitulate the history of man" (79). According to Page, the Camp Fire Girls and the Girl Scouts facilitate a pseudo-return to a more primitive racial past. Furthermore, the Camp Fire Girls and the Girl Scouts "will tend to restore [woman's] original and true status; and prepare her subsequently to function in the domestication of the larger social community' (81). "The general aim of the Camp Fire Girls," Page writes, "is to help girls prepare for the new social order, and to enable them to overcome the grinding tendency of modern machine work; to develop in girls the power of cooperation, the capacity to keep step" (81). Page's words reveal a dark underside to scouting ideology. Girls participate in camping activities, build nature crafts, and engage in the rituals of the Camp Fire Girls (coining Indian names such as "Nyoda" and "Hinpoha," building campfires, and adopting pseudo-Indian rituals) so that they will be closer to their "original and true status," not so that they experience any feeling of personal agency or empowerment. Scouts are taught not to question modernization and technological innovation; instead, they must "keep step" with the "new social order."

Dr. Luther Gulick, co-founder of the Camp Fire Girls, had no intention of subverting social norms of gender behavior in his organization. "I believe the keynote [of the Camp Fire Girls]," Gulick stated, "is...that we wish to develop girls to be womanly.... to copy the Boy Scout movement would be utterly and fundamentally evil, and would probably produce ultimately a moral and psychological involution which is the last thing in the world that ...any of us want. We hate manly women and womanly men" (qtd. in Buckler 22). He continues, "The bearing and rearing of children has always been the first duty of most women, and that must always continue to be. This involves service, constant service, self-forgetfulness and always service"(22). In light of Gulick's comments, we must consider the many physical activities (hiking, camping, swimming, and other outdoor sports) offered to scouts as aimed at developing and encouraging traditional gender roles. Thus, it comes as little surprise to the reader that both the fictional and the actual Boy Scout is allowed much more physical freedom than the Girl Scout or Camp Fire Girl.[3]

In the first quarter of the twentieth century, scouting did not undermine the role of the woman as wife and mother, and encouraged domestic training as a part of scouting practice. *Campward Ho! A Manual for Girl Scout Camps* (1920) insists on domestic training for all girls; "There are many young women with homes of their own whose houses are badly run because they have no idea how the daily housework should be done. They cannot do it themselves and they cannot direct another. The camp is the one place where the Scout can learn what to do and how to do it" (45). Many of the Girl Scout training manuals emphasize that the Girl Scout should be both a good mother and a fanatic housewife. "Every Girl Scout knows the deep and vital need for clean and healthy bodies in the mothers of the next generation" (11), states the *Official Handbook of the Girl Scouts* from 1920. Furthermore, the *Handbook* informs us, the Girl Scout "is honor bound to have no dark, damp, hidden, dirt-filled corners in any part of her house, not even in shed or cellar" (121).

Such scouting ideology is mirrored in scouting fiction, which is very much aware of its responsibility to instruct young girls about socially correct gender behavior. Thus, in *The Girl Scout Pioneers* (Garis) the narrator remarks,

it may not be amiss to call attention here to the value of such training given almost in play, and without question in such attractive forms as to make character building through its influence an ideal pastime, a valuable investment, and a complete program for growing girls, who may emerge as...nicely trained little helpers for the home. (16)

In Jane Stewart's novel, *The Camp Fire Girls in the Mountains*, the Camp Fire leader is even more explicit about the future responsibilities of the Camp Fire Girl: "the job every girl ought to get sooner or later" is "running a home" (75). Scout training is a "valuable investment," but for whom? Certainly, scouting is a worthwhile investment for a society intent on reminding the increasingly independent women of the 1920s that they must not disregard their ultimate responsibilities as future American mothers and housewives. In addition, as I shall suggest next, scouting fiction promotes the socioeconomic hegemony of the Anglo-Saxon girl by portraying working-class girls, African-Americans, and foreigners as inferior citizens who deserve only condescension.

Americanization in Scout Fiction:
Constructing The Supremacy Of The Bourgeois, Anglo-American Girl
If Fussell thinks the ideology of Boy Scouts and Girl Scouts is

pliable and adaptable, he should read *Anne Thornton, Wetamoo,* in which
the Woodcraft girls work at a local community center "teaching the
foreigners and helping them to become good citizens" (Anthony, np), or a
similar story, *The Campfire Girls Flying Around the Globe* (DeVries), in
which a group of Camp Fire Girls spreads Camp Fire ideology to France,
China, Japan, Germany, England, Spain, and Brussels. Or Fussell should
examine Latharo Hoover's novel, *The Camp-Fire Boys in the Philippines,*
in which "three clean-minded American youths" are pursuing a "vile
leprous [*sic*] Chinaman" (229) who is planning to marry not one but *two*
"beautiful white girls" (229).⁴ Of course, the "vile" Chinaman is killed,
while the beautiful, white girls are saved by the stalwart Camp-Fire Boys.

The connections between American imperialism and scouting are
impossible to escape, both in fiction and in reality.⁵ For example, Jean
Large's *Nancy Goes Girl Scouting* openly proselytizes for United States
culture. Not only does Mrs. Herbert Hoover (honorary President of the
Girl Scouts) write the introduction for Large's novel, describing herself as
an "extremely enthusiastic Girl Scout" (v), but fictional Girl Scout Nancy
discovers "the numerous ways the people of the United States have
benefitted the world" (129). Nancy is only one of countless fictional Girl
Scouts or Camp Fire Girls who praise the superiority of American values,
while implicitly or explicitly downgrading the values of other countries. In
Margaret Vandercook's *The Camp Fire Girls by the Blue Lagoon,* one
Camp Fire Girl desires to go into social settlement work "to teach our
immigrants more of the spirit and opportunities of the United States" (31),
while in *The Girl Scout Pioneers,* the Girl Scouts of the True Tred troop
are elated that they can start a troop for some poor mill girls; "The girls of
True Tred were radiant with the prospect of their work—that of assisting
the mill girls and actually taking part in real Americanization" (63). Both
fictional and real Girl Scouts could earn a merit badge in
"Americanization." Whether in fiction or in actuality, scouting offers a
convenient way to export Anglo-Saxon values to the rest of the world. It
comes as no surprise in *The Campfire Girls as Federal Investigators* that
the first thing Mrs. Evans' Camp Fire Girls do when shipwrecked on a
South Pacific Island is establish a Camp Fire circle for the native girls, and
instruct this new circle in how to start other Camp Fire groups on the
neighboring islands.

In conclusion, texts that are by no means literary masterpieces can
still offer us valuable insights into the construction of gender roles and,
more generally, United States culture. Such texts, however, remain shallow
and one-dimensional if they are studied only as reflections or
representations of our own historical period. Thus, *The Official Boy Scout*

Handbook may be interpreted as a gauge "for measuring the gross official misbehavior of the seventies," but it also must be understood as a gauge of the rampant Anglo-Saxon imperialist nationalism of the interwar years. Similarly, the scouting movement undoubtedly has offered individual girls and women a sense of agency and autonomy; but, as we have seen, the Girl Scout and Camp Fire girl movements between the Wars were also actively engaged in convincing women that domesticity was the *sine qua non* for feminine happiness. Furthermore, the scouting movement, whether in reality or in fiction, helped perpetuate the idea that the "true" American girl was Anglo-Saxon and bourgeois.

Insights such as these would not be possible if critics ignored popular texts like these and studied only a "handful of teachable masterpieces." Although Fussell made his claim in the mid-1970s, it still has validity in the 1990s. Today, many scholars still have blinders on when it comes to recognizing the importance of texts that will never be touted as "good books." Of course, there are critics (Allen Bloom springs to mind) who condemn efforts to bring high and low culture together, and claim that popular culture studies should be excluded entirely from the academy, or, at most, given a marginal position. These scholars generally argue that a call for popular culture in the classroom is a call for cultural anarchy; thus, they wish to build an impenetrable barrier between the literary classics suitable for teaching, and the innumerable other popular texts would remain in an outer purgatory reserved for "bad" books. Even scholars who wish to see Agnes Smedley's or Sarah Orne Jewett's works taught in the classroom balk at the thought that Carolyn Keene's novels might also be included. These approaches to pedagogy are narrow, elitist, and they construct a skewed vision of the past. They fail to recognize that "bad" literature in all its myriad forms has just as much (if not more) impact on United States culture than does "good" literature. Moreover, excluding popular literary works from the classroom establishes a dangerous precedent for students, who are led to believe that critical thinking about texts should be limited to certain canonical or semi-canonical works, failing to recognize that a critical approach to popular culture is vitally important in a world inundated with countless popular art forms.

Combining popular literary works with more traditional texts in the classroom actually can enrich the academic experience. As cultural critics, we can better interpret the ideological density of any historical era by integrating popular works into our pedagogy (and, I would add, our own scholarship). The possible combinations of works to teach together are exciting: visions of the West in both Willa Cather's novels and Owen Wister's Western, *The Virginian*; images of the city in Theodore Dreiser's

Sister Carrie and in Raymond Chandler's detective novels; gender roles in Edith Wharton's society romances and in Girl Scout novels. By juxtaposing texts in this manner, we not only encourage new insights into United States culture, but also create a more nuanced vision of how society constitutes itself through literary representation.

Notes

[1]In England, there were also Girl Guide novels and Camp Fire Girl Stories published. For an account of these texts, see Mary Cadogan and Patricia Craig, *You're a Brick, Angela! A New Look at Girls' Fiction from 1839 to 1975,* (London: Gollancz, 1976) 140-77.

[2]Histories of scouting are typically saccharin and uncritical. For examples of works of this genre, see Helen Buckler, Mary Fiedler, and Martha F. Allen, *Wo-He-Lo: The Story of Camp Fire Girls 1910-1960* (New York: Holt, 19651); and Anne Hyde Choate and Helen Ferris, *Juliette Low and the Girl Scouts: The Story of an American Woman 1860-1927* (New York: Girl Scouts, 1928).

[3]Boy Scout series allow their boys much more physical freedom than do Girl Scout series. For instance, in Herbert Carter's *The Boy Scouts Along the Susquehanna* (New York: Burt, 1915), many of the troop members carry guns and go on more strenuous hikes than fictional Girl Scouts are ever allowed. Other Boy Scout books of interest include Thornton Burgess, *The Boy Scouts of Woodcraft Camp* (Philadelphia: Penn, 1924) in which the scouts go through what one character calls the "man factory" (343): a wilderness camp; Herbert Carter, *The Boy Scouts Afoot in France* (New York: Burt, 1917) (the Boy Scouts in World War I); Latharo Hoover, *The Camp-Fire Boys in the Philippines* (New York: Burt, 1930) ("three clean-minded American youths" complete with rifles, automatics, and twin machine-guns on their private airplane); Howard Payson, *The Boy Scouts at the Panama Canal* (New York: Burt, 1913) (Boy Ralphson, *Boy Scouts in a Motor Boat or Adventures on the Columbia River* (Chicago: Donohue, 1912) (Boy Scouts who camp, and also work for the United States Secret Service) and many others. A more comprehensive listing of boy scout series can be found in *American Boys' Series Books 1900-1980* (Tampa: U of South Florida Library Associates, 1987).

[4]Scouting fiction is openly racist: "Chinamen" are described as lepers; the Japanese are scornfully referred to as "Japs," and African-Americans and Mexicans are portrayed as foolish and lazy. The authors seem to have felt no qualms about perpetuating the worst stereotypes of ethnic groups. Thus, in Hildegard Frey's *The Camp Fire Girls Go Motoring*, Katherine, a widely admired Camp Fire Girl, nonchalantly describes negroes as looking "like apes, but they're quite harmless. They're shiftless to the last degree, but not violent. They're too lazy to do any mischief" (50). An article that analyzes this racism is J. Frederick

MacDonald, "'The Foreigner' in Juvenile Series Fiction, 1900-1945," *Journal of Popular Culture* 8 (1974): 534-48.

    ⁵Of course, both fictional and real Scouts were engrossed with war work during World War I, and strongly supported the pro-America jingoism of the war period. See Margaret Widdemer, *Winona's War Farm* (Philadelphia: Lippincott, 1918).

Works Cited

American Boys' Series Books 1900-1980. Tampa: U of South Florida Library Associates, 1987.

Anthony, Lotta Rowe. *Anne Thornton, Wetamoo*. Philadelphia: Penn, 1922.

Blanchard, Amy E. *The Camp Fire Girls of Brightwood: A Story of How They Kindled Their Fire and Kept It Burning*. Boston: Wilde, 1915.

_____. *In Camp with the Muskoday Camp Fire Girls: A Story of the Camp Fire by the Lake*. 1917.

_____. *Lucky Penny of Thistle Troop: A Girl Scout Story*. Boston: Wilde, 1920.

Buckler, Helen, Mary Fiedler, and Martha F. Allen. *Wo-He-Lo: The Story of Camp Fire Girls 1910-1960*. New York: Holt, 1961.

Burgess, Thornton W. *The Boy Scouts of Woodcraft Camp*. Philadelphia: Penn, 1924.

Cadogan, Mary and Patricia Craig. *You're a Brick, Angela! A New Look at Girls' Fiction from 1839 to 1975*. London: Gollancz, 1976.

Campward Ho! A Manual for Girl Scout Camps. New York: Girl Scouts, 1920.

Carter, Herbert. *The Boy Scouts Along the Susquehanna or The Silver Fox Patrol Caught in a Flood*. New York: Burt, 1915.

_____. *The Boy Scouts Afoot in France; or, With the Red Cross Corps at the Marine*. 1917.

Choate, Anne Hyde and Helen Ferris. *Juliette Low and the Girl Scouts: The Story of an American Woman 1860-1927*. New York: Girl Scouts, 1928.

DeVries, Julianne. *The Campfire Girls as Federal Investigators*. New York: World Syndicate, 1935.

_____. *Campfire Girls Flying Around the Globe*. 1933.

Duffield, Elizabeth M. *Lucile, the Torch Bearer*. New York: Sully, 1915.

Foucault, Michel. *Discipline and Punish: The Birth of the Prison*. Trans. Alan Sheridan. New York: Pantheon, 1977.

Frey, Hildegard G. *The Camp Fire Girls Go Motoring*. New York Burt, 1916.

_____. *The Camp Fire Girls on the Open Road; or Glorify Work*, 1918.

Fussell, Paul. "The Boy Scout Handbook." *The Boy Scout Handbook and Other Observations*. New York: Oxford UP, 1982.

Garis, Lilian. *The Girl Scout Pioneers or Winning the First B.C.* New York: Cupples & Leon, 1920.

_____. *The Girl Scouts at Rocky Ledge or Nora's Real Vacation*, 1922.

Hoover, Latharo. *The Camp-Fire Boys in the Philippines.* New York: Burt, 1930.

Hornibrook, Isabel. *Girls of the Morning-Glory Camp Fire.* Boston: Lothrop, 1916.

———. *Camp Fire Girls in War and Peace,* 1919.

Large, Jean Henry. *Nancy Goes Girl Scouting.* New York: Appleton, 1927.

MacDonald, J. Frederick. "'The Foreigner' in Juvenile Series Fiction, 1900-1945." *Journal of Popular Culture* 8 (1974): 534-48.

Page, James F. *Socializing for the New Order or Educational Values of the Juvenile Organization.* Rock Island, Illinois: Augustana College, 1919.

Payson, Howard. *The Boy Scouts at the Panama Canal.* New York: Burt, 1913.

Ralphson, G. Harvey. *Boy Scouts in a Motor Boat or Adventures on the Columbia River.* Chicago: Donohue, 1912.

Roy, Lillian Elizabeth. *Norma: A Garden Scout.* New York: Burt, 1925.

Scouting for Girls: Official Handbook of the Girl Scouts. New York: Girl Scouts, 1920.

Stewart, Jane L. *The Camp Fire Girls in the Mountains; or Bessie King's Strange Adventure.* New York: Saalfield, 1914.

Thurston, I.T. *The Torch Bearer: A Camp Fire Girls' Story.* New York: Revell, 1913.

Vacation Book of the Camp Fire Girls. New York: Camp Fire Girls, 1914.

Vandercook, Margaret. *The Camp Fire Girls by the Blue Lagoon.* Philadelphia: Winston, 1921.

Widdemer, Margaret. *Winona's War Farm.* Philadelphia: Lippincott, 1918.

The Oil Patch:
A Part of The Passing Parade

JIMMIE COOK

America's past is littered with artifacts of the past: buildings, activities, attitudes. Most can be viewed from the vantage point of history with greater objectivity and evaluation than they could while being experienced. Small-time wildcatting for oil is probably pleasanter now than it was then. But it is a part of American history and should be understood.

The crumbling foundations and remnants of sidewalks poke through knee-high weeds in ghost towns scattered throughout Oklahoma as monuments, or perhaps a better description would be tombstones, to a time and a place and a way of life that flourished briefly on the American scene before a quiet but painful demise. The time was the first decade of the 20th Century to the World War II years; the place was the Southwest wherever Black Gold was the magic word; and the people who lived there were "Oilies." Altogether they comprised the Oil Patch. The Oil Patch People had a terminology all their own that was colorful, descriptive, and completely foreign to the untutored ear. The families of the Oilies were in a class of individuals well deserving of the label of pioneers. And the men themselves who chose the Oil Patch as a way of life were a breed apart. The way they talked, the way they lived, and the way they worked provided a kaleidoscope of a culture richly deserving of a place in the passing parade of Americana.

I was an outsider to the Oil Patch and while I was to live among them for nearly early three decades, I never really understood them. They talked of "slappin collars" and "stabbin pipe." I heard phrases such as "breakin in," or "crumbin out." Somebody would "drag up" or "hit the hooks," "buck the tongs" or "roll pipe."

They used tools such as a "bean joint," a "caliper," or a "carrying bar." And what in the world was a "jack board," a "lazy board," or a "one-armed Johnnie"? (Carney 18)

I felt I was on more familiar ground with "doghouse," "bronco," "crow's nest," a "cat," a "boll weevil," and a "possum belly." Was I ever wrong?

241

And I was amazed at the mobility of these Oil Patch People whose children showed up in school any day, at any point in a semester. Their mother might explain, "We're Magnolia." Or Tidewater. Or Mid-Continent. Their "company" was their identity. The young people quickly moved into football spots, basketball position, and the band. They made friends quickly and easily, and did exceptionally well in geography; they frequently mentioned names and faraway places their classmates, and many of their teachers, had never seen. Their place of residence was simply "The Magnolia Camp." Or Tidewater. Or Mid-Continent.

I sometimes saw the Oil Patch wives at the laundromat and curiously observed the oil-stiffened work clothes they poked into the machines. A particularly heavily-coated garment which would have evoked dismay on my part would elicit no more than a quiet comment for the owner: "My, that must've been a good one." Oil Patch wives seemed to find each other in a crowded room and I heard mention of "shot-gun houses," "company picnics," and "the camp." They joined the Parent-Teacher Organizations and taught Sunday School classes. Then one day they would come to school to pick up their children and their books, announce they had been "transferred"; they said their goodbyes and went away. If there was time they would attend the covered-dish farewell dinner hastily put together for them at the church fellowship hall where they hugged and smiled and said, "Let's keep in touch!" There were no tears! More often than not, we never saw them again.

And if I found the women somewhat different and difficult to understand, the men were even more so. Their talk invariably turned to that magic word "oil." They laughed a lot and told stories of sleeping in the doghouse and of shooting the rats as the rodents stuck their heads up through holes in the floor. Their voices would usually lower when womenfolk walked by, and one might hear expressions such as "Ain't that a Darb!" which would be followed by raucous laughter and a lot of thigh-slapping. Their conversations were punctuated by references to "bush gangs," "back up men," "gang pushers," and "jack man." Phrases such as "stabbers," "snap grabbers," "collar peckers" and "sharp shooters" were common terms to the Oilies.

And then one day in July of 1982, the bits and pieces that comprised my impressions of the Oil Patch come together to form one clear picture, and I realized for the first time what I had failed to recognize in the three decades I had known the Oil Patch People that they were a unique clan of individuals who had carved a niche for themselves in the history of our country, our state, our community. Ironically enough, the moment of illumination came about, not in the Oil Patch, but on the National Mall in Washington, D.C.

Dr. George Carney, Professor of Geography at Oklahoma State University, had been asked to put together a demonstration for the Festival of American Folklife for the Smithsonian Institution and for the National Park Service. Carney had come to Drumright, Oklahoma, the heart of the oilfield pipeline area, to obtain a crew of oldtimers. He sought out Melvin Cook, who, though not connected with the oil industry himself, was in touch with those persons connected with the field. Cook sought out former pipeliner Bill Hester, Drumright, Clarence Merrill, retired pipeliner from Drumright, OK, the "collar pecker" who recalled "slappin' a few collars in my day," Brice Downing, Tulsa, Oklahoma, who compared the collar pecking rhythms to "listening to music." And there were Darrell Smith, Oilton, Oklahoma, oil pumper, Roy Smaltz, Cushing, Oklahoma, who demonstrated the "doodle-bug," Buddy Settle, the gauger; Cook himself went along as the "boll weevil" or sometimes known as the "bronco," and Virgil Anderson, the "cat" who rounded out the crew.

Other folklife exhibitions were scheduled for each day. A loud speaker announced the starting time and location for the folk music, dance, and craft demonstrations including crowd-pleasers such as quarter-horse racing, Oklahoma Indian stomp dances and western swing music. As the spectators toe-tapped to the old Johnnie Lee Wills and his Texas Playboys band, the veteran pipeliners geared up for their performance which would follow. The crew to lay a joint of pipe consisted of a "back-up man," "the collar pecker," the "hook hitters," the "jack man," and the "stabber." Additional men would move joints of pipe and "spell off" the others.

Their big moment had arrived and as the crowd circled and shouldered close to the roped-off area, the pipeliners faithfully re-enacted a scene that could have taken place seventy-five years ago. Dr. George Carney describes the event thus:

The procedure followed in screwing a joint of pipe included several steps.... The last joint on the line was held above the ditch by the lazy board, usually operated by the back-up man, who was positioned behind the collar. He also manipulated the back-up tongs with the handles on the ground to keep the pipe from recoiling while the new joint of pipe was being screwed into the collar. The joint of pipe to be screwed in was then picked up with pipe calipers resembling large ice tons, and placed with its threaded end ready to insert into the collar of the last joint laid. As the joint was set into the collar, the stabber threw his arms around the pipe and started the threads into the collar. For a large diameter pipe, the stabber used a stabbin' board (a board or pole stuck in the end of the pipe) to help hold the pipe straight....

As soon as the joint was lined up and threads started, the stabber shouted "Catch it!" This cued the jack man who quickly placed the jack and the jack board in position to hold the pipe. The jack stood on a growler board which provided stability and kept the jack and the jack board from sliding into the ditch.

When the pipe was secure, the stabber cried "Roll'er!" which indicated he was ready for the spinning ropes to be looped around the pipe two or three times. As one worker pulled back on the end of each rope to make it grip the pipe, several gang members pulled forward, causing the joint to rotate in the proper direction.

As the joint was being started and slack taken up by the spinning ropes, the collar pecker, who was seated behind the collar on the joint that had already been laid, began to pount rhythmically or slap the collar into which the pipe was being screwed. The cadence provided by the collar pecker's hammer(s) served two purposes: it made the pipe turn easier....; the collar pecker's action also set the work pace for other members of the gang. When the pipe began to turn hard, the collar pecker would "knock off" the spinning rope crew and they would immediately "hook on" with the lay tongs.

At the beginning, two sets of tongs turned the pipe; however, as it became more difficult to screw, more sets of tongs were "knocked on" by the collar pecker. In order to keep the pipe constantly rotating, the tongs were operated so that half of the sets were screwing while the other half recovered.... In this process, the tong men were hitting the hooks on alternating beats of the hammer ("break out") which could be done when the pipe rolled easily. When the pipe rolled harder, the collar pecker would "hit a lick" that called for all sets of tongs to stroke in unison ("break in"). When the pipe was made up, the collar pecker would "ring'em off" with a special rhythmic pattern and the laying crew would move on to the next joint of pipe. (Carney 17)

After observing the pipeliner's performance several times, I began to notice the anticipation they exhibited as the workers prepared for their next "show." They were intensely dedicated to an authentic presentation, and they seemed eager to exhibit their skills, but more, they seemed to want to convey to their audience the importance of their contribution to our heritage. I noticed how carefully they put away their equipment between acts. Never were the tools tossed casually aside until the next every-other-hour performance, but were packed away each time as tenderly as an accomplished violinist would care for his violin.

I began to see the Oilies in a different perspective. We talked; I listened. The performance they had given was one they might have given ten or twelve hours a day often in a grueling hot sun or below freezing weather. Their job required not only enormous strength and skill, but split-second interaction. "It was hard—mighty hard," they agreed, but even though they were of one voice in that respect, I sensed the pride, the camaraderie, the dedication of these hardy individuals who had laid pipe which reached from eastern Oklahoma to the Gulf Coast.

They were eager to talk about their experiences sometimes interrupting each other goodnaturedly to clarify a term or answer a question. About the expression "Ain't that a Darb?" I was told after considerable hemming and hawing, that Ruby Darby was an attractive young dancer who followed the Boom Towns;. she was remembered as having performed at The Hump, a popular night-spot in the robust, rowdy boom town of Drumright, Oklahoma. Sometimes Ruby used a pool table for her stage, and once was said to have performed from the deck of a drilling rig on location, and characteristically sans clothing. Thus, a stamp of hearty approval or amazement was a "Darb!"

I learned too that a "screw pipe Johnnie" was a hard, steady worker as opposed to a "snap grabber" who looked for the easiest job. A "one-armed Johnnie" was a hand-operated pump used to lift water out of a pipeline trench, and, of course, what else could a "possum belly" be but a metal box fastened underneath a truck bed to carry pipeline tools. These expressions are but a few of the many rich, descriptive terms associated with the Oil Patch. Most of the terms are now obsolete due to changes in materials, equipment, and methods.

Obviously, their being here was a sentimental journey for these veteran pipeliners, giving them one last chance to relive moments from a glorious period of discovery. At the same time, they were given one last chance to let the world know of their existence, and that they had made their mark; they had made a difference.

Each day the hugh Seismic Vibrator operation adjacent to the pipeliner's location went into action following the pipeliner's show and responded to the delicate flip of valves and switches with an impressive roar that literally shook the ground beneath our feet. Invariably, Mr. Hester would turn sharply toward the technical monster, shake his head disbelievingly, and say, "Things shore ain't like they usta wuz."

In the crowds that gathered around the pipeliner's arena I was soon able to recognize those who were veterans of the Oil Patch. The men with weathered faces appeared early, and they lingered. Sometimes they were accompanied by a younger person, perhaps a son or grandson, to whom they excitedly pointed out familiar objects. And their spouses waited, waited, as patiently as they had done so many days, nights, years, when dinners grew cold, holidays were missed, while the men were trying to "flange up" a job in order to be home for a special occasion. Some of the men stepped into the roped-off area and lovingly caressed the crude tools of the trade now obsolete. They reminisced with the workers, recalled mutual acquaintances, swapped stories, until they were reluctantly pulled away by a younger generation's eagerness to inspect the chrome and metal marvel nearby.

And I heard—after I learned to listen—the rhythm and the music of each performance. The cadency provided by the collar pecker's hammer was clearly discernible. Mr. Hill contended that the tong men developed an "ear" for the tones and tempo of the hammer and "if the pounder hit a sour note, the tong men would let him know about it." Occasionally the workers would dance a little jig as the performance rounded off with "Shave and a Haircut—Six Bits" and their act was "flanged up."

I realized there was an urgency to preserving this scene. To my knowledge there is no record of such a performance, and these workers would never have occasion, nor time, nor opportunity to come together again. So I spent the better part of the next two days frantically searching for a cameraman; Cook and Anderson shared the costs in order to record this unique bit of our heritage. To truly appreciate the show, one must truly not just hear, but listen, and not just look, but really see—.

My purpose in sharing this story today is not to offer a history of the Oil Patch, but, rather, to give an identity to that unique time, and area, for certainly volumes could be written about their rich, exciting period in time, and people who comprised The Oil Patch, and who in those brief four decades in this century left us such a rich legacy. Time has made the colorful vocabulary obsolete; government regulations dispersed the oilfield camps which fostered the "company-family" relationship; and technology has changed the methods of pipelining, but I should like for those few remaining members of The Oil Patch culture to know that we recognize their contribution to our heritage. They were a clan of courageous, hardy, colorful pioneers whose lives touched ours briefly, but who enriched our memories and our history. And it is my earnest plea that the Oilies and the Oil Patch People be given their well-deserved place in the passing parade of Americana.

Works Cited

A copy of the tape is now on a loan basis at the Drumright Oilfield Museum.
Carney, George. "Slappin' Collars and Stabbin' Pipe: Occupational Folklife of Old Time Pipeliners." *Festival of American Folklife 1982.* U.S. Government Printing Office, Washington, D.C.

A Cultural Weave:
Ben Botkin, Constance Rourke & the
Development of Progressive Regionalism

DAVID R. MOORE

As folkculture comes to be recognized more and more as just as much an integral part of our present as of the past, major folklorists of the past who charted the everyday culture are becoming more and more important. Such individuals were surely Ben Botkin and Constance Rourke, as they blended the three traditions of folk, popular and elite, as David Moore carefully points out.

In a recent issue of the *American Quarterly* devoted to Cultural Criticism in America, Werner Sollors raised a key question at the heart of any study of cultural criticism. He asked whether "one decade's conservatism" may "turn out to contain the next decade's radicalism, and, by the way, vice versa?" (173) This paper proceeds in the spirit as well as focus of this question in examining both the legacies and the social and aesthetic issues shaping and energizing the work of two prominent but, until recently, overlooked popularizers in the fields of Folklore and American Civilization during the 1920s and 1930s. Rourke and Botkin left two distinct legacies that confute any attempt to apply easy labels to the cultural criticism of this or any period. Of course, I cannot help but approach the subject through much excellent recent work: including Joan Shelly Rubin's almost single-handed rescuing of Rourke from the graveyard of the myth-symbol school; Richard Handler, Ronna Lee Widner, and Bruce Jackson's rescuing of Botkin from the intellectual limbo to which his rival folklorist Richard Dorson had consigned him; and finally John L. Thomas, Casey Nelson Blake, and Donald Miller's reconsideration of regionalism from the vantage point of post-Reagan America (Rubin 133; "A Convergence of Vision" 191-222; Hirsch 3-38; Widner 1-22; Jackson 23-32; Thomas 158-172; "The Uses of Catastrophism" 225; Blake; Miller). Each of these scholars, and many more besides, have been drawn by the various progressive impulses that were implicit in regionalist discourse but, until recently, overlooked. My own contention is that these impulses grouped themselves into two strains, or legacies.

Botkin's legacy was the ideas of "living lore" and "progressive regionalism" viewed as a forward-looking, community-building enterprise that was also "acculturative," by which he meant, among other things, multicultural in the pluralistic rather than separatist sense; Rourke's search for an "irreducible element" in American culture seemed conservative to radicals like Alfred Kazin then and to many Americanists being trained in graduate school by the late 1960s. Yet Rourke's legacy included the creation of a critical position or role that would rescue the study of American cultures once and for all from that tired old charge of "thinness," by both embracing popular culture and recontextualizing folk and fine arts within it. Together, their work attempted to embrace modernism by documenting the interaction between oral tradition and print and other media at a time when practicing regional writers like Sherwood Anderson and artists like Thomas Hart Benton were lamenting the decline of the "folk" arts before the power of the phonograph, radio, and movie house. Moreover, against the anti-modernist grain of much regionalist discourse, they attempted to extend folkloric research into the new urban and industrial groups emerging as creative cultural centers.

***

In May of 1933, Ben Botkin got a letter from Constance Rourke. The author of numerous articles and three volumes of cultural history, including *American Humor* (1931), the pioneering study of the roles of folklore and the popular stage in American culture, Rourke was already busily earning her designation as, in William Carlos Williams' words, the "Moses" of modern American intellectuals. Though their correspondence was brief, theirs was a meaty one that revealed much about the roles these two would play in what Lewis Mumford dubbed the "New Regionalism" (157-8).[1] In all of its multiplicity, the new regionalism represented a "cluster of ideas and values" whose common core articulated an anti-modernist alternative to what was perceived as a deracinated modern capitalistic society ("Use of Catastrophism" 225). A rhetoric of conservation, based upon the analogy between cultural and natural "resources," regionalism recognized the existence "of real groups and social configurations and geographic relationships" that were ignored and, indeed, threatened by the "abstract culture of the metropolis," and which opposed to the "aimless nomadism" of modern commercial enterprise the conception of a stable, settled, balanced and cultivated life (Mumford 157-8).

Appropriately, Rourke directed her first letter to Botkin to the subject of teaching history and literature to college students. She was "anxious."

she said, to discover whether there were college courses that stimulated "interest in the students' native region." In the same year that *American Humor* consolidated Rourke's reputation, Botkin's editorship of the regional miscellany *Folk-Say* (1928-1932), and a regional anthology of Southwestern verse called *The Southwest Scene*, had cemented his own reputation as a promoter of regional literature in the schools as well as the literary magazines. Products of elite Eastern colleges and universities, they viewed themselves as educators as much as intellectuals, and they maintained an unswerving loyalty to the ideals, if not always the actual hurly-burly, of academic enterprise throughout their careers.[2] In thanking Rourke for "breaking the ice," Botkin revealed that by 1933 he and Rourke were hardly unacquainted in all but the most formal sense. In Botkin, Rourke was fortunate to find an educator already engaged with colleagues in the social sciences indevising an interdepartmental "regional study of culture" through a series of seminars that would "break down departmentalization in the curriculum" and "integrate the whole culture of a single region." The previous semester, Botkin had introduced a course in folklore in the anthropology department and required students to read Rourke's friend Martha Warren Beckwith's *Folklore in America*. But Botkin could point to other pioneering academic folklorists as well, including Mabel Major and Rebecca Smith at Texas Christian University, Margaret Kennedy at New Mexico Normal University, his future mentor, Louise Pound, at the University of Nebraska, and Percy MacKaye at Sweet Briar College.[3] Such members of the expanding "coterie" still tended to treat each folk form discretely: Pound and Mackaye focusing on folksongs and speech, and Kennedy and Smith and Major on folk expression in literature. It would rest with Botkin and Rourke to weld these forms together into a unified theory of folklife.

In the most significant epistolary exchange, Botkin solicited Rourke's contribution to a symposium on "Aspects of Regionalism." Botkin told Rourke that he had noted "a very intimate relation between American humor...and regional life and character, especially in their local-color and occupational aspects." Rourke's task for the symposium would be simple, Botkin assured her. All she would "have to do is treat the humor from the point of view of American regionalism instead of the regionalism from the point of view of American humor."[4] Rourke replied that she had always seen an "underlying basis for regionalism" in *American Humor*, which had, moreover, already provided "the early groundwork for a regional approach to American literature."[5] Both Botkin and Rourke had come to regionalism through literary criticism, whose dedication to cultivation of a taste and public dovetailed nicely with regionalism's call for the "creative conservation of human resources." Yet, this exchange marked, as well, a key point of departure, if not quite outright disagreement.

During the late 1920s and early 1930s, Botkin's tenure as editor of regional anthologies like *Folk-Say*, *Space* and *The Southwest Scene* alerted him to the limitations as well as successes of a literary approach to cultural criticism. In "reckoning up" his ventures' losses and gains, Botkin could applaud a progression from a certain quaintness and old-timeyness to an increasingly "crisper note of lusty, hard-boiled youth," whose emphasis was upon contemporary cultural, racial, and class conflicts rather than survivals, and whose forms were "experimental rather than traditional." Moreover, *Folk-Say* and *The Southwest Scene* played important roles as medium for the discovery of talent and for "the free expression of personality and of social ideals in connection with the theme of the relation of individual to environment." In this latter role, *Folk-Say* further provided a model for other regional publishing ventures in the South, Midwest and Northwest (*New Mexico Quarterly* 157). By the middle of the decade, however, Botkin had taken his contribution to regionalist discourse, the idea of "folk-say," about as far as it would go and was obviously dissatisfied. In Botkin's hands, Mumford and Howard Odum's ideas of cultural renewal and cultural conservation had proven useful tools for suggesting a path toward cultural diversity based upon the assertion of the essential richness of the country's many folk cultures. Yet, the regionalist belief, shared by Botkin, that expressive culture must be rooted in an organic, "bottom-up" process of transmission was belied by its tendency to impose its own aesthetic framework upon the intended producers of these cultures. Calling his own "strenuous efforts at welding a great mass and diversity of material into a semblance of unified sequence" less a progression than an "unholy progression," Botkin struggled with his own new version of that most elusive American myth, *e pluribus unum*.[6] Still missing was the glue of a realistic and compelling ideology, rooted in the *social*, that would accurately reflect actual American society and, just as important to Botkin, provide a role for the folklorist-intellectual. And it was precisely this deeper and wider access to the social that the field of folklore would provide, though it would also require a new setting and a more radical shift from the academic to the very public world of the cultural wing of the New Deal.

As folklore editor in the New Deal's Federal Writers' Project, Botkin found a new agency through which he could pursue studies he thought would contribute to a celebration of diversity and cultural integration (Hirsch 3-38). The roots of conflict between the professional and popular, may have reached back to his regional anthologies, but they became even clearer in Botkin's intended use of the texts and phonograph disks gathered from his small army of field workers. The archival material *would* be made available to scholars, educators, and writers all over the country. But publications of the material would be designed "to meet the needs of the general reader rather than the specialist," though a "high standard of accuracy as well as interest "would be "aimed at" throughout. The collections would contain lore in its "literary" and "popular" states in magazines, newspapers, calendars, catalogues, and poetry and would, moreover, "by means of large, cheaply printed editions, pamphlets, and school readers," be expected to reach a large audience and to find increasing use in the education of Americans to "a new understanding and appreciation of its cultural heritage" (*Supplementary Instructions* 3-5).

By the late 1930s, the rhetoric of progressive regionalism had relocated individual identity and the "good life" from its earlier, more mystical "community of impulse" to a new, explicitly class-conscious "community of interest" (Hart 140-57). A full-blown cultural politics, progressive regionalism viewed the celebration of American diversity and the criticism of social injustices that violated democratic principles as interrelated tasks whose articulation would be best served through folklore (Hirsch 26). As an "acculturative" fact of modern life, regionalism needn't resort to setting up the myths of lost causes like those Boktin saw underlying the credos of the Southern Agrarians, or the false dualisms underlying Mary Austin's opposition to the "sophisticated." In the parlance of cultural pluralism, to which progressive regionalism bore the closest resemblance, the tendency of the provinces—conceived either geographically or ethnically—to substitute their local myths for the national myth of Americanism was preferable to what Donald Davidson had called that "all-destroying abstraction, America." From Mumford, Botkin derived the notion that regionalism was capable of solid contemporary and forward-looking significance as a "valuable social adjunct to literature, along with ethnology, folk lore, and Marxist economics." The protean conception of a regionally differentiated and inter-regionally related culture had something to offer to literature, Botkin believed.

And this "something" included a subject matter (the physical and cultural landscape, local customs, character, speech, etc.); a technique (folk and native modes of expression, style, rhythm, imagery, symbolism); and a point of view in the social ideal of a planned society and the cultural values derived from tradition as the liberator rather than the confiner. As a guide to a complete picture of the American scene and the American folk, regionalism pointed to the new ideology and mythology emerging alike from the country's "buried cultures" and "submerged classes" ("Regionalism: Cult or Culture?" 181-85).

While Botkin became increasingly interested in class, Rourke focused on America as a land of myth-makers. Beginning with *Trumpets of Jubilee* (1927) and *Troupers of the Gold Coast* the following year, Rourke traced out the cultural construction of great characters like the Beecher family, Horace Greeley, P.T. Barnum, and Lotta Crabtree. A "humble student of character" who believed that human character remained an "inexhaustible matrix," Rourke hoped to draw exquisite portraitures of figures who had "commanded superlatives, in the numbers which they drew to themselves, in the praises which they received, in the huge tumultuous reverberations which they produced in the public situation" (*Trumpets of Jubilee* viii). By the time she discusses Greeley and Barnum, however, her figures push in and out of a foreground increasingly crowded by the "great instinctual purpose" of a migratory people trying to shape a social identity in a centrifugal society. In the end, her figures become submerged within the configural, the personal within the public it addressed, and their "linked utterances" become signposts charting out a path among the noisy, defiant and unappeased popular movements of nineteenth-century America.

"Americans love a rogue," Rourke had written of Barnum in *Trumpets of Jubilee*, and in *American Humor*, published in 1931, Rourke made that roguery (we might call it *Voguery* today) a unifying concept for explaining the development of cultural forms and behaviors in a nation of self-promoters. Here, at the intellectual crossroads where Johann Gottfried von Herder, Frederick Jackson Turner, and Ruth Benedict offered a definition of folklore as a both a subject and a method of inquiry that focused on the "many layers of cultures of peoples" rather than on so-called "peaks of achievement," Rourke worked out her own contribution to progressive regionalism. In the songs, ballads, folk-theater, travel sketch, local history and chronicle that emerged from the mists of the early Republic, Rourke found the popular strains of American myths. The "ground thought" (Beckwith 313)[7] of *American Humor*—and of all Rourke's books and articles in the thirties—was that great writers had often embraced popular moods and formulations even when they seemed to range "furthest afield," and that without such sources "for fresh life and continuance," even the most complex literature could scarcely exist at all. Rourke's idea of an holistic approach to culture, weaved together by popular, folk, and fine arts thus defined expressive culture as multivalent forms created by and for specific audiences in what the folklorist Henry Glassie would call "public culture" (Dorson 258).

As Joan Shelley Rubin has argued, though Rourke pioneered the field of American Civilization by stimulating interest in myth, she was never more than an "intellectual second cousin" to writers like F.O. Matthiessen, Henry Nash Smith, R.W.B. Lewis, and Leo Marx (*Constance Rourke and American Culture* 133; Rubin 191-222). The myth school were synthesizers willing both to take a single or small cluster of mythic constructs to describe a fundamental *American experience*, and to invest these constructs with the power of historical explanation. Rourke, on the other hand, was far more interested in opening up avenues and assembling myths in their dynamic unfolding as part of ritual behavior. Certain of Rourke's assumptions—a seemingly uncritical enthusiasm for the minstrel tradition, the repeated references to an "homogeneous" American "mind"—have long ceased to provide us with compelling models for understanding cultural change and conflict. Yet in focusing on myth not as a chronological string of references in a plot for a story whose ending is already known, but as a dramatic mode of *ritual behavior*, a "habit of self-scrutiny," Rourke assigned to myth an integrative, community-building function among competing regional, ethnic, and even sexual groups. Thus, in the humorist's ritual "masking," Rourke discovered more than an amusing device made famous in Twain's "How to Tell a Story." She located the source of cultural forms in the psychic tensions attending the process of community building. In *Shadow and Act*, Ralph Ellison referred specifically to Rourke's discoveries in characterizing America as a "land of masking jokers," whose humor served the numerous and often ambivalent purposes of "aggression as well as defense," of "projecting the future as well as preserving the past" (*Shadow and Act* 54-5).

By the time she finished *The Roots of American Culture*, the first volume in an extended cultural history she would not live to finish, the flexibility of her method allowed Rourke to discover a new set of culture heroes and configurations. These included the educator, novelist, and dramatist Susannah Rowson, who trained her "young ladies" in the art of "public declamation" and to become "women of the great world," and the Shaker religious sect. Though Rourke the historian could claim that this communal organization "concentrated essential purposes" and "popular movements" of the mid-nineteenth century, it reflected as well her own utopia of democracy, sexual equality, an accomplished handicrafts tradition that was progressive and functional, and an agrarian, communitarian society shorn of the excesses of individual competition (*The Roots of American Culture* 195-237).

Ironically, the eclipse of Botkin's "progressive" wing of the regionalist movement in the post-War era tells us most about its possible interest to us today. Regarding matters of style and method, Botkin and Rourke's sprawling interests and commitment to balancing the professional demand for intellectual rigor on the one hand, and the more general reader's demand for accessibility and relevance on the other would become increasingly inimical to the demands of specialization in the academy. Botkin's belief that folklore should be interdisciplinary as well as cooperative and "experiential" drew the devastating charge by Richard Dorson that Botkin was peddling in "fakelore." Second, the viability of cultural pluralism, to which the *cultural weave* and its emphasis upon oral tradition contributed directly, was displaced by the growing dominance of a cosmopolitan ideal that opposed the nurturing of "provinciality" of any kind, while substituting, in place, its own kind of parochialism.[8] At the same time, the so-called "mass-culture critique" would, by the 1950s, carry forth with greater effectiveness the more conservative regionalists' claim that popular culture was little more than an aberration born of commercial greed and public ignorance.[9]

By the end of *The Roots of American Culture*, in a meditation that would be her last, posthumously published words, Rourke left a suggestion of how she and Botkin's understanding of the budding field of folklore could stand as a model for cultural criticism in the age of postmodernism and multiculturalism. "A prodigious amount of work is still to be done in the way of unearthing, defining, and synthesizing our traditions," wrote Rourke, in what remains truly a standard conclusion to many a scholarly effort. In what has become less standard practice, however, she urged her colleagues to make these traditions finally known through "simple and natural means." For, "beneath this purpose must probably lie fresh reconstructions of our notion as to what constitutes a culture, with a removal of ancient snobberies and with new inclusions" (*RAC* 295).

Notes

I want to thank John Thomas, Bruce Rosenberg, and Kent Ryden for their generous and insightful help with this paper.

[1]Botkin and Rourke would exchange roughly sixteen letters, mostly between 1933 and 1934.
[2]CR to BB, 15 May 1933, MSS.
[3]BB to CR, 17 May 1933, MSS.
[4]BB to CR, 16 June 1933, MSS.
[5]CR to BB, 19 June 1933, MSS.
[6]Botkin's retrospective appeared as "Folk-Say and Space: Genesis and

Exodus," in Southwest Review, v. 20, no. 4 (July, 1935), p. 321-335.
⁷This summation appeared in Martha Beckwith's glowing review of American Humor in Journal of American Folklore, v. 44, no. 173 (July-Sept, 1931): 313. Beckwith taught at Vassar College, Rourke's alma mater.
⁸For a useful distinction between cultural pluralism and cosmopolitanism, see David Hollinger's "Ethnic Diversity, Cosmopolitanism, and the Emergence of the American Liberal Intelligentsia," American Quarterly v. XXVII (1975): 133-151.
⁹Herbert Gans summarizes the mass culture critique as a four-pronged attack upon the negative character of popular culture creation, its negative effect upon high culture, upon pop culture audiences, and upon the whole of society, in *Popular Culture and High Culture: An Analysis and Evaluation of Taste* (New York: Basic Books, 1974): 19.

Works Cited

Blake, Casey Nelson. *Blessed Community: The Cultural Criticism of Randolph Bourne, Van Wyck Brooks, Waldo Frank, and Lewis Mumford.* Chapel Hill: U of North Carolina, 1990.
Botkin, Benjamin A. "Regionalism: Cult or Culture?" *The English Journal.* XXV: 3 (March 1936): 181-185.
_____. *Supplementary Instructions to The American Guide Manual: Manual for Folklore Studies.* MSS, Benjamin A. Botkin Collection, Love Library. U of Nebraska, Lincoln, Nebraska: 3-5.
_____. "The New Mexico Round Table on Regionalism." *New Mexico Quarterly* (Aug. 1933) 152-157.
Cantwell, Robert. "Conjuring Culture: Ideology and Magic in the Festival of American Folklife." Journal of American Folklore. 104:412 (Spring, 1991): 148-163.
Dorson, Richard M. ed. "Folk Art." *Folklore and Folklife: An Introduction.* Chicago: U of Chicago, 1972: 258.
Ellison, Ralph. *Shadow and Act.* New York: Random House, 1964: 48; 54-55.
Hart, Henry, ed. "Regionalism and Culture." *The Writer in a Changing World.* New York: Equinox Cooperative P, 1937: 140-157.
Hirsch, Jerrold. "Reassessment" of Botkin "Folklore in the Making: B.A. Botkin." *Journal of American Folklore* 100:395 (Jan.-Mar. 1987): 3-38.
Jackson, Bruce. "Ben Botkin." *NYFQ.* XII:3-4 (1986): 23-32.
Miller, Donald L. *Lewis Mumford: A Life.* New York: Weidenfeld and Nicolson, 1989.
Mumford, Lewis. Botkin's second *Folk-Say: "Toward a New Regionalism." The New Republic.* 25 March 1931: 157-158.
Rourke, Constance M. *The Roots of American Culture and other Essays.* Ed. Van Wyck Brooks. New York: Harcourt, Brace & Col., 1942: 195-237.

_____. *Trumpets of Jubilee: Henry Ward Beecher, Harriet Beecher Stowe, Lyman Beecher, Horace Greeley, and P.T. Barnum.* New York: Harcourt, Brace & Co., 1927: viii.

Rubin, Joan Shelley. "*A Convergence of Vision: Constance Rourke, Charles Sheeler, and American Art.*" *American Quarterly* 42:2 (June 1990): 191-222.

_____. *Constance Rourke and American Culture.* Chapel Hill: U of North Carolina, 1980): 133.

Sollers, Werner. *American Quarterly.* "Of Mules and Mares in a Land of Difference; or Quadrupeds All?" 42:2 (June 1990): 167-90.

Thomas, John L. "The Uses of Catastrophism: Lewis Mumford, Vernon L. Parrington, Van Wyck Brooks, and the End of American Regionalism." *American Quarterly* 42:2 (June 1990): 225.

Thomas' John L. "Lewis Mumford: Regionalist Historian." *Reviews in American History* (March, 1988): 158-172.

Widner, Rona Lee. "Lore For the Folk: Benjamin A. Botkin and the Development of Folklore Scholarship in America." *New York Folklore Quarterly* XII:3-4, (1986): 1-22.

Totems, Flight and Fetishes:
Shamanic Elements in Biker Culture

NORMAN LANQUIST

Americans have always taken to the open-road with the gusto and freedom voiced by Walt Whitman in his "Song of the Open Road," "Afoot and light-hearted I take to the open road," where he is "strong and content." The ecstasy was made even more intense with the invention of the motorcycle. From the 1950s on some Americans would say that the motorcycle, with its lure to particular kinds of people, has become a curse. But, as Norman Lanquist points out, this culture has developed its own totems, fetishes and shamanic elements, with roots in the most ancient of archetypal imagery and practice.

American Harley biker culture has evolved many tribal traits to reinforce social cohesion. Among these are several elements of shamanism endemic to primeval belief systems. These include reverence for metalwork, skull fetishism, bird totemism and an intense identification of the rider with his mount. Most important, though, is the "technique of ecstasy" making possible transcendent spirit flight into other levels of reality, and the resultant sense of liberation.

Biker culture is an authentic contemporary sub-culture like those of ethnic populations or other highly cohesive same-interest groups within North American mass culture; there is no aspect of activity for the hard-core biker that does not have an artifact of material culture or attitudes of non-material culture in terms of biker imagery distinct from those of mass society. These include distinguishing costumes and hairstyles, "tribal" markings—tattoos—and decorative/symbolic icons. Furthermore, its exoticism, cohesiveness and atavistic ferocity hold a continual and irresistible fascination for the "straight" citizen. Its strength is in its continuity and energy—its weaknesses in its marginality, alienated despair and dependence on consumer-oriented manufactured goods. And what is a biker? Some self-definitions from *Easyriders*, the premier biker magazine:

...the tattooed, bushy bearded, long-haired chopper rider in his grubby clothes and cut-off Levi jacket with all the patches and pins on it...the freedom exhibited by

257

258 Continuities in Popular Culture

the biker as he flies down the highway with his long hair blowing wildly in the wind, with his chick tucked in behind him...

....Bikers is a driftin' bunch. Most wouldn't be caught dead in one place for more'n the time it takes fer'm to wash the dust down the gizzards with a few cold beers....Then that old road fever gits a new holt on their minds, draggin' m someplace new.

...The girl is infatuated with choppers and the guys who ride them. To her, such guys are some kind of gods, riding winged horses—all supermen.

One area of biker culture is of particular and somewhat surprising interest—that of shamanism. Fundamentally and originally, the term was assigned by anthropologists to magical/religious folk practices of tribal Siberia, but exhaustive ethnographic research has shown shamanism to be not only universal but of such age as to have given rise to substantial speculation that it lies at the root of all subsequent belief systems involving the supernatural, including organized institutional state religions.Moreover, biker culture, having, as it were, synthesized a pseudo-tribal way of life, exhibits an intriguing number of cohering shamanic elements, giving credence to the atavism and strength of shamanic beliefs and practices.

There are a few fine sources on shamanism, some hoary classics, others recent and moderately obscure. Halifax's *Shaman: The Wounded Healer* is a passionate and concentrated summary, assiduously illustrated with tribal art from throughout the world; *Stones, Bones, And Skin: Ritual And Shamanic Art* provides detailed text and rare photographs of the Canadian tribal experience with articles focussed on special areas. Czaplicka's text of 1915 is awesome in that she must have read absolutely everything available for her *Aboriginal Siberia* in several languages, but her compilation is, after all subtitled *A Study In Social Anthropology* and not specifically focussed on shamanism, as is, finally, Mircea Eliade's key work in the field, simply entitled *Shamanism*, that deals centrally and interpretively with the topic on a world-wide basis. Mention should also be made of R.G. Cleland's *This Reckless Breed Of Men: The Trappers And Fur Traders Of The South West* for a startling look at biker precursors on the frontier, and Colin Wilson's pioneer work of the 1960's, *The Outsider*, since reprinted.

Perhaps it'd be helpful to try to establish the biker culture as being tribal, but comparisons to preliterate rural folk of modest technologies may seem far-fetched, and parallels of bikers and Navajos, for example, hard to explain. Jan Yoors' book, *The Gypsies* suggested several points of parallel between gypsy life in Europe of about 50 years ago, and the biker lifestyle of the last 40 years in America. First , the gypsies have a unique and private language, not only to speak to one another, but for the mystification of outsiders. Similar is the function of biker argot. More to the point, however, is the single strong theme of profound alienation from the so-called dominant culture. Irresistible nomadism is also a common trait of the two, exhibited persisently in the *Easyriders* short stories. There are also periodic gatherings for feasting and reaffirming of group solidarity. A distinct manner of dress is vital to each, again for the dual purposes of unifying the group and distinguishing its members from sedentary citizens. Unlike bikers, gypsy society actually is composed of tribes—about five of them, world-wide.

But let's see what the biker and the shaman have in common, starting with a minor but fascinating issue. Eliade makes reference to the affinity between the role and function of the shaman and the metal-smith, noting the forging of numerous heavy symbolic iron fetishes that hang from the costume worn while shamanizing. He notes the mystery and fear historically connected in the minds of the non-initiated with the working of metal. One need only recall the ill-tempered Vulcan, husband of Venus, and the irrascible earth-bound dwarves of German legend and Wagnerian opera. The magic allure of metal-working can be demonstrated without effort in examples from silver casting among Navajos to bronze and iron work in the civilizations of the 18th century coastal Africa, such as the Benin. But the contemporary biker craftsman has become a magical artist in two inter-related realms: as mechanic, intuitively and non-verbally—magically—repairing and perfecting the potential performance of the Harley Davidson engine, though a less romantic and more common occurrence is actually that of the trained and respected mechanic, schooled in one of the two factory-sponsored institutes, a magician of sorts nonetheless, who is called upon to heal an ailing mount or often as not resurrect a dead one. Secondly, is the custom bike builder whose concern is almost entirely with the visual appearance of the motorcycle; hence, he's a sculptor, a genuine pop artist in a very real sense exemplified by the eccentric genius, Ron Finch.

But what is the essense of shamanism? To Eliade it is the "technique of ecstasy" the ability to "ascend to the sky...to descend to the underworld." He notes the shamanic experience as an "ecstatic experience...the Primary Phenomenon" of religious experience. I believe it apparent in biker writing, to some extent only partially successful in the poetry, but mainly expressed in the fiction, that this is the experience that is at the foundation of the biker's quest and life-style and is found in motorcyle riding as the bikers' principal activity and reason for being: the biker's basic article of faith—"Live to Ride; Ride to Live."

At the initiation of the Siberian tribal shaman, a typical theme is that

260 Continuities in Popular Culture

of symbolic death and dismemberment and the shaman candidate's contemplation of his own skeleton, seemingly as a rebirth into another order of being, different from ordinary men, but there is also the theme of *memento mori* present, too, it seems to me, and could be seen as well as a strong element in Aztec traditions and in a curious sub-genre of 16th century Spanish painting, too. The fact remains that the skull specifically, is one of the biker's primary icons. A hasty scanning of a catalogue of biker jewelry—a highly developed area of merchandising—would show at once that perhaps over half of the pins, earrings, necklaces and patches are of skulls. *Easyriders* decided to investigate the iconography themselves, in an article "Symbolism of the Skull." Fundamentally though, I believe the skull provides a constant reminder of the biker's—man's—own mortality in a fashion uncomfortable to the "citizen." One aspect of this, of course, is the relative fragility of a man or woman on a bike in the context of two-ton automobiles on the open road. Both the popular press and the biker press are constantly replete with tales of "downed brothers" or "motorcyclist killed." I suspect another aspect of the skull fetish is the urge by many bikers to associate with the "dark side" of life, related to the theme of death and diabolism with which so many bikers obsessively associate.

However, there is no element more central to the shamanic experience than that of flight. To Eliade, "All over the world the same magical power is credited to sorcerers and medicine men." In trance-like states induced by hypnotic drumming, chanting and hallucinogens, the shaman and those around him are convinced of the reality of his soaring; to the observer the movements are limited, and earth-bound, frequently consisting of nothing more than climbing a notched log a few yards above the ground, but the shaman's accounts are of unmistakeable flying; the very best are the aerial views of the earth on Black Elk's spirit flight in Neihardt's books. What has this to do with the Harley-riding biker? The biker literature is permeated with descriptions of the motorcycle riding experience that express the yearning for ecstatic flight that is shamanic in nature and that frequently are intense enough to replicate that experience.

What gives a little more credence to this is the persistent bird imagery in tribal shamanics and in biker or Harley culture, too. In Eliade's words, "All this makes us think of the ornithomorphic symbolism of the Siberian shaman's costume." It should remind us unavoidably of the obsessive eagle iconography of the biker. Naturally, to begin with the trade-mark emblem of the Harley Davidson motorcycle company has always been the eagle surmounting the Harley Davidson escutcheon, or "bar and shield," what the company calls its "traditional" eagle. Not incidentally, Eliade notes that the bird usually chosen world-wide as the shaman's totem is the eagle. In his words, "..we must also consider the mythical relations that exist between the eagle and the shaman...The eagle, it will be remembered, is held to be the father of the first shaman...Nor must we forget that the eagle in a manner represents the Supreme Being...." Thus the identification. And here is as good a juncture as any to indicate the meaning of the shaman and the biker's yearning for flight, its archetypally mythical nature and the importance of it all for everyone. As Eliade puts it, "According to many traditions, the power of flight extended to all men in the mythical age; all could reach heaven, whether on the wings of a fabulous bird or on the clouds." Eliade further notes that "...among the Yakut shamans, their costume displays a complete bird skeleton of iron." (Note here the relation to the metal-working motif.) And that "....the bird costume is indispensible to flight to the other world...." In sum then, the most conspicuous aspect of the Harley rider, other than his motorcycle itself, is his use of the Harley eagle in the forms of a profusion of pins and patches, in half a dozen sizes, a variety of colors and design variants.

Now interestingly enough, the Harley Davidson eagle is not typically shown in flight, but perched. There are shamanic analogues for this particular iconography. Eliade again:

The bird perched on a stick is a frequent symbol in shamic circles. It is found, for example, on the tombs of Yakut shamans. A Hungarian 'taltos' had a stick or post before his hut and perched on the stick was a bird. He sent the bird wherever he would have to go. The bird perched on a post is already found in the celebrated relief as Lascaux (bird-headed man) in which Horst Kirchner has seen a representation of a hypnotic trance. However this may be, it is certain that the motif 'bird perched on a post' is extremely archaic.

But what really is the meaning of this ornithomorphism? Obviously, perched eagles are familiar to us all outside of biker culture and tribal ethnology in the form of national emblems—the U.S., Germany, Imperial Russia—and the key to meaning is in archaic bird images. Eliade:

.....for did they not evince and emphasize the shaman's superhuman condition, his freedom, in the last analysis, to move safely among the three cosmic zones and to pass indefinitely from 'life' to 'death' and vice versa, exactly like the 'spirits' whose abilities he had appropriated?

And this is not only the heart of shamanism—the shaman as psychopomp in Eliade's terms—but fundamental to biker culture. Eliade:

"...to rise to higher spheres and descend into the lower, and distinguish there the things which it would be proper to do..." And as the tribal shaman moves between the three worlds, so biker fiction conveys the same theme. There is a defined subgenre of these stories that deal with after-death experiences, some grimly humorous, some merely grim, as bikers encounter God, and about as often, the Devil.

This diabolic element in biker culture is very pronounced, particularly in its iconography, and in club names like Hell's Angels, Satan's Slaves. At the risk of over-simplifying a complex psychosocial issue, I also suspect this conspicuous identification with the *outre*, the shocking, has its origins in a couple of factors—the desire to be as much set apart from the citizenry at large by espousal of the evil and shocking, and by a real sense of worthlessness and self-loathing on the part of many. Note here the strength of this theme in Hunter Thompson's *The Hells Angels* and *Freewheelin' Frank: Secretary Of The Angels*, co-authored by poet Michael Mc Clure.

A study of biker culture would be incomplete without some mention of drugs, taking for granted the pervasiveness of drugs at all levels of American culture. First, there's the history of the formation of biker culture in its present state as growing out of '60's counter culture. Another factor is a practical one for riders making long runs: use of stimulants for staying awake on the road. Compare here Linda Ronstadt's truck driver song ".....weed, whites, and wine, then show me a sign..." In a sense, both bikers and the traditional shaman are "involved with drugs." However, Eliade doesn't put much credence in the importance of drugs on shamanic practice, in contrast to Michael Harner, who believes them not only central to, but the very origin of shamanism! Harner has credible field-work experience in ethnopharmacology in Latin America as accounted in his *Hallucinogens And Shamanism*. He has also written an instructional manual for shamanic practice.

One of the arresting common elements of the shamanic I've discovered is that of the horse, and the curious practice of horse sacrifice which seems very widely distributed in both hemispheres among tribal peoples, like the Siberian Altaic. And while Eliade does not give this emphasis, it seems that the sacrificed horse symbolized a spiritual mount for the shaman in his role of psychopomp— conductor or recoverer of lost souls. What seems of crucial interest here for our purposes is the intense and fanatic identification of the Harley rider with his mount. His touchy defensiveness regarding his Harley is well-known. There are allegations that the fatal stabbing at the Altamont Raceway rock concert during the Stones' performance was triggered by the victim's jostling the Harley of one of the Angels hired for "security." Aside from all this though, there are documented instances of "horse sacrifice" among bikers—"downed bros" buried with their motorcycles.

An extremely interesting aspect of horse sacrifice in shamanic rites is the erotic. In Eliade's account,

Among the Kumandin of the Tomsk region the horse sacrifice includes an exhibition of wooden masks and phalli, carried by three young men; they gallop with the phallus between their legs 'like a stallion' and touch the spectators. The song sung on this occasion is distinctly erotic. Among the Teleut when the shaman, climbing the tree, reaches the third *taptys* the women, girls, and children leave and the shaman begins an obscene song resembling that of the Kumandin; its purpose is to strengthen the men sexually. This rite has parallels elsewhere, and its meaning is the more explicit because it forms part of the horse sacrifice....

The erotic mount is a major motif in biker culture, too. The sexual allure of Harley riding is without question one of the great attractions for the rider or the "wannabe" or would-be rider. Here are some expressions from *Best Biker Fiction* #1, an anthology of the best of the first ten years of the *Easyriders* fiction:

There's something about a man with a quarter-ton of noisy, high-powered steel between his legs that gets to chicks. They seem to mix the two, the man and the machine, together into some sort of super sex-fantasy, which, it must be admitted, is one of the better points of riding a chopper.

As I straddled her to give her one hell of a kick on the starter pedal, I remember that some hotshit college chick once told me that a bike was a sex thing for freaks like me. She vibrates, purrs when she's running free on the road, and roars when I squeeze her.

Reno listened, smiling. He wondered what sensations had been aroused in Jean and Marjorie—by anything other than the ride itself. For instance, the stroking hands, the brute power of the machines they straddled, the unaccustomed vibration that shook them tinglingly from head to toe. He wondered if they'd ever admit to those thrills, even to themselves. No car could ever get a chick that shook up.

In sum, shamanism and the biker mystique are worth our attention because, in Eliade's words:

an analysis of the 'imagination of motion' will show how essential the nostalgia for flight is to the human psyche. The point of primary importance here is that the mythology and the rites of magical flight peculiar to shamans and sorcerers confirm and proclaim their transcendence in respect to the human condition; by flying into the air, in bird form or in their normal human shape, shamans as it were proclaim the degeneration of humanity. For as we have seen, a number of myths refer to a primordial time when *all human beings* could ascend to heaven, by climbing a mountain, a tree, or a ladder, or flying by their own power, or being carried by birds. The degeneration of humanity henceforth forbids the mass of mankind to fly to heaven; only death restores men (and not all of them) to their primordial condition; only then can they ascend to heaven, fly like birds.

In our larger social order it is the biker who more earnestly than others attempts continually with each ride to seek and to attain this experience—for Eliade, the "...ecstasy—which induced the experiences that were expressed as 'magical flight.'..."

In the end, it seems that the salient element —the very reason to ride—in biker culture is the sense of freedom, closely allied with the sensations of riding itself that we've looked at. *Easyriders* says it best:

The endless ribbon of asphalt, that's what makes all the hassles, all the pain, and even the dark-night glooms of bein' a scooter tramp worthwhile.

Ours is a hard life, a harsh life. At the same time, on a heartening level, it is a wonderful and idyllic kind of life, a gypsy existence, having no ties that bind and reveling in the magic-carpet freedom of being able to take off any time, for anywhere, on any whim. Most people can't handle that kind of freedom. It's too intense. It scares them.

We live the way I think most men would want to live if their blood flowed hot enough to let them dream of so much freedom. Our lives have a majesty that has passed beyond the ken of most of the world around us.

Bikers flaunt a glimpsed heraldry of envied ritual embodying apparent mystery to mere citizens in cars; yet their ways are a complex of traits for those who, in the words of poet Gary Snyder, "...hold the most archaic values on earth. They go back to the Paleolithic...the magic of animals...the power of vision and solitude...terrifying initiation and rebith..."—our longest and deepest continuities of culture.

Contributors

Ronald J. Ambrosetti is Chairperson of the Department of English at the SUNY—College at Fredonia. He is currently writing a book on Eric Ambler for Macmillan-Twayne.

Nadine Brewer an Associate Professor of English at Buena Vista College in Storm Lake, Iowa, teaches British and Comparative Literatures, Literary Criticism and Linguistics. Devoted to Women's Studies and Literature, she has taught and lectured on such in France, Romania, Croatia, Slovenia and the Netherlands, as well as here at home. She has also presented programs in various countries on American folkloric and gospel music, and has published in numerous journals and trade magazines, including *National Geographic*. At present, she is revising a book on Elizabeth Madox Roberts for a university press and hurrying to finish an annotated anthology of literature by women writers of the Eastern Bloc nations, 1946-1989.

Ray B. Browne is founder of the Popular Culture Association, and editor of the *Journal of Popular Culture* and the *Journal of American Culture*. He is also Chair emeritus of the Department of Popular Culture at Bowling Green State University, and the author/editor of more than 50 books on culture and the humanities.

Jimmie Cook is a veteran of the Department of English at Oklahoma State University, Stillwater, Oklahoma; she retired from the teaching profession in May of 1993. Cook resides in Drumright, "A Town of Oil Repute." She has written a number of scholarly articles, and is a freelance writer of stories, poems, and articles for numerous newspapers and periodicals. Cook regularly writes a weekly newspaper column, and presents a weekly ten-minute radio spot for KWHP-KUSH. Cook has presented numerous papers at national and regional Popular Culture Conventions.

B. Lee Cooper is an internationally recognized scholar in the realms of lyric analysis, rock bibliography, and contemporary music discography. While serving as Academic Vice President and Professor of History at three different colleges during the past two decades, Dr. Cooper has authored seven books, nearly 100 articles, and more than 250 book and record reviews. His recent publications include *A Resource Guide to Themes In Contemporary Song Lyrics, 1950-1985* (Greenwood Press, 1986), *Response Recording: An Answer Song Discography*, with Wayne S. Haney (Scarecrow Press, 1990), *Popular Music Perspectives: Ideas, Themes, and Patterns In Contemporary Lyrics* (Popular Press, 1991), and *Rock Music and American Popular Culture: Rock 'n' Roll Resources* (Haworth Press, 1993). Dr. Cooper is currently completing a book-length manuscript tentatively entitled *Doo-Wop Stylists: A Bibliographic Resource Guide.*

David Crouch is Reader in Cultural Studies and Geography, Anglia University, Cambridge, U.K. He researches and writes widely about popular culture, landscape and leisure that people make themselves—how we make our own culture. This includes the diverse topics of allotments (including the book *The Allotment; Its Landscape and Culture*), Stonehenge; the British countryside and popular culture; people celebrating their local place. Current research includes culture and space in terms of caravans, small holdings and orchards; back gardens and intentional communities.

Morris B. Holbrook is the W.T. Dillard Professor of Marketing, Graduate School of Business, Columbia University, 504 Uris Hall, New York, NY 10027. The author gratefully acknowledges the support of the Columbia Business School's Faculty Research Fund. He is the author of *Daytime Television Gameshows and the Celebration of Merchandise: The Price is Right* published by the Popular Press.

W.J. Hug is an Associate Professor of English at Jacksonville State University, Jacksonville, AL. He has been involved in the ACA/PCA since 1985, and is currently ACA chair in Ethnicity.

Sherrie A. Inness is a Ph.D. candidate at the University of California, San Diego, where she is completing a dissertation on turn-of-the-century representations of the college-educated woman. She has essays on a wide range of topics published or forthcoming in *American Literary Realism 1870-1910, Journal of American Culture, Journal of Popular Culture*, the *NWSA Journal*, and *Women's Studies*, as well as in an anthology of nineteenth-century girls' culture.

Gary L. Jones is an Associate Professor of Political Science at the University of Nevada, Las Vegas. Author of numerous studies on the politics of popular culture, he is currently engaged in writing a book on the political theory of Noah Webster and editing a collection of Webster's political writings.

Margaret J. King was the first to earn a graduate degree in Popular Culture from the Center for the Study of Popular Culture. Her Ph.D. is in American Studies and cross-cultural research from the East West Center, with field study in Japan. She writes and consults as a cultural specialist in theme parks, museums, the popular arts, creativity and lifestyles and teaches on the faculty of General Studies at Thomas Jefferson University in Philadelphia.

Norman Lanquist gave up his proprietary interest in the Children's Lit and PCA/Conjoint sessions of the Rocky Mountain MLA in the mid 1980s when he defected to the PCA/ACA where he presented papers on Rituals, Fetishes & Icons and on the Pornotopic Vision at the Montreal and New Orleans conventions and read from his fiction and poetry at the conferences in Stillwater, Bowling Green, Las Vegas and San Antonio. Publications have appeared in *JPC. Goldsmiths Journal* and in the poetry, tattoo, biker and Namvet press in the U.S. and U.K. He has written a novel, *Long Roads, and* teaches college writing in southeastern Arizona.

George H. Lewis is Professor of Sociology and Anthropology at University of the Pacific, Stockton, California. Author of numerous articles and books on popular culture, his most recent project is a book entitled *All That Glitters: Country Music In America*, available from the Popular Press.

David R. Moore earned his Ph.D. from Brown University's Department of American Civilization in 1992 and has worked as Adjunct Lecturer in English at Brown University. He is currently at work revising his dissertation, *Exiled America: Sherwood Anderson, Thomas Hart Benton, Ben Botkin, Constance Rourke, Arthur Raper, Paul Schuster Taylor and the Great Depression,* for publication.

David Prindle is Associate Professor of Government at the University of Texas at Austin. Among his other publications are *The Politics of Glamour: Ideology and Democracy in the Screen Actors Guild* (University of Wisconsin Press, 1988), and *Risky Business: The Political Economy of*

Hollywood (Westview Press, 1993). He also teaches an upper-division undergraduate course entitled "The Politics of Hollywood."

Stephen J. Pullum is an Associate Professor of Communication Studies at the University of North Carolina at Wilmington. He has published several articles on religious discourse, including televangelism and pentecostal rhetoric. He received his Ph.D. in 1988 from Indiana University, Bloomington.

Will Rockett is Dean of the School of Fine Arts and Professor of Film at the University of Wisconsin-Milwaukee. He is the author of *Devouring Whirlwind: Terror & Transcendence in the Cinema of Cruelty* (Greenwood-Praeger, 1988) and of articles in such journals as *Clues, Post Script, The Journal of Popular Film & Television,* and *The Journal of Canadian Theatre History.* Currently, he is writing a study of Peter Weir for Macmillan-Twayne.